SURVIVING AND THRIVING IN CARE AND BEYOND

Systemic Thinking and Practice Series

Charlotte Burck and Gwyn Daniel (Series Editors)

This influential series was co-founded in 1989 by series editors David Campbell and Ros Draper to promote innovative applications of systemic theory to psychotherapy, teaching, supervision, and organisational consultation. In 2011, Charlotte Burck and Gwyn Daniel became series editors, and aim to present new theoretical developments and pioneering practice, to make links with other theoretical approaches, and to promote the relevance of systemic theory to contemporary social and psychological questions.

Other titles in the Series include

(For a full listing, see our website www.karnacbooks.com)

Innovations in the Reflecting Process
Edited by Harlene Anderson and Per Jensen

The Performance of Practice: Enhancing the Repertoire of Therapy with Children and Families
Jim Wilson

The Dialogical Therapist: Dialogue in Systemic Practice
Paolo Bertrando

Systems and Psychoanalysis: Contemporary Integrations in Family Therapy
Carmel Flaskas and David Pocock

Intimate Warfare: Regarding the Fragility of Family Relations
Martine Groen and Justine Van Lawick

Being with Older People: A Systemic Approach
Edited by Glenda Fredman, Eleanor Anderson, and Joshua Stott

Mirrors and Reflections: Processes of Systemic Supervision
Edited by Charlotte Burck and Gwyn Daniel

Race and Culture: Tools, Techniques and Trainings: A Manual for Professionals
Reenee Singh and Sumita Dutta

The Vibrant Relationship: A Handbook for Couples and Therapists
Kirsten Seidenfaden and Piet Draiby

The Vibrant Family: A Handbook for Parents and Professionals
Kirsten Seidenfaden, Piet Draiby, Susanne Søborg Christensen, and Vibeke Hejgaard

Culture and Reflexivity in Systemic Psychotherapy: Mutual Perspectives
Edited by Inga-Britt Krause

Positions and Polarities in Contemporary Systemic Practice: The Legacy of David Campbell
Edited by Charlotte Burck, Sara Barratt, and Ellie Kavner

Creative Positions in Adult Mental Health: Outside In–Inside Out
Edited by Sue McNab and Karen Partridge

Emotions and the Therapist: A Systemic–Dialogical Approach
Paolo Bertrando

SURVIVING AND THRIVING IN CARE AND BEYOND

Personal and Professional Perspectives

edited by

Sara Barratt and Wendy Lobatto

KARNAC

Excerpts from Jackie Kay, *Darling: New & Selected Poems*
(Bloodaxe Books, 2007) www.bloodaxebooks.com
Reproduced by kind permission of the publisher

First published in 2016 by
Karnac Books Ltd
118 Finchley Road, London NW3 5HT

British Library Cataloguing in Publication Data

A C.I.P. for this book is available from the British Library

ISBN 978 1 78220 301 8

Edited, designed and produced by The Studio Publishing Services Ltd
www.publishingservicesuk.co.uk
email: studio@publishingservicesuk.co.uk

Excerpt from Dewan, V. (2003). A truer image. In:
A. Douglas & T. Philpot (Eds.), *Adoption: Changing Families, Changing Times*
(pp. 120–126). London: Routledge. Reproduced with permission.

www.karnacbooks.com

CONTENTS

PART III
THE VOICES OF ADULTS WHO HAVE BEEN ADOPTED OR EXPERIENCED THE CARE SYSTEM EITHER AS CHILDREN OR AS THOSE WHO ARE CURRENTLY PARENTING CHILDREN

ACKNOWLEDGEMENTS

We would like to thank Gwyn and Charlotte for their support and patience during the development and fruition of this book. Particular thanks also to Sally Hodges, who has been steadfastly supportive and encouraging at times when we wondered if we would ever finish it. Thanks to all the colleagues and trainees we have learnt from and worked with in the Fostering, Adoption and Kinship Care, First Step, and Tavistock Haringey Services.

For Sara, my thanks to my family, John, Daisy, Luke, Sam, Alex, Vicky, Edith, Jimmy, and Eddie who have shown patience, tolerance, encouragement, given ideas, read drafts, and shown me the importance of belonging.

For Wendy, my thanks to my children, Anna and Joe, who have enabled me to find the mother in me and to Maureen, Stanley, Ralph, and Diana who support me to work and use my creativity and my will to make a difference.

Our thanks also to Mat Sparrowhawk, who designed the cover, Agata Morgan for her illustrations, John and Kate Hills, Betty Sheridan, Mike Napier, Sue Pearson, Eleanor Anderson, and other friends, for suggestions, support, and stimulating and interesting conversations. Thanks also to Jackie Kay and Bloodaxe Books for their permission to publish extracts of Jackie's poems.

We are very grateful to all who have contributed to this book, for their hard work and patience. This book would not be possible without the personal stories of adoptive parents, kinship and foster carers, and children and young people who have shown so much openness and generosity in telling their stories. Personal and clinical information has been anonymised and, where appropriate, permission to use material has been sought and granted.

Identifying information has been changed so that any resemblance to a child or family is coincidental.

Finally, our thanks to you, our readers. We hope you find something of interest in this collection that will help you understand and inspire you to go on.

ABOUT THE EDITORS AND CONTRIBUTORS

Sara Barratt is a consultant systemic psychotherapist and social worker who worked in the Fostering, Adoption and Kinship care team at the Tavistock and Portman NHS Trust since its inception and subsequently managed the service. She also teaches on the Masters and the Family Therapy Supervision courses. Sara has worked for most of her career with children who are looked after, adopted, and in kinship care, and their families. She also works as a psychotherapist in general practice and consults to social service teams and individual practitioners. She co-edited *Positions and Polarities in Contemporary Practice: The Legacy of David Campbell* with Charlotte Burck and Ellie Kavner and has contributed to a number of books and papers on systemic psychotherapy, fostering and adoption, and systemic work in general practice.

Mark Brownfield studied medicine at Charing Cross and Westminster Medical School (London), trained as a GP in High Wycombe (Bucks) and has been a full time general practitioner at Kings Langley Surgery since 1994. Additionally, he worked for nine years as a GP in Accident and Emergency and four years as a professional member on a PCT Executive Board. Currently, he is a senior appraiser for NHS

England, working to support GP colleagues through appraisal and revalidation. His special interests are in diabetes, minor surgery, and, particularly, mental health. During his psychiatry training, he was able to observe and learn from professionals offering family therapy and explore the concepts of systemic work. As a GP of twenty-two years' standing, he values joint working and sees positive results in using this approach to help vulnerable individuals increase their sense of safety and enable them to contemplate emotional recovery. Within the current constraints that bind modern-day general practice, he prefers to pause, listen, and search to understand patients, even if this means running over time.

Chloe Charles is a student at London Metropolitan University, studying English Literature. Chloe has a passion for creative writing and youth; she is now on the journey to completing her degree in the hope of doing a PGCE, allowing her to teach English in secondary schools. Her future goal is to set up a creative writing programme in youth offending prisons across the UK, which she hopes will help to encourage youth to channel their emotions into something constructive and creative, while also giving them some skills to go towards other educational goals.

Julia Granville is a consultant systemic psychotherapist and social worker who worked for many years in the Fostering, Adoption and Kinship Care Team at the Tavistock Clinic. Julia has over twenty years' experience in working with families in the voluntary and statutory sectors. She has a particular interest and experience in working with adopted and looked-after children and their families and with families who have non-traditional family forms. Julia has trained Masters level family therapists and teaches a range of mental health courses for professionals on systemic approaches to working with families. In addition, she is currently developing mindfulness-based approaches in therapeutic work in the Tavistock Clinic.

Perlita Harris is a registered social worker with a background in adoption support. Her research interests focus on child welfare, adoption, and service user perspectives, particularly Black, LGBT, and seldom heard voices. She has written a number of journal articles on adoption support. Her edited books include: *In Search of Belonging:*

Reflections by transracially adopted people (BAAF, 2006), *The Colours in Me: Writing and Poetry by Adopted Children and Young People* (BAAF, 2008), *Something That Never Went Away: Reflections on Adoption, Being in Care, Adoption and Searching for Family Members* (Adults Affected by Adoption, NORCAP, 2009), and *Chosen: Living with Adoption* (BAAF, 2012). She also co-authored the research study, *Pathways to Permanence for Black, Asian and Mixed Ethnicity Children* (BAAF, 2010) and contributed to the DVD, *Readings from The Colours in Me* (BAAF, 2009). Her most recent publication, is the co-edited book, *Safeguarding Black Children: Good Practice in Child Protection* (JKP, 2016). On a voluntary basis, Perlita co-facilitates workshops for adults with an international element to their search for information and/or birth family (hosted jointly by the Transnational and Transracial Adoption Group, and the IAC: The Centre for Adoption). Perlita holds a PhD in Social Work and is Senior Lecturer in Social Work at Goldsmiths, University of London.

Gillian Hughes is a consultant clinical psychologist and systemic psychotherapist who currently leads the Child and Family Refugee Service at the Tavistock and Portman NHS Foundation Trust. Throughout her career, she has worked in the NHS in inner city locations with marginalised communities as a practitioner and trainer, where she has developed innovative community psychology, systemic, and narrative approaches. She has recently edited a book, *Liberation Practices: Towards Emotional Wellbeing Through Dialogue*, with Taiwo Afuape.

Wendy Lobatto is a social worker and family therapist, and currently manages First Step, an innovative psychological health screening and assessment service for looked-after children in the London Borough of Haringey, which is commissioned from the Tavistock and Portman NHS Foundation Trust. She has worked in the child mental health/ social care field for over twenty-five years. Wendy has a particular interest in working with others to create and deliver integrated systemic service models, which allow us to make a real difference to the lives of vulnerable children.

Val Molloy qualified as a social worker in 1972 and, after ten years working with adults in the Criminal Justice system, changed direction to work with a charity placing so called "hard to place" children for adoption. After a career break when her children were young, Val returned to working with children and families in adoption and to acting as an independent chair for adoption and fostering panels. The last fifteen years of her working life were spent working with adults who had grown up in adoptive families, or in care, and who wished to access information from their childhood records. Val is now retired but retains links with the agency in which she spent a good deal of her working life.

Graham Music is a consultant child and adolescent psychotherapist and an adult psychotherapist in private practice. His publications include *The Good Life: Well-being and the New Science of Altruism Selfishness and Immorality* (2014), *Nurturing Natures: Attachment and Children's Socioemotional, Cultural and Brain Development* (2011), and *Affect and Emotion* (2001). He has a particular interest in thinking about the interface of developmental science and clinical work. Formerly Associate Clinical Director of the Tavistock's Child and Family Department, where he currently teaches and supervises, he has worked therapeutically with maltreated children for several decades, and managed a range of services concerned with the aftermath of child maltreatment. He currently works clinically with forensic cases at the Portman Clinic. He teaches, lectures, and supervises on various psychotherapy and other trainings in Britain and abroad.

Valerie O'Brien is a College Lecturer at the School of Applied Social Science at University College Dublin and is an Associate at Clanwilliam Institute, Dublin. She is a social worker and a registered systemic psychotherapist and supervisor. She has a particular interest in action-based research and has been at the forefront in aiding numerous developments in the child welfare system in Ireland. Her main areas of research interest are family group conferencing, kinship care, and adoption practice and policy. Clinically, she works predominantly with complex blended families (kinship, adoption, re-formed) and consults on complex multi-party cases.

Neil Rees is a consultant clinical psychologist and the Programme Director (Clinical) of the Professional Doctorate in Clinical Psychology at the University of East London. He also works in the NHS at the Child & Family Consultation Service in Newham, East London, which serves a very diverse borough with a significant population of refugee families and separated children and young people seeking asylum. Other activities include psychosocial emergency response overseas with the British Red Cross.

John Simmonds is Director of Policy, Research and Development at CoramBAAF, formerly the British Association for Adoption and Fostering. Before starting at BAAF in 2000, he was head of the social work programmes at Goldsmiths College, University of London. He is a qualified social worker and has substantial experience in child protection, family placement, and residential care settings. He is currently responsible for CoramBAAF's contribution to the development of policy and practice in social work, health, the law, and research. John has published widely including, in the 1980s, the first social work edited book on direct work with children. More recently, he edited, with Gillian Schofield, the Child Placement Handbook and drafted BAAF's Good Practice Guidance on Special Guardianship. Recent research studies have focused on unaccompanied asylum-seeking children in foster care with the Universities of York and Bedfordshire, a study of 100 women adopted from Hong Kong into the UK in the 1960s with the Institute of Psychiatry, and a DfE funded study on Special Guardianship with York University. John sits on the Adoption Leadership Board, the Expert Advisory Group on Adoption Support, and the Expert Group on Special Guardianship. John is the adoptive father of two children, now adults. He was awarded an OBE in the New Years Honours list 2015 and an honorary doctorate in Education from the Tavistock NHS Foundation Trust /University of East London.

SERIES EDITORS' FOREWORD

Charlotte Burck & Gwyn Daniel

This volume, edited by Sara Barratt and Wendy Lobatto, breaks new ground in a practice area which calls out for an approach to delivering services to children, their families and carers which is collaborative, which is integrated, and which holds systemic thinking at the core. The editors have achieved the remarkable feat of producing a volume that not only advocates these principles, but weaves them into the book's very texture.

The book comprises a series of contributions that are multi-levelled, multi-vocal, and draw upon different modes of representation. Whether authored by practitioners or consumers of services, they keep the perspectives of children and parents/carers at the centre. The effect of foregrounding these voices is to enhance the emotional impact for readers as we engage with the long term repercussions of living within the "care system" and with the complexity of the systems within which decisions are made and lives are lived. The volume attends rigorously to many levels of context: from the changing political, social, and legal landscapes which frame the lives of families and children and the positions taken by professionals, to the intricacies of family interactions, and to the ways that early experiences of deprivation, cruelty, abuse, and disruption are inscribed on mind and body, requiring constant vigilance and revision over time.

Yet, while many of the practitioners and family member authors gaze unflinchingly into the shameful and shaming practices that have been visited on children in the "care system", from outright abuse and exploitation to the erasure of crucial aspects of racial and cultural identities, this book, as its title suggests, is, above all, about resilience and about those creative actions that make a difference. These range from the power of autobiographical writing and of the poetic imagination to the development of playful practices with children, and to therapeutic interventions that engage with the particularity of human experience and elicit the unique lived experiences and coping strategies of individual children and their carers, rather than follow any kind of normative or developmental template.

The contributions of users of services will be especially helpful for practitioners, as they provide so much to learn from, including the importance of attending to feedback and of responding to the changing needs of families as they evolve over time. Unusually for a volume written mainly by therapists, their attention to the views of family members involves taking a position which is, at times, sceptical about the desirability of therapy itself as the preferred solution for troubled and traumatised children. This questioning and flexible attitude is one of the hallmarks of a volume that is both compassionate and rigorous and which attends both to the patterns that connect the lives of children in the care system and to the nuanced details of individual narratives.

We are proud and delighted to include this volume in our series.

FOREWORD

Peter Fonagy

As a parent of adopted children, I am all too aware of the complexities (a euphemism for pain, disappointment, and conflict, mixed with unadulterated joy) that taking a person into your life whose biological background is different from your own invariably entails. As our knowledge of the genetic and biological basis of behaviour expands, it becomes harder and harder to adopt a naive environmentalist view that all predispositions can be modified and that epigenetic effects will mitigate temperamental variations. To balance biological reductionism, we need a high level of sophistication that helps guide professionals as well as carers and adoptive parents to identify what they can expect to be able to achieve in circumstances that, in many instances, are very challenging, to say the least.

Part of the problem of fostering and adoption is that it is a social system put in place to deal with a problem. The problem may be extreme poverty, severe mental disorder, cruelty, societal violence, such as war, or individual loss. Children in care do badly, and the outcomes of adoption are also often suboptimal. The reasons for this are well known but solutions are lacking. This means that those who are brave enough to offer care to babies, children, and teenagers are taking on board not simply the care of this person, but also the sometimes complex sequelae that the possibly horrific experiences bring.

Added to this are the difficulties that attachment imposes. The paradox of attachment is that without the creation of a secure base and a privileged emotional relationship that attachment provides, fostering and adoption stand no chance of healing any of the psychological wounds that the child has sustained. However, the activation of attachment undermines the capacity to be able to think clearly about the perspective of another person. We only need to conjure up the last time we felt intense romantic love for another: that was not a time in which perspective taking or the judgement of social trustworthiness could be readily undertaken. Intense attachment obscures rather than clarifies the mental state of the person we are with. It is far easier to deal with other people's children than one's own and, unsurprisingly, one's own children seem to find little difficulty dealing with other people's parents. Thus, the creation of the essential bond between carers and the child in some respects undermines the carer's capacity to provide the emotional support that the child needs. Attachment creates a challenge for mentalization.

All this is just to say that there is much need for this book. It is a unique collection of perspectives by those with the deepest understanding of this multi-faceted yet urgent problem. The book provides a theoretical framework—in fact, several—for understanding the challenges faced by those who are part of an aspect of the process our society has put in place to remedy the effects of trauma and abuse on young children. It is a book that does not shrink from political commentary, and one that faces head on the unsatisfactory experiences of all the protagonists within the current system, be they the biological parents, the carers or the child—and, indeed, the professionals who surround the family, offering their assistance. As the book shows, in order to be adequately evaluated, the outcomes have to be seen in the context of the shaping of adult lives.

The problem of care is multi-layered. It involves the responsibilities of the society we live in and the way professionals discharge these on behalf of all of us. The instruments, however, are the foster carers and adoptive parents who have to cope with what is thrust upon them, which, as the book describes, may be an amalgam of biological predisposition, the neurodevelopmental challenges that early trauma brings, and the mixture of emotions that we may anticipate a person who has escaped from a life-threatening situation, but has been thrust into an environment that is far from their own choosing, to have. The best way of representing this difficult situation is through narratives—stories that those who have experienced one or other aspect of this situation can tell.

This is what makes this book unique and, in the most aesthetic sense of the word, beautiful. The stories are not pretty, but the determination of all the protagonists to put right what was so wrong, to survive and thrive in the face of adversity, to confront the inconceivably cruel experiences and find imaginative and uplifting solutions, gives one courage to carry on with this work. The options available are best understood through individual examples, and the stories that emerge from the pages are all moving and succeed where another medium could only reveal selective aspects of the experience. Personal experience is more persuasive than statistics, as many writers know. It is these stories that will offer the reader a comprehensive picture of the current state of the field of adoption and fostering better than any number of government reports and research papers.

Everything that is presented here is real and, as the reader will find, some issues raise significant problems to which, currently, we have no solutions. None of the chapters is superfluous; each conveys one or more messages that require our urgent attention. While some chapters describe substantial achievements that have made the lives of children and carers more productive and happier, others focus on elaborating the depth of the problems from either a neurobiological or a social standpoint. Some chapters that consider racial issues are particularly painful, and the picture that the lifelong perspective offers is indeed challenging. The legacy of institutional care has appalled—and continues to appal—many. Clearly, we are doing better than those running children's homes half a century ago, when sexual abuse was rife, but evidently we are not doing well enough. Maybe we never will. This book, however, is a landmark contribution creating a platform of hard-won insight that, if conscientiously read, should make all those who are part of the process of foster care and adoption better at what they do—which is probably the most important thing that any of us can.

Peter Fonagy, PhD, FMedSci, FBA, OBE
Professor and Head, Research Department of Clinical,
Educational and Health Psychology, University College London;
Chief Executive, Anna Freud Centre, London.

Introduction

This is a book about children who have to grow up apart from their biological families, the impact of this on their lives and on those who look after them, and how we can respond to the challenges this poses in order that they can grow and develop in healthy directions.

We use a systemic framework to describe working with children and adults who are or have been in care or adopted, and with their adoptive parents and carers, highlighting their own narratives as well as those of professionals working with them.

We have tried to make space for multiple voices to speak and describe aspects of the care system and life beyond. There are contributions from those who have been brought up away from their biological families, their adoptive parents, and foster or kinship carers. There are contributions from researchers and professionals with expertise in working with children in substitute care, who will describe their theoretical and clinical approaches, privileging the voices of those with whom they work. We have been deeply influenced by the people we have worked with over the years and hope that this book gives a flavour of the remarkable ways which carers, adoptive parents, and children have found in order to stay together while in the presence of so much pain and loss, and the trust that they have to develop to be able to grow to love one another. This book will bring their voices to the fore. We are also mindful of the position of the biological parents who are not part of this work, their grief and despair at the loss of their children and the yearning that they and their children might be feeling for one another, no matter how much they know that this might not be best for the children if they cannot meet their children's needs.

Sara's voice

For the past fifteen years, following a lengthy career in social work, I have been working both as team manager and family therapist at the Fostering Adoption and Kinship Care team at the Tavistock & Portman NHS Foundation Trust, a specialist CAMHS for children who are not living in their biological families. I started working as a trainee social worker in 1968 and, on qualifying in 1972, worked in a generic team. At that time, the relationship between social workers, children, and their families was considered important and I was able to work with families in child protection, take children into care where necessary, work with them in foster care, while also working with their biological parents. I also assessed and selected adoptive families and followed children through their journey towards adulthood. I remember them very well and sometimes bump into young adults who update me on their families because, for better or worse, for many years I was an integral part of their lives. I was part of the Jane Rowe and Lydia Lambert study which reported on decision-making that led children to languish in foster care (Barratt, 2010; Rowe & Lambert, 1973) and have seen many changes in the way social workers are expected to work with families.

I have been privileged to work with children and their carers/parents, and have learnt so much from them; in trusting me enough to talk about their lives, they have greatly enriched my life. The inspiration for this book came from many conversations with children who have been separated from their birth families and brought up in kinship, foster, or adoptive families.

In many years of work, both as a social worker and a family therapist, I have realised that children who have been abused are very unlikely either to have the language to describe their experiences or the confidence to let people know about life in their birth families. Many years ago, as a social worker, I was working with a young person who was subsequently in care and adopted. As there were concerns about his safety, I took him out for a burger to talk to him separately from his mother and stepfather. I was aware that he was not safe at home and took him into care shortly after I started working with him and his family, but it was not until some three years later, when he had been in care for two years and was living with his adoptive family, that he told me that he was badly beaten after I saw him on his own. He was unable to talk about his life in his birth family until he felt safe from further abuse. I learnt from him to be very careful to pick up signals from children, to liaise closely with their schools, and to try to understand what is happening by attuning myself to the way parents talk about or to them, rather than seeing them alone or asking them questions that it would be dangerous to answer.

More recently, when I have worked with adoptive parents whose children start to display various signs of abuse some time into their lives in the family, I am reminded that most children do not talk to anyone about abuse they might have suffered until they start to feel safe. This view is corroborated by Grayson Perry in the biography written by Wendy Jones (2007), in which he describes a visit from the NSPCC after he had told his grandmother of his stepfather's violence towards him. He describes his confusion when the social worker arrived and spoke initially to him on his own. He goes on to describe the family meeting in which she asked him in front of his stepfather, who was abusive to him, whether he loved him. He says that he could only say "Yes" because she would be leaving him with the person who: "held the sword of Damocles hanging over me so I wasn't going to reply, 'No! He's an f…ing bastard! He's a f…ing Bastard! The woman was going to leave but I was going to have to go on living with the old man'" (pp. 70–72).

In editing this book. we hope to show that children's experiences can be appreciated and made sense of despite the complicated nature of their reality, not just in their biological families, but in their lives going forward. We endeavour to show how children can move on to positive developmental pathways through good and trusting relationships with carers, and that this can be a lifelong journey.

For many years, I have been involved in training family therapists and one of my supervises during the 1990s was Wendy, also a social worker, who later moved into working with children in the care system and whom I asked to work with me on this book.

Wendy's voice

Like Sara, I was also trained as a social worker, and then later as a family therapist. Unlike Sara, I did not spend years working with children and families in a context where relationships were understood as key to positive change. By the 1990s, when I qualified, children's social work was taking a more bureaucratic and procedural shape. When I was able, I was happy to move into therapeutic social work in a child mental health context, which is where I have worked ever since.

By chance really, I was offered a promotion in a specialist child mental health team for looked-after children in 2003, at a time when the government was investing significantly in child mental health services and new models of good practice were being developed. I began to meet children, young people, foster carers, birth parents, and social workers and to appreciate the complexity, struggles, and small triumphs that mark the lives of those in the care system and those who care for them. I was astonished, time and time again, at the selflessness, courage, and determination of the adults involved in caring for children and young people in care. At the same time, I was also struck by the energy of those children and young people who are growing and moving forward, despite enduring the bitterest of life's pills, the loss of their parents.

We have attempted to incorporate a variety of perspectives in depicting a landscape of life in and after care to enable those who work and live in this land to appreciate more of its features. We hope that the reader will find this a rich and textured collection of writings, which will hearten and support us in this varied and complex terrain.

Outline of the book

We have organised this book into three sections; the first part offers an overview of the organisational, political, and clinical context for alternative family care.

In Chapter One, "Family placement: continuity and discontinuity over time", John Simmonds, from CoramBAAF, gives an overview of the subject. His theme is continuity and discontinuity and he talks from a personal and professional perspective. John looks at some of the current national debates, including recent legal judgments, which have altered practice and decision-making in the adoption field, as well as investigating the tension between the UK's non-consensual approach to adoption and the attempts of the state to promote co-operation with parents. John frames these big issues alongside a conversation with his young adult son about the development of his identity. It combines a broad conceptual approach with a warm and personal account of the impact of these issues at the family level.

In Chapter Two, "Working with professional systems", Wendy Lobatto looks at how to facilitate the creation of functioning parenting teams for children and young people in care. It is not straightforward to provide high quality, child-centred care as a group of disparate workers from various agencies, but she shows how this can be supported and enabled. It is so important for children that the key adults in their lives find ways of working coherently together to make good decisions for them, yet there are many pressures, which constrain our ability to do this. Wendy looks at how to make a difference in these processes, illustrating with some moving case examples.

In Chapter Three, "Approaches to working with foster carers and children", Sara Barratt talks about ways of working with foster carers and their different approaches to engaging with CAMHS services. She outlines the "needs led" approach in which therapists draw on different ways of working with children and their carers at different stages of the work, based on what they feel would be most helpful. She describes the importance of their engagement in helping children to attend the service and the different ways in which they approach their role. Some see themselves as parenting children and attune themselves to their children emotionally, while others feel they can be more containing by responding on a behavioural level. Carers and children contribute their own remarkable descriptions of their experience of attending CAMHS.

In Chapter Four, "Under our skins: developmental perspectives on trauma, abuse, neglect, and resilience", Graham Music describes the importance of an understanding of neurodevelopment for children who have suffered early trauma. He examines the ways in which adverse early experiences can affect our psychological, emotional, and physical lives. He looks at some of the fascinating recent brain science and developmental psychology research, and what it tells us about how the early family context of a child affects the way his brain is sculpted, his autonomic nervous system develops, his hormonal systems are programmed, and how children are, as a result, likely to relate to other people and the social world. Although this perspective can help us understand why some children can suffer as a result of their early experience, it also shows us that there remains hope for positive outcomes as our brains grow and mature.

In Part II, we move on to looking at particular examples of clinical work with children and young people.

In Chapter Five, "Adoption stories", two sets of adoptive parents with Sara Barratt describe their experiences of becoming an adoptive family and of attending the Fostering, Adoption and Kinship Care Service (FAKCT). They talk about their experiences of assessment and of bringing their children to CAMHS. Each family is headed by a same-sex couple. One couple adopted three siblings and describe the challenges of meeting the needs of three young children and their experience of help and the different work undertaken, such as assessment, sibling work, family work, and then parent work, which, they say, at the time was bewildering but, in retrospect, was helpful. They speak of the need for professionals to give more explanation or rationale for their interventions. The other parents describe the help they received at the time of placement of their son and the work undertaken with our team and the challenges they faced. They have now adopted a second son and speak about the boys' different needs arising from early life experiences.

In Chapter Six, "Working with vulnerability and resilience for separated children seeking asylum: towards stories of hope", Gillian Hughes and Neil Rees describe the painful work undertaken with asylum seeking young people who arrive in the UK. For these young people, the experience of multiple losses and dislocation presents a huge challenge to their sense of identity, with the obvious negative impact this has on their emotional wellbeing. The authors describe how this is amplified by political agendas seeking to reduce immigration, which feed public perceptions of asylum seekers as people to be feared and mistrusted. However, Gillian and Neil refuse to take a pathologising view of these young people, describing some positive and life-affirming approaches to helping them survive and thrive in their adopted country.

In Chapter Seven, "'The best thing is the lunch! My friends! Being with other people in the same situation! Oh, and the slow walking! The Fostering, Adoption and Kinship Care Team Children's Group", Julia Granville describes a group that is run with colleagues in FAKCT for children aged between seven and eleven years old. The group runs during a week of either half-term or a holiday. The programme is manualised, using frameworks such as mindfulness and EMDR, and offers opportunities for children to reflect on their responses while also having fun. This heart-warming chapter describes the group, the work with parents, and involves children in describing their experiences.

In Chapter Eight, "The strength to smile behind my mask", Chloe Charles shares some of her experiences of being brought up by an extended family member in a kinship arrangement and has written some powerful poems which we are privileged to include in this collection. She says, "My poems were written as a form of anger management. I was an extremely angry foster child who was torn between the loyalty and love for my biological mother and learning how to accept the love and care from my foster mother. I had to leave a mother who was young, troubled, and struggling and felt forced into a situation I wasn't happy with! I lived with my younger brother's aunt, which was difficult for me to accept, especially coming from parents who made it very clear that they were my parents and weren't going to be replaced. I acted out and pushed away all forms of kindness, even though deep down all I wanted to be was loved. I didn't want to be happy knowing that my mother was all alone and probably unhappy."

In Chapter Nine, "Helping children through working with their adoptive parents", Sara Barratt, together with three sets of adoptive parents, describes how families can be helped without working directly with their children. The first parent came initially with his daughter, but continued on his own when she dropped out of the work. He talks about the failures of professionals to understand and respond to his family's needs and his feeling of being on his own with the problem. The other parents talk about the importance of being seen without their children, whom they feel would be traumatised by attending the clinic with the fear that another rejection was coming. While there had been plans to include the children at some stage, the parents felt that the work without them provided sufficient help and support.

Then there is a brief interlude, which features extracts from the poems of Jackie Kay, who writes movingly about her experience of being transracially adopted.

In Part III, we hear the voices of adults who have experience of the care system, either when they were children or from their position as the carers of children currently.

In Chapter Ten, "The lived experience of transracial adoption", Perlita Harris draws on many of the ideas in her book, *In Search of Belonging*, to describe the political drivers for a colour-blind approach to transracial adoption and the experiences of adults who were adopted transracially. In the voices of those adults who talk about their experiences as children in the care system, we can hear their pain and confusion and we are offered the opportunity to understand more about the nature of these experiences.

Chapter Eleven, "Never too late", is written collaboratively by an older woman, Janet, who spent her childhood in care, together with her GP, Mark Brownfield, and Sara Barratt, and tells an inspiring story of how it is possible to move towards recovery and healing later in life. Janet had suffered a lifetime of mental health problems and suicide attempts and her GP felt there was something behind them that she had not talked about. In an initial session, she described physical and sexual abuse while in care in the 1940s. This chapter is written from three perspectives, in which the GP talks about his work, Janet describes the effect of her experiences in residential care on her life, and Sara talks about her work with her, using EMDR and linking closely with the GP. The care agency who supported this work and were involved in going through Janet's records with her also comments.

In Chapter Twelve, "Positioning and respectful professional interventions for working with the legacy of Irish institutional care", Valerie O'Brien describes the effect of being brought up in the industrial schools in Ireland, the political context, and the power of the Catholic Church. The chapter draws on Valerie's research and talks about the legacy of the experiences on survivors. It offers a moving and informative account of a traumatic period of Irish history in which generations of children were hurt and abused.

In Chapter Thirteen, "Co-creating a coherent story with adults who have been fostered or adopted", Val Molloy describes her work in undertaking life story work with adults who were in care. She uses case examples to describe the issues that those applying for knowledge of their birth families come with and the pain and distress when the responses are not those they hoped for. She also talks about their criticism of the agency when their care experiences have not been positive and her work in helping them with the fallout of their experiences.

In Chapter Fourteen, "'It turns your whole world upside down . . . but still it brings immense pleasure': perspectives on kinship care", Julia Granville describes her work, both in running a group and in her clinical practice with kinship carers. She explores some of the issues that arise in work with this client group, drawing on experience of facilitating a support group for kinship carers over a number of years, and includes interviews with four members of that group. The themes are those of hard work, the relationship with the parents of the children, and the poverty and lack of support from social care. This chapter offers a fascinating account of how carers cope in this complex position between their own families and statutory agencies.

We are very grateful to all the contributors who have added their perspectives to our wide portrait of life in care and beyond. We have reflected on how our own relationship, which began with Wendy's professional dependency under Sara's supervision, and then developed over time into a collegial connection, mirrors the hopes of all of us that children can find the parenting they need, despite the complexity and difficulty of their lives, and take their social place in time as functioning adults. In creating this volume, we have enjoyed our collaborative debates from which we hope that we have produced something of interest to you, our readers.

References

Barratt, S. (2010). Test of time: children who wait (1973), by Jane Rowe and Lydia Lambert. *Clinical Child Psychology and Psychiatry, 15*(4): 627–631.

Jones, W. (2007). *Grayson Perry: Portrait of The Artist As a Young Girl.* London: Vintage Books.

Rowe, J., & Lambert, L. (1973). *Children Who Wait: A Study of Children Needing Substitute Families.* London: Association of British Adoption Agencies.

PART I

OVERVIEW OF THE SOCIAL, POLITICAL, AND CLINICAL CONTEXT FOR ALTERNATIVE FAMILY CARE

CHAPTER ONE

Family placement: continuity and discontinuity over time

John Simmonds

Ten years ago, I drafted a note to myself.

"My adopted son has just turned eighteen and finished his A-levels. He is currently on a gap year and due to start at university next year studying 'Product Design'. His plans for this year are to train as a chef. This marks a long-standing ambition of his. His flow in the kitchen is quite remarkable to the benefit of the family that can have a Jamie Oliver meal on a Monday night. His kitchen cleaning skills are not quite so remarkable. On the cooking front, his girlfriend is undoubtedly outclassed—in fact none of his friends can compete with him in this area. He has recently been taken on as an assistant chef at one of our local well-known modern European restaurants in London after a short trial.

"In a fairly academically orientated family, his flair and motivation in the kitchen stand out and as with many families, the question is asked 'Where does this come from?' Is it his early life experience of watching *Ready, Steady, Cook* or indeed being given Jamie Oliver cookbooks as presents? All of this might be true, but can't explain why he took to actually cooking rather than just passively watching the TV programmes as many of his friends have done. Did he pick it up from us? Well not really—my wife can turn out an excellent meal but like many working families, this tends to be on special occasions rather than Monday nights. And cooking was not something that his school prized or encouraged at all.

"It might not come as a complete surprise to hear that his birth mother was a cook. He knows this but I am not clear what this means to him. Is this his way of staying in contact with her emotionally—he hasn't had any contact with her given he was adopted 18 years ago so this does seem a bit far-fetched. Is this something that he has inherited from her? This also seems a bit but not completely far-fetched. In one way the explanation doesn't really matter—he needs to fulfil his own ambitions, build on his aptitudes and energise his motivations. Who he takes after in this respect and where this comes from is interesting and sometimes emotionally charged but if he 'finds himself' over the next few years, then that is what I want for him."

Where are we now? My son graduated as planned. University was a bit up and down as it probably is for most undergraduates. The process of finding oneself in the late teenage years and early twenties is complex—highs and lows, uncertainties and anxieties, achievements and successes. One success among a number of others was being employed to run a small cafeteria on campus that reinforced the cooking ambition. It was a downside, if not a nightmare, to graduate at a time of economic crisis. However, an opportunity to be employed as a chef at a "pop up restaurant" averted the problem that thousands of other graduates were experiencing and that was quickly followed by a fairly lengthy period of employment as a chef at a well-known restaurant in the West End of London. It was a period of learning, challenge, and exhaustion—a life of afternoon/evening and weekend hours is not the most familial or socially conducive.

How does this personal story connect with the theme of this chapter? First, this is the story of an adoption of its time and maybe has little direct connection with what I know about adoption today (Simmonds, 2012). Our experience was rooted in a particular social structure where illegitimacy was still subject to stigma, resources to support single parenthood accompanied by significant ambivalence, and adoption agencies were geared up to place babies quickly when they were relinquished by their birth parents. It was also an era that had just emerged from the view that "secrecy" was best and adoption should be thought of as similar to "born to family life". Telling children that they were adopted had started to be accepted as necessary and being open about origins was regarded as helpful. In some circumstances, there might even be communication and the exchange of information through "letterbox contact" (Howe et al., 2003; Triseliotis et al., 2005). Similar issues were being raised about children in foster care and their understanding of why they were in care and what the plans for them were. Research by Rowe (1983, 1984; Rowe et al., 1989) identified serious issues resulting from the lack of openness and clarity in these placements, which amounted to "drift". These issues reflect significant themes in adoption and all other types of family placement: that of continuity and discontinuity, the many questions that arise about how individuals, families, and society address their thoughts and feelings between the past, present, and future. Where did I come from? Who am I? Why did this happen? Could something have been done then that would have prevented me from finding myself in the position I am today (Harris, 2006, 2008, 2012)? This chapter explores the complexity of establishing continuity in the context of discontinuity within the changing professional and social discourses that influence policy, practice, and family life.

Issues of continuity and discontinuity are fundamental to our experience. There is little doubt that the pathway of family life is marked by the need for continuity. Indeed, its strength is seen as the continuity of relationships throughout life in providing stability, commitment, and protection. Adults undoubtedly benefit from this continuity and it is a key underpinning of marriage, civil partnership, or non-legally framed long-term relationships. Children, in particular, require continuity. This theme has been well and deeply articulated through the concept of attachment (Bowlby, 1968, 2005). The emotional and social connection between young children and their parents (and, indeed, a small number of other adults over time), driven by sensitivity to the thoughts and feelings of the child at its core, is profoundly important. This is the secure base for building children's sense of who they are, their connection with the world around them, and their confidence to explore that world. However, we know that there is much more to it than this. Continuity might be desirable in adult and child relationships but discontinuity is likely to be a significant experience. Indeed, the rates of divorce bring us close to having to regard continuity as unusual in adult relationships and family life.

However, this is only one part of recognising that change, dislocation, uncertainty, and loss are a core part of human experience and the secure psychosocial base that lies at the heart of attachment enables us to address these feelings.

As important as attachment has become as a core concept in understanding child development, there are many factors that promote the healthy development of children and these are subject to lengthy and complex debate. No one concept can do justice to the variables involved, especially when there is complex interaction between what happens inside people, what happens between them, and what happens when they are members of groups (Sroufe, 2005). As much as the study of child development has become a serious and substantial scientific subject, it cannot avoid the deeply embedded value issues or choices that human beings make when striving to create meaning in a social world. Over a generation, the Western world has shifted its perspective from identifying heterosexual marriage and the nuclear family as the only foundation for healthy development. There are many other family forms, which are socially sanctioned and which offer both benefits and challenges to their members and to society as a whole, where there continue to be dominant discourses about how families should be. These are discussed by Julia Granville in Chapter Fourteen.

Taking too limited a historical perspective on individual development and family life is unhelpful, as the greater span of human development indicates the significant adaptability of human beings to the changing physical and social environment. There are two key themes in this. First, co-operation is necessary for procreation and the survival of the species in creating the next generation. Second, co-operation enables human beings to respond to threats or challenges in the environment to ensure that our species survives. The capacity to adapt, to be flexible, to learn from experience, to transmit what has been learnt to other people and to the next generation, plays a huge part in the capacity to survive. The key significant issue in this is the development of the capacity of human beings to co-operate and to trust (Fonagy & Allison, 2014; Koenig & Harris, 2005; Sperber et al., 2010). The ability of one individual to work with another individual or group is central to survival, with trust being a key component. The combined efforts of people to respond to, and solve, a new challenge or threat is usually significantly better than where the problem is worked on by just one person, but working with other people requires appropriate levels of trust based on experience and a belief that this is a safe and effective strategy. The need to co-operate to survive often means dealing with the possible threats posed by other people, whether these are individuals, small groups, or whole populations.

Learning to co-operate is a complex psychosocial activity that involves balancing the pursuit of self-interest with the belief that fulfilling the needs of the other is not a threat but an advantage. Trust is difficult to reliably establish when it is based on a single experience that might be transitory. In most situations, trust develops through experience repeated over time. For a child who has experienced unpredictable parenting, it takes time for him to trust that his carers will be there when he needs them and, for example, provide food when he is hungry. Tensions and anger can erupt at mealtimes and patience and calm predictability are required before children can begin to rely on the adults around them. Successfully negotiating these events over time is important to the establishment of a trusting relationship. Repetition binds people together and the absence of trust will become a major issue in the continuity of relationships and all social groupings. When it becomes established, it is of such importance and value that it is defended through complex psychosocial processes, which extend to every aspect of life, such as believing that your parent or carer will be there when you expect them to be. Experience, belief, and trust established over time, become embedded in institutions. This is an important part of survival; human beings need to create joint memory that serves the function of releasing them from continuously having to rediscover and re-create trusting and reliable structures that enable them to survive.

Whether as individuals, groups, families, or communities, co-operation is enabled by identification with others unified by nationality, religion, culture, language, or location. We co-operate with people we believe to be the same as we are. If we are not sure about this, they might pose a threat. This might not be immediately obvious and might not even be true, but so important is the need to survive that it would be foolhardy to ignore it. At times of danger, our instinct tells us that we need to know who our friends are and these are most likely to be the people that are "like us". As uncomfortable as this might be when it becomes the source of racism, religious intolerance, or other forms of discrimination or oppression, what individuals, groups, and whole communities might do when they are threatened cannot be lightly dismissed under pleas of tolerance or understanding. Adaptability comes with the price of a deeply embedded capacity to both defend and attack. These factors lie at the heart of many issues in family placement. Maltreatment may be thought of as a fundamental breach of trust between the child and their parents. Removing the child might be necessary to protect them but might, for the child, indicate a further source of danger with unknown people and, therefore, can elicit a heightened need for self-protection through attacking the new parent figures. The process of resolving these issues and establishing a workable new family are, furthermore, likely to be full of uncertainty and delay. The child's capacity to trust could be the overarching casualty and, even when a resolution is being approached, might continue to present painful feelings for the child and her carers: for example, mealtimes might continue to be a source of tension because these processes become activated.

Co-operation, then, relies on an individual's belief that "the other" is a source of help and support and not a threat. Trust in the other cannot be naïvely assumed; making sense of one's own mind and the minds of others needs to be reliable, accurate, and insightful. The room for error is significant because human perception and judgement is fallible: misunderstandings occur, accidents happen, and threats are perceived and might be real. Prior experience is likely to play a key part, as the example above of children in care and the anxiety and tensions around mealtimes illustrates. The recent development of the concept of reflective functioning (Aber et al., 1985; Slade, 2005; Steele et al., 2008) has been particularly important in articulating this. Reflective functioning recognises the unique capacity of the human mind to accept and understand that relating to others means learning that:

- the minds of other people are opaque: "Sometimes, I can't quite understand what she wants. She seems to be hungry but any suggestion I make about food seems to spark off a mixture of fear and anger—or at least that is what I think it is";
- one's own mind is difficult to understand: "I am not sure that I really know what I feel about her when this happens. Am I too sensitive in just wanting to be seen as a good mum?";
- mental states change, and change over time: "I was feeling very upset about what happened at supper yesterday but having

thought about it, I can see why mealtimes are so stressful for you";
- the process of relating influences mental states: "I feel very upset about what has just happened but maybe we can talk about it when you have calmed down a bit to see if we can sort this out."

It is important that parents and carers can facilitate children to understand that their mental states are opaque, subject to change, change over time, and are influenced by others during the process of relating. Subjectively, children need to experience their own minds as a reasonably safe place that they can trust in steering them through the world, using opportunity, experiencing the challenge of learning, managing risk and threat, adapting to new circumstances, and facing transition and loss. In turn, their own experience and development will set them on a path to being able to relate to the minds of others. Being able to co-operate and work together is the outcome, which drives adaptability and the capacity to survive. When children have been maltreated, there are serious issues in rebuilding the capacity to trust and the mental processes that enable this.

The threat in family placement

Family placement across the board finds itself embroiled in complex issues of survival, threat, adaptability, and co-operation. As one example, on 27 May 2015, the *Daily Mail* published a piece in which Denise Robertson, their agony aunt, "after a lengthy investigation", "reveals the 'rotten' side of the adoption system in Britain". The investigation was based on 450 letters received over the previous year "from desperate families". The headline identifies the piece as the "Blood-chilling scandal of the thousands of babies stolen by the State" (Robertson, 2015) There could not be a more direct evocation of the perceived threat that the state poses to some families in removing their children to be placed for adoption. It is difficult to square the claims of this article with the framework of law that governs the adoption system. The European Convention on Human Rights is central to this, with two key Articles providing an overarching framework to ensure that the state acts fairly and justly. Article 6 establishes the right to a fair trial and Article 8, the right to respect for one's private and family life, one's home, and one's correspondence, with no interference with this right by a public authority except in very specific circumstances. This is supported by various judgements of the European Court of Human Rights (ECHR). It is important in the way that domestic legislation is framed in England and Wales, in particular, the Human Rights Act 1998, the Children Act 1989, and the Adoption and Children Act 2002. Domestically, the Supreme Court, High Court, and local courts determine each case in accordance with the law with local authorities, the Children and Family Court Advisory and Support Service (CAFCASS), and others preparing the evidence according to the law and regulatory and professional protocols. If there is a scandal, as Robertson argues, it is not one that is legally sanctioned.

The issue with adoption is complex in the UK, as, unlike the rest of Europe, it does not restrict adoption to those situations where birth parents give their lawful consent to their child being placed for adoption. If the court is satisfied that there is no alternative plan for the child to secure his or her needs and welfare, including returning the child to his or her parent/s or wider family, then an Order can be made which authorises the local authority to place the child for adoption. The legal availability of non-consensual adoption, sometimes described as "forced adoption", is a child-focused solution to a serious issue: the absence of a safe and loving family life for a child—the key to their future.

The very existence of non-consensual adoption, as strong as the argument might be in terms of a child's long-term development, raises serious questions about the theme of adapting and co-operation in order to survive. If the identified threat to the child is from the parent/s and their lack of capacity to successfully and appropriately provide a family life for their child, resulting in State intervention, then, from the parent/s point of view, the threat is from the state. The dynamic interplay between the parents, the wider family, the child, and the state is driven by the issue of threat, but where the solution is still intended to be framed by co-operation: assessing the degree of risk and opportunity, finding solutions to the parents' problems, discussing possible plans, enabling them to participate and play their part in the plan. That might include the return of the child to the parents with appropriate support, placement with family members possibly framed by Special Guardianship, and it might include adoption. The intended outcome is to establish a plan for the child that ensures a family for life, established in law. Working co-operatively in partnership should drive this process for it to be effective but significant uncertainty might hang over every aspect of it.

These issues have recently been explored by the Supreme Court in a way that has had a profound impact on adoption. In Re B (A Child) (2013) UKSC 33, the court was asked to consider the plans for a child who had had been removed at birth and placed in foster care. The parents had significant problems; the mother had suffered serious abuse herself and was in a highly vulnerable position with a range of psychological difficulties. She had spent time in prison. The father also had a range of problems, including a series of criminal convictions. He also had four other children in whom he had taken very little interest. Because the child B had been removed at birth, she had not suffered directly from her parents' care or lack of it and, in fact, they had been seen to be very caring of her during contact visits. The legal threshold, therefore, was one of "likelihood of significant harm", a predictive evaluation based on the serious issues in the history of the couple. The local authority's plan was that the child should be placed for adoption, but the experts who gave evidence differed in their view of the plan for the child. One argument was that B should be returned to her parents with a comprehensive package of safeguarding and support services, building on the positively observed care of the parents during contact. The other was that the parents did not accept their need for help and there was no evidence of their capacity to co-operate with services that might be arranged—indeed, quite the reverse. Lord Justice Rix in the prior Court of Appeal judgment (B (A Child) [2012] EWCA Civ 1475) concluded:

> I also wonder whether this case illustrates a powerful but also troubling example of the state exercising its precautionary responsibilities for a much loved child in the face of parenting whose unsatisfactory nature lies not so much in the area of physical abuse but in the more subjective area of moral and emotional risk.

Judge Hedley, in Re L (Care: Threshold Criteria) (2007) 1 FLR 2050 states clearly,

> It follows inexorably . . . that society must be willing to tolerate very diverse standards of parenting, including the eccentric, the barely

> adequate and the inconsistent. It follows too that children will inevitably have both very different experiences of parenting and very unequal consequences flowing from it. It means that some children will experience disadvantage and harm, while others flourish in atmospheres of loving security and emotional stability. These are the consequences of our fallible humanity and it is not the provenance of the state to spare children all the consequences of defective parenting. In any event, it simply could not be done. (para 50)

These are complex issues. On the one hand, these judgements clearly articulate deeply entrenched belief in the benefits that come from the continuity of family life in all its various forms, whatever dilemmas there are for the child in experiencing low standards of care from the parent/s. The role of the state is not to socially engineer by removing children into more beneficial family and social environments. However, there are particular circumstances where the state is authorised to intervene and this is set out in law: evidence of the likelihood that the child will suffer, or has suffered, significant harm, together with the court's responsibility to ensure that, in any decision it makes, the child's welfare is paramount and the long-term consequences are fully explored when it comes to decisions such as adoption. This is made difficult where there are issues of judgement about lifestyle choices or personal standards, as Judge Hedley and others set them out.

In Re B, by a majority of four to one, the Supreme Court accepted the local authority's plan for adoption on the grounds of the parents' inability to co-operate with services to ensure their daughter's welfare. But the impact of the argument in that judgment and a series of subsequent judgments have introduced significant doubt about the place of non-consensual adoption. There has been no change in the law as such, but a summarising paragraph by the President of the Family Division, Lord Justice Munby, in Re B-S (2013, EWCA Civ 1146) makes it clear what the standards are that must be met by local authorities and the courts in considering adoption:

> Orders contemplating non-consensual adoption—care orders with a plan for adoption, placement orders and adoption orders—are "a very extreme thing, a last resort", only to be made where "nothing else will do", where "no other course [is] possible in [the child's] interests", they are "the most extreme option", a "last resort—when all else fails",

> to be made "only in exceptional circumstances and where motivated by *overriding requirements* pertaining to the child's welfare, in short, where nothing else will do". (para. 22)

In addition, a further issue was identified about the standards of current practice:

> We have real concerns, shared by other judges, about the recurrent inadequacy of the analysis and reasoning put forward in support of the case for adoption, both in the materials put before the court by local authorities and guardians and also in too many judgments. This is nothing new. But it is time to call a halt. (para. 30)

Both of these summary paragraphs restate the standards required of local authorities and the courts when planning and considering adoption and centre on three issues:

1. The local authority and the courts taking the least interventionist approach while continuing to support families and placing the child at the centre of any decision.
2. Exploring all the feasible options: return home, placement with extended family members or friends, foster care or adoption, and demonstrating in evidence why they might or might not be in the child's best interests.
3. Identifying and providing those services which might be needed to support the parents and family in rebuilding themselves to adequately care for the child in the immediate and longer term.

These are sound principles, but the impact of the quoted case law on the number of children with adoption as the plan in England has been dramatic, with a fall of some 50% in the two years since the judgment. It is difficult to predict whether this signifies a longer-term fall, but the vulnerability of planning and decision-making in adoption is clearly demonstrated in what has happened since these judgments.[1]

The legal framework sets out a powerful institutional response to what is at the core a set of fundamental beliefs about human beings, their survival, and the relationships and other processes that enable this. It is also a powerful reminder of the complex role of the state. It has a responsibility to be supportive of, and engaged with, individuals and families in providing safe and effective structures and services which enable society to prosper in the present and survive through to future generations, with the family at the centre of this. At the same time, the state must identify any significant threats within and from the family and take action to address these where children are concerned. Co-operative and supportive engagement, the capacity to adapt and change and the ability to experience loss and incorporate this into learning are critical parts of this process. At an individual level, it lies at the heart of Re B, where the parents' inability to openly and positively co-operate and engage with services in order to create the conditions where their daughter could thrive was the primary question. Rather than the parents experiencing the offer of services as supportive engagement, it was experienced as an unnecessary, unwelcome, and probably a significant threat. Trust was non-existent and the predicted impact of that on B as a child was such that the parents in turn could not be trusted to provide the care she needed. From a psychosocial perspective, the evidence about parental capacity and competence in Re B can be explained as a failure of reflective functioning. The detail of the judgment identifies that the mother did seek help on numerous occasions, but the problems she perceived were seen by professionals to be, at best, a false construction of her difficulties. They were concerned about the consequence of these false beliefs on her daughter's well-being and development. The consequential impact on her daughter to trust, to work co-operatively, to learn, and to adapt might then be severe. Children need to directly experience the relationships that they have with their parents or carers as supportive and companionable (Simmonds, 2010) as they begin to engage in the world around them. It is essential that, as they increasingly explore the world of opportunity, they develop the mental capacities to enable them to engage with that personal and social world based on an increasing familiarity with the qualities outlined in the concept of reflective functioning. At the same time, children need to know that when the going gets tough, they can return to a reliable, safe haven of relationships where, whatever the nature of the problem, there is a sensitive, thoughtful, reassuring, and encouraging response, framed by the principles of reflective functioning. Whatever the placement type, or the legal framework that supports it, this issue is fundamental.

The theme of continuity and discontinuity is a powerful issue across all family placements, whatever the form of the legal order:

adoption, special guardianship, care orders or child arrangement orders. The involvement of the state and its capacity to act in removing children from their parents wrestles with the intention to be supportive and companionable, but with the real risk that it will be experienced as the state being dominating and expecting submission from the family. The consequences of this movement between the supportive–companionable and the dominant–submissive (Heard & Lake, 2009) can be confusing.

The beginning of this chapter described adoption and other placements emerging from a perspective where they were thought of as a new beginning for the child unencumbered by whatever had preceded it. As is now well known, information and knowledge about all the factors that resulted in an alternative form of family life created by the state are seen to be essential to the child—a right to know, a right to explore, a right to be consulted, and a right to be listened to. In fact, information about, and contact with, birth parents, siblings, or others is seen as increasingly significant in state-arranged family life although disputes about its benefits continue (Loxterkamp, 2009; Neil, 2010; Neil et al., 2014, 2015; Selwyn et al., 2015). Over this time, there has been a significant change in adoption in particular, with a move from understanding the structural arrangements for contact—who with, where, and when—to the concept of "communicative openness". Brodzinsky (2005) explains what it is that makes a difference: "the creation of an open, honest, non-defensive, and emotionally attuned family dialogue, not only about adoption related issues" and a willingness in that dialogue for family members

> to consider the meaning of adoption in their lives, to share that meaning with others, to explore adoption related issues in the context of family life, to acknowledge and support the child's dual connection to two families, and perhaps to facilitate contact between these two family systems in one form or another. (p. 149)

Although developed in relation to adoption, communicative openness is a concept that readily lends itself to all forms of family placement. As such, Brodzinsky is essentially describing a state of mind—how one thinks, feels, and talks about something that is emotionally charged. These thoughts and feelings do not easily lend themselves to resolution by rules or procedures and may be experienced in different ways by different people at different points in their lives. Communicative openness relies on those qualities identified in reflective functioning as well as a belief in, and the operation of, a supportive and companionable form of relating. It also means recognising the continuities and discontinuities in a child's life and those of her current parents or carers, as well as those that have played a part in the past. What has the child learnt, how has she adapted, and how does she experience herself in the intimate world of relating and relationships, whatever form her family placement takes?

What communicative openness cannot mean is an idealised version of the issues related to the placement of the child, the new family, or the birth family. The experiences and memories from the past, especially of poor, if not dangerous, care, abandonment, and loss, of the failure to establish forms of relating that engender epistemic trust, are likely to be significant issues for the child and new carers as they rebuild a foundation from which to build a new future. However, where there are campaigns supported by the media that portray adoption, in particular, as a conspiracy on the part of the state to remove children from parents who are "too slow" or "too poor", then this is likely to create a toxic mix. When this then appears to be supported by government targets and cash incentives, the question becomes: does this then result in local authorities being on a spree of child snatching to grasp the pots of gold on offer? As portrayed by the *Daily Mail*, it is a scary and sinister story. Yet, there are critical issues about the impact that this kind of story has on children placed by the state. What might they be asking themselves lying in bed at night—was I stolen by a group of thieving magpies organised by the state? What impact does this have on adoptive or foster families—was this child who was presented to me with a painful and disturbing history of abuse and neglect really removed from their birth family to meet my local authority's overspend?

While these headlines must be understood for what they are—the media at work—the issues they raise are complex although not in quite the way that the *Daily Mail* is trying to get at. Carers, whether adopters, foster carers, kinship carers, or others, children and birth families are confronted with a powerful and painful set of issues. Nobody is likely to be involved in this complex unravelling and reconstruction of family out of choice. Neither are they likely to have planned or anticipated that this was a pathway on which they would find themselves. Uncertainty and loss have already been identified as common and these might well be expressed with a sense of injustice, anxiety, and feelings that important aspects of life are out of control. The headlines indicate something of the sense of scandal and outrage that might be experienced by those directly caught up in trying to find a solution to the most painful of human circumstances—the need to re-create a family life for a child who, without state intervention, is in danger of never having that family life.

The process of rebuilding will inevitably mean establishing a positive sense of continuity—acknowledging in a meaningful way the significance of the past for the present—on beliefs, on thoughts and feelings, and on behaviour. But this will inevitably mean acknowledging the likelihood that discontinuities are a part of that experience as well: in one sense, a new beginning, in another, a significant break from the past. The impact of these daily reminders of discontinuities and dislocations can be unexpectedly disturbing. They have an impact on everybody. For carers, these discontinuities and dislocations will have been imported into their lives from elsewhere. For a grandparent carer, there will be the advantages of the continuity of family history and culture, but the discontinuity that directly results from one's own child not being able to care for the child that he or she brought into the world. For the child, there will be the discontinuity from inadequate care or the effects of maltreatment and also the continuity of the associated memories and experiences of this. Preferences and choices will play their part as well. Integrating continuities and discontinuities to build a new family life will be a continuous challenge, with some of the fears and anxieties that are generated along the way never finding expression in a tolerable way because they are too painful and threaten the integrity and safety of the individual and the family unit. Some might be expressed in an intolerable way and, indeed, threaten the integrity and safety of the individual child or the carer/parents or entire family (Selwyn et al., 2015). It is remarkable that ordinary people find the resources and resilience to manage these challenging and highly emotive issues creatively and positively and with determination and commitment, but it cannot be surprising that sometimes this is a real struggle.

It is the reason why support is so central to any placement. Support needs to be planned and made available from the point at which an alternative family life for the child is being considered and that it continues through family finding, to the legal order, and then beyond as a lifelong issue.

I recently resumed my discussion with my son about the issues of continuity and discontinuity as I sought his views about sharing the note at the beginning of this chapter. I wanted to know whether he felt comfortable with my plan in submitting for publication. In one sense, he was very pleased that I thought enough of these issues to actually put something in writing. At another, he used our conversation to express his frustration at the excessive demands on him by his current employer—he looked exhausted! "Yes, why did I become a chef?!" he said with a real sense of exasperation. It felt that there were significant questions in his mind about the impact and meaning of continuity and discontinuity. "Had a turning point been reached", I thought, "and are we about to embark on something unknown and completely new?"

Note

1. The government has published a new policy paper that seeks to address these questions—Department for Education (2016) Adoption: A Vision for Change, available from https://www.gov.uk/government/uploads/system/uploads/attachment_data/file/512826/Adoption_Policy_Paper_30_March_2016.pdf

References

Aber, L., Slade, A., Berger, B., Bresgi, I., & Kaplan, M. (1985). The parent development interview. Unpublished Protocol: City University of New York.

Bowlby, J. (Ed.) (1968). *Child Care and the Growth of Love* (2nd edn). Based by permission of the World Health Organization on the report Maternal care and mental health. London: Whitefriars Press.

Bowlby, J. (2005). *A Secure Base: Clinical Applications of Attachment Theory* (new edn). London: Routledge.

Brodzinsky, D. (2005). Reconceptualizing openness in adoption: implications for theory, research and practice. In: D. Brodzinsky & J. Palacios (Eds.), *Psychological Issues in Adoption*. London: Praeger.

Fonagy, P., & Allison, E. (2014). The role of mentalizing and epistemic trust in the therapeutic relationship. *Psychotherapy, 51*(3): 372.

Harris, P. (2006). *In Search of Belonging*. London: British Association for Adoption and Fostering.

Harris, P. (2008). *The Colours in Me: Writing and Poetry by Adopted Children and Young People*. London: British Association for Adoption and Fostering.

Harris, P. (2012). *Chosen: Living with Adoption*. London: British Association for Adoption and Fostering.

Heard, D., & Lake, B. (2009). *The Challenge of Attachment for Caregiving*. London: Karnac.

Howe, D., Feast, J., & Coster, D. (2003). *Adoption, Search and Reunion: The Long-term Experience of Adopted Adults*. London: British Association for Adoption and Fostering.

Koenig, M. A., & Harris, P. L. (2005). The role of social cognition in early trust. *Trends in Cognitive Sciences, 9*(10): 457–459.

Loxterkamp, L. (2009). Contact and truth: the unfolding predicament in adoption and fostering. *Clinical Child Psychology and Psychiatry, 14*(3): 423–435.

Neil, E., Beek, M., & Ward, E. (2014). *Contact after Adoption: A Longitudinal Study of Adopted Young People and their Adoptive Parents and Birth Relatives*. London: British Association for Adoption and Fostering.

Neil, E., Beek, M., & Ward, E. (2015). *Contact after Adoption – Summary Report – A longitudinal Study of Adopted Young People and their Adoptive Parents and Birth Relatives*. London: British Association for Adoption and Fostering.

Neil, E. C. (2010). *Supporting Post Adoption Contact in Complex Cases: Briefing Paper*. London: Department for Education.

Robertson, D. (2015). Blood-chilling scandal of the thousands of babies stolen by the State. *Dail Mail*. Accessed at: www.dailymail.co.uk/news/article-3098468/Blood-chilling-scandal-thousands-babies-stolen-State-TV-agony-aunt-Denise-Robertson-s-spent-years-investigating-says-s-monstrous-injustice-age.html - ixzz3bXahZLdB.

Rowe, J. (1983). *Fostering in the Eighties*. London: British Agencies for Adoption & Fostering.

Rowe, J. (1984). *Long-term Foster Care*. London: Batsford Academic & Educational in association with British Agencies for Adoption & Fostering.

Rowe, J., Hundleby, M., & Garnett, L. (1989). *Child Care Placements: Patterns and Outcomes*. London: British Agencies for Adoption and Fostering.

Selwyn, J., Wijedasa, D., & Meakings, S. (2015). *Beyond the Adoption Order: Challenges, Interventions and Adoption Disruption*. London: British Association for Adoption and Fostering.

Simmonds, J. (2010). Relating and relationships in supervision: supportive and companionable or dominant and submissive. In: G. Ruch, D. Turney, & A. Ward (Eds.), *Relationship Based Social Work: Getting to the Heart of Practice*. London: Jessica Kingsley.

Simmonds, J. (2012). Adoption: from the preservation of the moral order to the needs of the child. In: M. Davies (Ed.), *Social Work with Children and Families*. Basingstoke: Palgrave Macmillan.

Slade, A. (2005). Parental reflective functioning: an introduction. *Attachment & Human Development*, *7*(3): 269–281.

Sperber, D., Clément, F., Heintz, C., Mascaro, O., Mercier, H., Origgi, G., & Wilson, D. (2010). Epistemic vigilance. *Mind & Language*, *25*(4), 359–393.

Sroufe, L. A. (2005). *The Development of the Person: The Minnesota Study of Risk and Adaptation from Birth to Adulthood*. New York: Guilford Press.

Steele, H., Steele, M., & Busch, F. (2008). On the origins of reflective functioning. In: F. N. Busch (Ed.), *Mentalization: Theoretical Considerations, Research Findings, and Clinical Implications* (pp. 133–158). New York: The Analytic Press.

Triseliotis, J., Howe, D., Feast, J., & Kyle, F. (2005). *The Adoption Triangle Revisited: A Study of Adoption, Search and Reunion Experiences*. London: British Association for Adoption and Fostering.

CHAPTER TWO

Working with professional systems

Wendy Lobatto

Introduction

Children and young people coming into the care of the state are likely to have suffered painful and chronic experiences of deprivation, neglect, abuse, and complex trauma in their birth families which have played a part in shaping their neurophysiological and emotional development, as Graham Music goes on to discuss in the next chapter. Such children have had to adapt to the conditions in which they found themselves, to develop strategies and defences to enable them to survive. These children additionally now find themselves without an adequately functioning birth parental figure and their parenting needs are to be taken over by agencies of the state.

Parenting is a highly complex, multi-faceted, and emotionally involving task which is demanding for parents living in ordinary circumstances. Fostering children who have been hurt and damaged by the adults who should have been caring for and protecting them, and with whom there is no primal "blood" familial connection is an especially demanding task. Social workers are required to make quasi-parenting decisions in the midst of legal disputes, high caseloads, and organisational constraints of various kinds. Creating a good enough parenting team out of a group of paid professional workers requires a particular commitment and approach, especially when this parenting team has to work closely together within contexts of trauma and secondary trauma, profound organisational pressures, and the frequent replaying of trauma-induced organisational dynamics which militate against the provision of good, healthy, and integrated care.

In this chapter, I intend to look more closely at how to facilitate the creation of a functioning parenting team for children and young people in care. First, I look at supporting foster carers, then at working alongside social workers, and, finally, at linking the professional network in order to enhance the care given to the children and young people. I have worked within Child and Adolescent Mental Health Services for Looked After Children for a number of years, and currently manage a multi-disciplinary team integrating therapeutic approaches that provides universal psychological health screening and assessment service for looked-after children, commissioned by an inner city local authority.

My grateful thanks go towards the carers, social workers, children, and adults who have worked alongside us. All the case examples that follow are composites, although many readers working in this field will, I expect, recognise the issues that they illustrate. My thanks, too, to my team, the members of which are the context in which these approaches have been developed and provide the creativity, commitment, and energy that is needed to make a positive difference to the lives of children and young people.

Working with the inner world of the child and supporting the foster carer

Children and young people, when they arrive in care, are likely to be preoccupied with their birth family, their fear and anxiety about its collapse, confusion about what might happen next alongside the emotional and developmental particularities that living and growing in that birth family have created. They are likely to be intimately connected to their birth parent or parents and birth familial context, in complex and charged ways, and to bring their entire history, experience, and expectations to the new relationship with their current carers.

In her classic paper, Henry (1974) describes a psychotherapeutic process with a fourteen-year-old boy, Martin, who had been placed in residential care when he was two months old, who had then endured a number of failed placements, the death of his birth mother, and a suicide attempt at the age of eleven. She writes about his "double deprivation",

> firstly the one inflicted upon him by external circumstances of which he had no control whatsoever, second the deprivation derived from internal sources: from his crippling defences and from the quality of his internal objects which provided him with so little support as to make him an orphan inwardly as well as outwardly. (p. 16)

Henry's description of Martin is extreme and disturbing to read, and yet she draws attention to the difficulties in parenting children who have been both deprived by the conditions of their early lives and then, as a consequence, by their inability to receive the ordinary love and care that can be provided by ordinary loving parents, this being the second deprivation.

Furthermore, ordinary loving parents bring their own history of relationships, needs, and vulnerabilities to the parenting relationship. As Rustin writes,

> Once humans get close to each other, their internal worlds are in dynamic relation to each other. All of the earlier experiences of each member of a significant intimate relationship . . . contribute to the landscape of the new relationship. (Rustin, 1999, p. 55)

So, foster carers are asked to parent a child or children who continue to exist in living, internal, concealed relationships with their significant parental figures. This relationship is represented in Figure 2.1.

The foster carer provides the first layer of parenting and everyday care to children and young people in the care system. Both the literature and clinical practice offer multiple examples of foster carers struggling to care for children because they

> are faced with a baffling array of destructive behaviours—lying, stealing, hitting, soiling, wetting, hurting pets, hoarding food, absconding—to name just a few . . . foster carers can quickly become disillusioned, despairing and debilitated by the situation in which they find themselves. (Caw, 2014, p. 98)

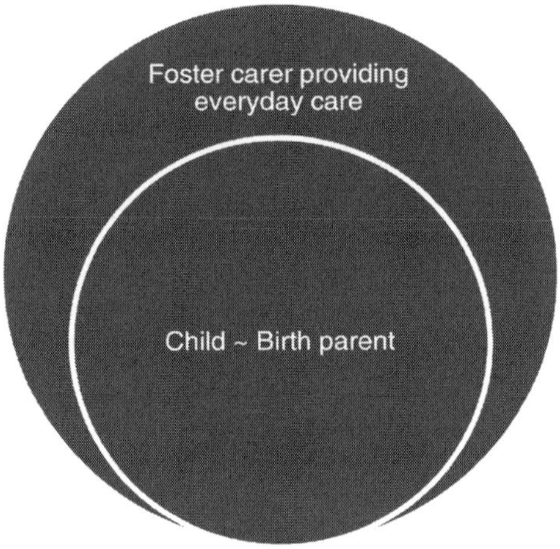

Figure 2.1. The external relationships between foster carers and children and the internal, concealed relationships between children and their birth parents).

Working to support carers to provide high quality everyday parenting is, then, the first layer of intervention with professional systems.

In Chapter Four, Sara Barratt describes many of the issues and approaches that are relevant to the task of supporting foster carers from a CAMHS perspective, and there are various other models and descriptions. Caw (2014) describes the "team parenting" approach to supporting foster carers within a specialist fostering agency. She describes the three areas of support, knowledge, and skills that are required. First, fostering support workers need to be able to listen, to hear in an open and non-judgemental way, to provide a containing and soothing space for the carer to air their worries, and to accept their highly aroused and intense emotional states. Over time, this relationship offers a "secure attachment" for the carer (Bowlby, 1979) in which "being able to reflect on the struggles being presented in a coherent and meaningful way allows . . . the foster carer to assume a meta-perspective to the difficulties in which they can otherwise feel embroiled" (Caw, 2014, p. 101). Second, the fostering worker offers a psycho-educational perspective in which they teach, and think with, the foster carers about attachment theory, projective identification, and findings from neuroscience in relation to complex trauma. These theories offer a way of making sense of the foster carer's experience of their foster child, allowing empathy with that child's experience and offering an understanding of the way to go on. Third, the fostering worker teaches the three skills that are components of therapeutic parenting: attunement, reflective function, and self-regulation/affect regulation. Maintaining these stances on a twenty-four-hour basis in one's own home is a demanding task and one that requires commitment, maturity, and abundant support and consultation.

In our service, we offer another kind of shorter-term foster carer support for those carers who are not receiving ongoing support from a CAMHS team or a fostering support agency. This support is based on joint observation of the child's play over about six sessions. It is particularly suited to working with younger children who are still able to communicate and express their preoccupations and experiences through the medium of play. This case example illustrates some of the profoundly difficult dynamics that can be enacted in relationships between traumatised children and their carers, and also how a supportive therapeutic relationship, even briefly, can make a significant difference to the care that well-meaning and good-hearted adults can offer.

Two-year-old Shelley came into care with her older sister, five-year-old Anna, after experiencing chronic neglect and abuse in their mother's care. Their mother was a refugee from a war-torn African country and struggled with severe depression and ongoing substance abuse problems within the context of long-term family relationship difficulties and suicide.

In the first few weeks of the foster placement, their foster carer, Barbara, reported that at least once a day Shelley had episodes when she hit and punched her sister. These attacks felt quite forceful and when she was restrained, she began to hit or kick the carer instead. It took several months before the attacks lessened and for Shelley to be able to accept comfort or affection from Barbara. Shelley often disrupted interactions between Barbara and Anna but tended to reject Barbara's attention when it was offered. In common with many looked-after children, Shelley lacked stranger awareness.

We started to work with the foster carer after the children had been with her for about six months. Other professionals had described her as "cold and rejecting" towards the girls. We can only imagine how difficult that situation was for a single carer to manage for all those months. On her first home visit, the therapist, my colleague, observed that the carer did not respond when Shelley was insisting on being lifted on to her lap,

> although she was rueful in describing how Shelley had made a good start at nursery, not showing any difficulties in separating from her. She seemed quite brittle and close to the end of her tether, explaining that she was not receiving enough support from her agency, and was finding Shelley really demanding. She was reluctant to commit to offering any regular one-to-one time with Shelley, as she would not want to disappoint her or let her down if she could not keep it going. When it was tidy-up time, Shelley became fractious and tearful, and Barbara was unable to distract or soothe her and, in fact, perhaps escalated the situation by telling her several times in a loud voice not to throw things. The therapist found herself comforting Shelley, who then approached Barbara and touched her face, naming the parts, but Barbara was unable to respond with a cuddle or soothing words. It seemed as though things had become so difficult that Shelley had to manage her own moods and then approach Barbara in a way that would be acceptable to her. The therapist left with a feeling of lostness and bleakness.

Although this account so far also makes for bleak reading, it is important to remember that these observations took place within a particular context. The children had been placed with Barbara on an emergency basis after they were discovered at home by themselves, and continued to live with her all these months later. She was traditionally a respite carer for young people, and did not receive psychological support from her fostering agency. As a single carer with little support, she might have picked up on the children's trauma and be showing signs of "secondary trauma" herself. She agreed to engage in a brief support intervention with the therapist, and they met on five occasions, during which they watched Shelley play. They discussed how her communications and her experiences with her mother might have affected her relationships now. In between sessions, the therapist and Barbara talked on the phone and made links with Shelley's early history and relationship patterns.

> In the first session, Shelley came across as a sturdy toddler, warmly and attractively dressed with a pretty hairstyle. She appeared rather self-sufficient and it was hard to believe she was only two years old. She played readily with the toys in the playroom, mostly with a serious and, at times, sombre facial expression. The therapist observed her to smile only once, when Barbara sang a song with her. In this moment, her whole body seemed to relax and she looked more her age.

The therapist heard that in their foster home Shelley had begun to play with a baby doll, sometimes insisting that Barbara hold it while Shelley watched. It seemed important for Shelley to be able to see Barbara's predictable safe response over and over again. Barbara also described the fighting between the sisters and the level of rivalry between them that felt stressful to manage. They thought together about the neglect both children were subjected to, and how Shelley must have been often hungry, frightened, or in discomfort, with no one to reliably help her manage her feelings. Under the influence of both substances and severe depression, their mother is likely to have responded to Shelley in ways that were unpredictable and, at times, frightening. Thinking about these experiences allowed Barbara to make links with Shelley's current behaviour.

The therapist heard that as Shelley became used to mealtime and bedtime routines, there began to be times when she regressed and crawled and vocalised like a baby. She explained that she thought Shelley might have powerful experiences of infantile needs that were unmet in her first months of life. These were now being understood and met with a response. These moments of regression can be opportunities to catch up on missed early experiences and she advised Barbara to "think younger" and respond to Shelley as to a younger child at these times.

Barbara was able to observe and take an interest in Shelley's play. During the sessions, they were able to see a pattern of Shelley being able to accept comfort and nurture in indirect ways, for example, as represented by the baby doll. Unlike a typically developing child with a secure attachment, Shelley might find direct attention threatening because, in the past, her mother's responses might have been unpredictable and, of course, her big five-year-old sister could not provide her with the parenting she needed.

The therapist and carer also discussed how quickly something might feel "too much" for Shelley. Interacting with her needs had to be done in a particularly sensitive way. There were many instances of Shelley rejecting help from Barbara, while, at the same time, seeming to need affection and physical closeness. As the sessions continued, it was encouraging that Shelley began to seek and accept more closeness with Barbara, sometimes sitting in her lap and sometimes playing out scenes like a bedtime routine with increasingly lively smiles and real sense of enjoyment. There seemed to be signs of a developing trust and intimacy between them.

Barbara described having felt isolated while trying to establish relationships and routines with Shelley and Anna. In the first weeks there had been times when Shelley had "iced her out" or suddenly scratched her, behaving like an older child and leaving Barbara feeling as though there was nothing she could do to help. These emotional patterns or communications are characteristic of children with insecure or disorganised attachments. These attachment patterns, established in the first months of life, make it difficult for children to elicit or accept the nurturing care they greatly need (the "crippling defences" referred to as Henry's "double deprivation"). It is important to address these ways of relating as soon as possible so that the child's psychological needs for comfort, trust, intimacy, and interaction can be met.

This close attention to the child's behaviours, responses, and feelings and the attempt to make sense of them in terms of his or her experiences can help carers appreciate the child's position and deal with challenging situations. Carers who receive the right kind of support are clearly more able to continue to provide sensitive, attuned, and loving care to children who can be difficult to care for, and, therefore, children and young people are less likely to experience further placement disruption and be exposed to another set of damaging relational breaks and rejections. Offering support to foster carers is, then, the first level of supporting the parenting function for looked-after children. The next level is working with the social worker, who has an important decision-making function in planning for the present and the future direction of children's lives.

Enhancing thoughtful decision-making: consulting to social workers

The foster carer looks after a child within a complex context of legal decision-making, social work care planning, and ongoing birth family contact, where many agencies are likely to be involved and all of them dealing with painful and disturbing family situations. The social worker is the key professional in terms of steering that child's life through the difficult and unstable current situation in order to create safety, stability, predictability, and a loving family context. Most social workers work alone with these situations, with more or less organisational support. This, then, is the next layer of the parenting function (illustrated in Figure 2.2) that needs support in order to be effective.

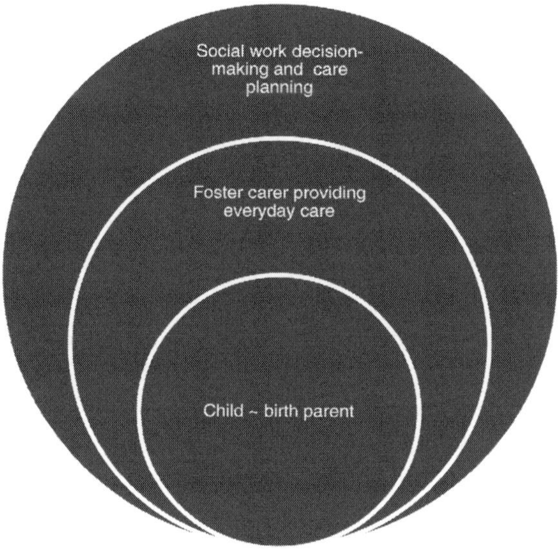

Figure 2.2. The second layer of the parenting function.

We offer individual consultations to our colleagues to support them in taking account of the child or young person's experience in performing their role. Often, social workers are preoccupied with co-ordinating a number of different factors, including the current situation and difficulties, the limitation on resources, the needs of the birth parent and the legal process, and organisational pressures to "get it right". Consultation meetings allow for a reflective space, where the history and experience of the child in his family can be considered and their context brought into view, which can begin to allow for the possibility of meaning to emerge and can then guide the way ahead. This approach has a number of parallels with the systemic reflection advocated by Professor Munroe as a good practice requirement for social workers (Munroe, 2011).

Eleven-year-old Jasmine and her younger brother Benny, aged five, had recently been moved to an agency emergency respite placement after their agency foster home had disrupted after five years. The children had come into care after experiencing chronic neglect and domestic violence in their birth family; their mother had learning difficulties and both children had some developmental delay. Jasmine had learning difficulties and was of small stature. Benny had severe physical and learning needs.

> Shortly after they came into care, their mother had moved away and there had been no contact with her for some years. The new Independent Reviewing Officer, working to best practice guidelines, was keen to reinstate contact and so had succeeded in reaching the mother and contact had been resumed during the summer that Jasmine finished at primary school. There was no record on the local authority files of how this contact had gone and there had been three social workers in the intervening period. At around the same time as this contact had occurred, Jasmine made an allegation that the carers had hit her. These allegations were investigated and shown to be well founded. It seemed possible that the carers had been largely focused on the profound physical needs of the younger child and had little time or warmth for Jasmine. The children were removed immediately from this placement and placed with respite carers. Jasmine was showing signs of high anxiety, was refusing to attend school or be apart from her new carer for any length of time, and was showing her distress in violent and destructive behaviours in the new foster home. She was refusing to wash and this did not seem possible to tackle, since the fostering agency prohibited the carer being in the bathroom with her to protect the carer from any further allegations. She "looked like an angel" but was described as "violent" and controlling towards her brother. The new carer was coping well but the social worker was rightly concerned at the possibility of another disruption. The local authority was reluctant to agree further permanency arrangements with a private fostering agency carer due to its relatively high cost.

Thinking about this upsetting history and current situation, we attempted to put ourselves into Jasmine's shoes. We imagined that she felt responsible for the welfare of her brother and that it was up to her to control his behaviour to safeguard their current placement. At the same time, her experience might have been that adults who looked after her were prepared to let go of her very easily. Her mother had disappeared and then her foster carers had disappeared as well. Her wish to be looked after might have coincided with a deep sense of powerlessness that she could succeed in realising this wish and this is likely to have created a profound sense of being out of control and in despair. Small wonder, then, that she was so adamant that she would not be separated from her current carer, to the extent that she refused to go to school without the carer staying with her all day. Furthermore, she was in Year 7, adjusting to a large and complex institution where her need for learning support and her developmental delay might render her vulnerable and uneasy.

Attempting to appreciate Jasmine's experience led us to formulate some child-centred direction. First, it was clear that Jasmine was highly anxious and aroused and it seemed clear that she needed to be able to relax and feel safe. The carers were apparently willing to provide a long-term home for the children and were seen as able to provide appropriately for the children's differing needs. Jasmine was still commuting to the school that had been selected as local to her previous foster home and this might have contributed to her sense of instability and perhaps to her anxiety that she would have to go back when she had disrupted/"rejected" the placement by "telling" on her carers. It was important to focus on re-creating permanency again at this point, and, if with these carers, then a move to a local school.

The children's need for psychological continuity had been disrupted again by this precipitous move with no permitted contact with the previous carers although they were requesting it. Although the agencies were nervous about the consequences of enabling contact with carers who were seen to have failed the children, it was curious that no one had picked up their need for ongoing contact with the family who had cared for them for the majority of their lives. At the same time, there was a continuing move to re-engage the birth mother for another contact without any impetus from her to do so. We agreed it would be helpful to consider how to arrange contact with both the birth mother and the previous foster carers. We can only speculate how Jasmine experienced these breaks in relationship, and we can imagine that she felt guilty and immensely powerful to have got rid of all these adults. We imagined it would be reparative for her to re-establish contact and be helped to understand that it was not her fault that these disruptions had occurred.

So, by "putting our heads together", the social worker was able to formulate some ideas to attempt to avoid drift and secure permanency for these children, to think with others about the most child-centred way of re-establishing contact in order to make links for the children between their past and present and lessen Jasmine's anxiety about the extent of her destructive power, to ensure that the current carer was receiving helpful and supportive consultation from their agency (as discussed above), and, finally, to consider a CAMHS referral for the children once their situation was clarified.

This situation, aspects of which will be familiar to many professionals working with looked-after children, could be an example of how our systems can lose sight of the child when operating under certain conditions. Each party had its own personal and organisational agendas; thinking about each party's position can help us gain a richer understanding of the dilemmas faced by the social worker, and is one aspect of how systemic theory can illuminate this field of work.

So, from the very scarce information presented above, we might conjecture the following, which might help us think about the dilemmas presented to social workers in these situations.

Let us imagine that Jasmine's preoccupation was in getting herself and her brother looked after in a reasonable way while staying loyal in her mind to her birth family, so maybe she was relieved not to have to get too close to another mother figure, which might feel disloyal. At the same time, she needs to feel very much in control because adults cannot be trusted and, therefore, everything is up to her.

The previous carers, where the female carer came from a nursing background, might have been organised by the need to provide loving care to the younger disabled boy, and may not have given the same level of care to the older child who appeared to function better. In fact, if Jasmine did hold herself away from this family as an attempt to stay loyal to the birth mother, this might have made it hard for them to know how to approach her and habits of little or harsh interaction might have developed over time between them.

The fostering agency are keen to provide high quality childcare at the same time as being commercially organised by the importance of retaining the block contract with the local authority and the need to preserve their reputation. The perceived "failure" of the initial placement might have been "embarrassing" for the agency and there could have been a need to expel the not-good-enough carers and to work hard to avoid any formal sanctions by turning away from them.

The new carers are likely to have known about the "failure" of the previous placement in their agency, and might have been captured by the agency preoccupation with offering something better to the children this time. They might be working hard to show that they can manage these children's significant differential needs but the description of Jasmine's anxiety makes us wonder how anyone could manage this situation over the longer term.

The social work management are preoccupied with cost in the current ongoing stringent financial conditions in the public sector, and reluctant to agree expensive independent agency permanency carers if there are "equivalent" carers in-house. They might wish to stall decision-making until all in-house options have been explored. Despite the pressures on costs, the senior management are likely to be concerned about the formal agency operations and attempt to ensure that the letter of the law is followed in decision-making processes.

The birth mother might have felt that she has so damaged her children—the younger being born with such significant needs—that she might feel the need to stay away so as to harm them less, or she might have felt so intimidated and blamed by the legal process and by her own failures of care that she cannot bear to maintain the occasional contact which was granted. The IRO, trying to do her job and mindful of the needs of children to have ongoing contact with birth parents, has been pressing for this contact to be reinstated.

The social worker, in trying to make sense of the current situation and decide what is best in the children's interests, is faced with a complex array of needs, pressures, and constraints, as illustrated in Figure 2.3. The social worker is required to juggle the conflicting needs of all these players and in such circumstances, it can be challenging to keep the needs of the child in view. We have found that offering a reflective space, focussing on these unique children's needs and attempting to appreciate their experience is one way to find a path through the confusion.

As part of a recent service evaluation (Kanfizer, 2014), a researcher collected feedback from social workers and foster carers about their experience of consultation sessions. Respondents described feeling "listened to", the reassurance of "someone else seeing what I have been seeing" (foster carer), and receiving "encouragement" (foster carer). The sessions seem to provide an opportunity to formulate and develop a psychological understanding of the child through historical events: "[it was useful] looking at the children's needs and presentation in the context of life events" (social worker) and "I found the exploration of the client's past and issues very useful" (social worker). In addition, some reported it helpful thinking about systemic elements: "[it is useful] going through the family history—genogram" (social worker) and "very good advice and detailed analysis of the relationship between foster family and the children" (foster carer), as

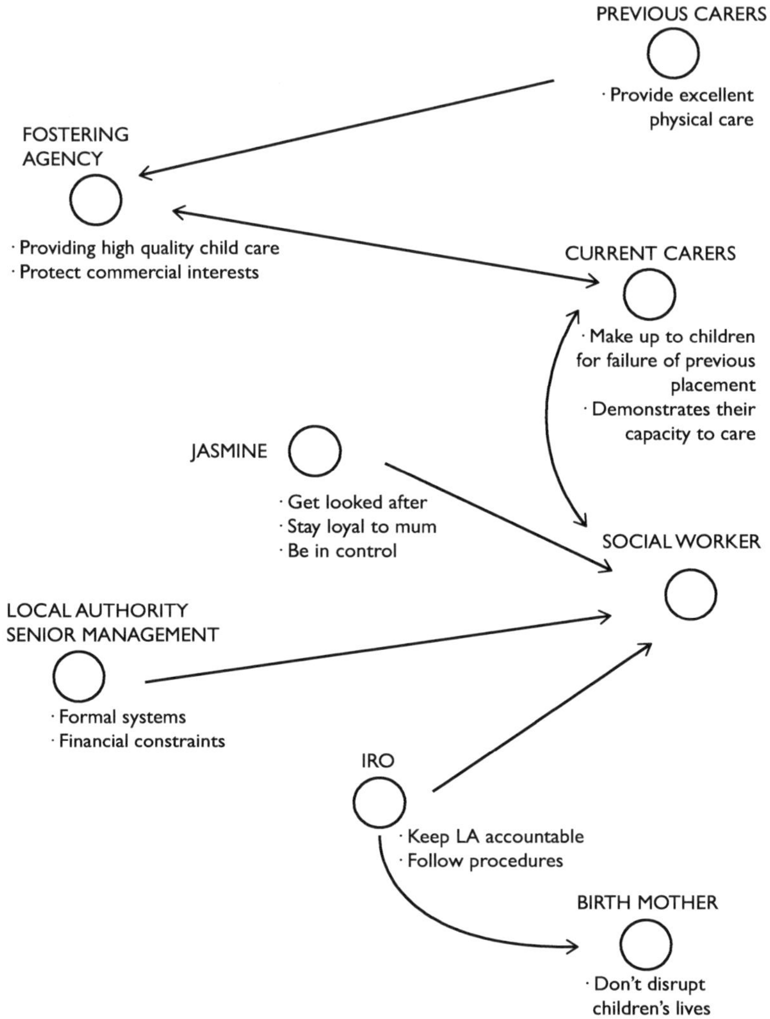

Figure 2.3. A representation of the pressures on the social worker in Jasmine's case.

well as specific theoretical components: "[it is useful] discussing child development as related to x".

The researcher commented that

> the sessions seem to offer valuable reflective space that extends social workers' clinical supervision: "I think about the case a bit more in

depth from a different angle . . . it looks into the case more holistically and it reminds you why you work with this child in the first place" (social worker).

The clinician's ability to contain the social worker's concerns were noted: "it's like a therapeutic session, we can offload and they provide a good sounding board" (social worker). For some this supports how they work with children: "it provides me with a different perspective about the case so it does inform how I work" (social worker). (p. 14)

As we have seen, then, supporting the social worker and the foster carer in performing their parenting function can help create more sensitive, attuned, and child-focused care. The next level of support required is in collating the various aspects of the parenting role by bringing together the people in child-focused network meetings. This, then, is the next level of intervention with professional systems.

Linking aspects of the parenting function: child-focused network meetings

For those of us parenting our own birth children, it is generally helpful to have the perspective of the other parent, or, if they are not available, other trusted members of the child's parenting network: a grandparent, a friend or partner of the parent, or a worker. We discuss the child's progress, plan for immediate arrangements and longer-term decisions, enjoy thinking about them together, and feel supported in our role. When the state parents a child, the various parenting functions are specialised and split off from each other. The person who feeds and clothes and tends to them is not the same person who makes decisions about where they will live or whether they can sleep over at a friend's house after school, and neither is it the same person who remembers their birth or with whom they share a genetic inheritance. Thus, it is especially important to provide opportunities for the different people/aspects of the parenting function to come together to form a parenting team (see Figure 2.4). The 2007 White Paper, *Care Matters: Time for Change* (Department for Education and Skills (DfES)) urges effective multi-agency working for looked-after children.

However, another significant difference between ordinary parenting and parenting children in the care of the state is the way in which

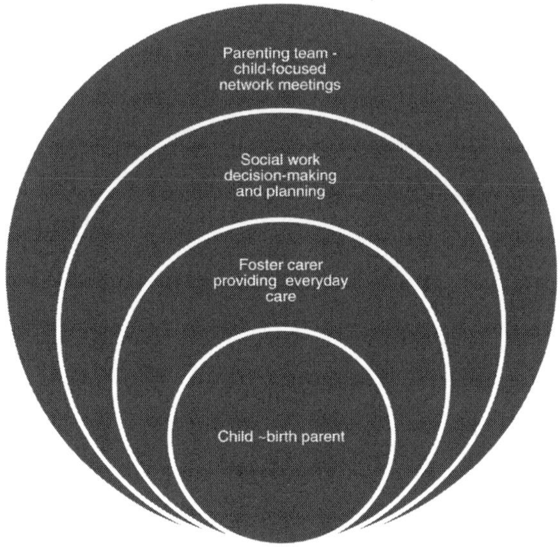

Figure 2.4. A parenting team for a looked-after child.

the experiences of children are communicated, enacted, and re-enacted throughout the system. Conway (2009) uses the psychoanalytic concepts of splitting and projection to explain why the complex systems around looked-after children can develop "fault lines" which damage our best intentions to work together. She explains that children who have had poor care in infancy develop fragmented inner worlds which they struggle unconsciously to communicate through the processes of splitting (in which the world is separated into separate, often hostile groups), and projection (which fills up others with the powerful feelings that cannot be borne). If we think back to Barbara's experience of feeling "iced out" and helpless in her interaction with Shelley, we see an example of the operations of projection, and if we consider the way the system positioned Jasmine and Benny's former carers as bad while the new carers were seen as good, we may recognise the operations of splitting. Conway holds that the operation of these dynamics can be fatal for effective communication within professional systems, and this means that "the child's real need for a parental couple who can put their heads together and think about his needs is lost" (p. 26). Emanuel (2002) describes this process as "triple deprivation", extending Henry's idea of "double deprivation" discussed earlier to include the deprivation that can be wrought on children's lives by the re-enactment of these processes within the systems designed to care for these vulnerable children. Emanuel (2002) suggests that one way in which these disturbing feelings find expression in organisational life is when social workers become paralysed by the often conflicting demands and feelings of parents and children, as well as by the conflicting demands of their managers, as we saw illustrated in the case of Jasmine and Benny above.

Through a clinical research study of therapeutic observation of a child in foster care, Wakelyn (2011) goes on to distinguish further patterns of organisational functioning that can be seen over time in the carefully observed interactions around children in care. Experiences of emotional connectedness and containment are denoted as "matrix" functioning. Experiences of confusion, pressure, and fragmentation are described as "tornado" functioning, while those of dissociation are called "machine" functioning, and drift or provisionality are identified as "limbo" functioning. Matrix functioning is thought of as a healthy developmental mode for the organisation, whereas tornado, machine, and limbo are described as trauma-driven organisational functioning.

So, if we consider the case examples discussed so far, we might notice matrix functioning occurring in the linking conversations made by Barbara, Shelley's foster carer, and the therapist. An example of tornado functioning might be the sudden removal of Jasmine and Benny from their permanent foster placement after Jasmine's allegations of physical abuse appeared to have been substantiated, but without arranging a proper goodbye or making arrangements for contact. An example of machine functioning might be the search for an "equivalent" in-house carer for Jasmine and Benny, despite their desperate attachment to their new, but costly, agency carer, as though relationships are interchangeable and it does not matter which adult is looking after which child.

Moving from the psychoanalytic to the systemic domain, an alternative language for understanding and describing these processes comes from Seikkula and Arnkil (2006), who describe their practice of convening "open dialogue" and other types of meetings for working with people suffering with psychosis and extreme mental ill health

> When professionals who are in contact with complex interaction patterns through their client/patient relations meet to discuss cases, it

> is not exceptional that the experienced interaction is carried over to the relations between professionals. A central dimension in this process is identification . . . and it is not a professional flaw. However it can produce peculiar processes in network sessions, even deadlocks. (p. 44)

A central assumption here is the systemic notion of isomorphism, the idea that if they connect, different levels of a system will co-evolve and become alike (Maturana & Varela, 1980). The core process at work is the "contagion of emotions" (Arnkil & Eriksson, 1995). In order to understand one another, we identify with the other, we sense and feel each other's emotions, either with or without an accompanying internal dialogue. By doing this, we can understand what direction the interaction is taking and orientate ourselves in the relationship. It is, therefore, no surprise to find these emotions accompanying us into discussions with colleagues or thinking about the child's situation. "Network meetings that deal with considerable worries are particularly prone to isomorphic processes . . . meetings that discuss emotionally touching, worrying, professionally difficult situations without panacea are particularly charged . . ." (Arnkil & Eriksson, 1995, p. 46).

Both the psychoanalytic and the systemic frameworks thus offer theories to help us begin to understand the complex operations that create systemic tensions. In order to support the professional system, we need to appreciate and be mindful of these dynamics in order that we can achieve a matrix in a developmentally functioning organisational form rather than a trauma-driven one.

> Fourteen-year-old Janice had recently been placed with a single carer after leaving her previous foster placement at the same time that her older sister, May, had left for university. Janice remained at a distance from her new carer and was cutting herself, and her foster carer felt anxious about how to help her. The social worker, unusually, had known the two children for a number of years. She had taken them into care when they were younger, and returned them home after a number of professionals recommended rehabilitation. It was not until May disclosed sexual abuse from a friend of her mother's that the children were removed again when she was fourteen and Janice was nine.
>
> The children had progressed well educationally with the foster carer but there were concerns about Janice's care. The foster carer's grown-up son was hostile towards her, and she was punished excessively. However,

the carer was very loving and proud of May and so the children remained in this placement with a planned move for Janice when May left the foster home.

Janice was now struggling in school and her teachers were concerned about her unco-operative attitude and her academic performance slipping. She had few friendships, although she was friendly with one girl, another vulnerable child. She now lived at some distance from school and it was difficult for her to organise a social life with other young people there.

Janice had had only occasional contact with May since she had moved. She kept up contact with her mother, who was keen to be linked with her youngest child, whereas May had stopped contact after the sexual abuse and seemed to have put her mother far from her mind.

Dialogical approach

We agreed to offer a child-focused network meeting to support the parenting function for this vulnerable and troubled young person. Our approach is derived from a social constructionist stance, which holds that our experience of social reality is constructed between us through the language that we agree to use together. This approach, thus, "positions us to view therapeutic process as a conversation or dialogue" (McNamee, 2005, p. 78). The emphasis is on co-ordination of meanings rather than on agreeing one shared meaning. This approach has been extensively used in Finland by Seikkula and colleagues (Seikkula, 2011; Seikkula & Arnkil, 2006) in their development of the practice of dialogical meetings. The aim of these is not

> unanimous understanding of the problem as the basis of a plan for action. The point of departure is, on the contrary, that each person has his/her own specific view on the matter. It is important to try to understand each point of view. The new understanding is created at the boundary of the parties, as no one person's point of view takes precedence as the single and correct definition. (Seikkula & Arnkil, 2006, p. 91)

So, our meetings are predicated on the assumption that everyone present has a valuable perspective that, if placed alongside the other perspectives, might thicken and enrich our understanding of the child's situation.

In practice, we invite and welcome all participants into a comfortable and receptive meeting space with tea and biscuits. We hope that this approach will incline people towards taking a more active stance in the meeting rather than acting as passive onlookers. We have already allocated the role of conductor to a person not closely involved in resolving the live dilemmas who can facilitate the presence of all the voices in the room. Issues of who feels entitled to speak in professional meetings are outside the scope of this chapter, but the conductor remains mindful of allowing all voices and perspectives. We collect the hopes of all participants for the outcome of the meeting. The conductor then moves the meeting through its phases and holds the time so that it feels like a safe space for the participants.

We invite those people who have frequent contact with the child in their day-to-day life. In Janice's case, this included her social worker, her new carer, the supervising social worker, the SENCO and Head of Year at her school. Those people are invited both in their professional roles and as living human beings who are touched in some ways by the child we wish to care for. As Seikkula and Arnkil put it, "understanding emerges between individuals, not between institutions" (2006, p. 90). The hope is to create something more than a cognitive process, but an embodied emotional experience. By experiencing this together, groups of professionals can become more than the sum of their parts and can reach closer to being a parenting team.

We do not generally invite the child or young person to attend, on the grounds that children are not necessarily expected to be present when their parents or carers are discussing them and that there are things the adults need to sort out together. Nevertheless, we try to centre the child's perspective throughout the meeting, as we would if we were discussing our birth children. We like to invite the birth parents if they are involved and supportive of their child's emotional well-being but, unfortunately, the non-consensual statutory processes of the care system (see Chapter One) often leave them positioned at some distance from the adult networks caring for their child.

Importance of context and history

In these meetings, we offer the possibility of creating rich meanings together. When workers become isolated and affected by trauma-driven organisational functioning, it is easy to lose track of the idea that sense can be made of our concerns. So, we introduce a child-centred perspective via the introduction of a family tree at the outset of the meeting, gathering together the child's history from the participants. In Janice's case, we heard about her mother's abusive childhood and string of violent, substance-abusing male partners. We imagined what it might have been like for the girls to live in this household, what it might have been like for them when they spent a considerable period in care as younger children, and then what it was like when they returned home to their mother. What did May have to go through to disclose the sexual abuse to the teacher as she did? How might have that affected the relationship between the girls? How did their different decisions about contact with their mother affect them and their relationship with each other?

We knew that this little family had been through a life transition recently. Both Janice and May had left home, in different ways. How did Janice cope with the loss of her sister, who might have protected and mothered her all her life? What did this new relationship with a new carer mean to her? What sense had she made of her relationship with the old, now lost, carer? As we talk and think together, with each contributing their unique perspective and understanding, new levels of comprehension begin to dawn. No longer is this just a child creating anxiety for professionals because of her worrying and inexplicable behaviour; this is now a child who has survived and endured and is struggling to cope with the new, uncertain landscape.

Managing trauma-driven organisational processes

As we speak and listen to each other, various emotional processes begin to surface. The social worker felt protective of the previous carer, as she had been influential in the decision to leave the girls there despite the mixed reports about their relationship with the foster family. She was highly concerned about Janice, as she might have worried that she had "sacrificed" her needs for the good of her sister, who did so well in that placement. She bristled when the supervising worker mentioned "favouritism". In fact, she retorted, the mother had always shown favouritism towards the younger child. She had treated May like a co-parent, and also as a sexual stand-in. The level of emotional heat generated over the topic of which child was the favourite and which had needed protection more alerted us to the possible operation of trauma-driven emotional processes. The supervising worker wished to safeguard the new carer as the good carer and she clearly viewed the old placement as inadequate and damaging. It was important for the conductor of the meeting to make space to allow and hear these different views clearly and without judgement and appreciate that all parties had been trying to do their best in an impossibly difficult situation for children with different needs.

Generating plans

As we tracked the various strands of development and identity which we imagined Janice might have been experiencing through all these complex events, the carer began to acquire a sense of her need to be treated as a younger child. Initially, she had complained that her bed slats were broken, but later she began to wonder whether Janice needed to jump on her bed as though she were a much younger child, as though moving to her home and losing the presence of her sister had almost given her a moment to start again with her development. At the same time, listening to the social worker's account of poor experiences in her former foster home sensitised her to the level of fear and uncertainty that Janice might be feeling, wondering whether it would be the same this time and perhaps feeling the need to protect herself from having too high expectations of what the carer could provide for her. She resolved to use the support available from the supervising worker to look at providing a more therapeutic approach to this big, but small, fourteen-year-old.

The education staff were stunned to hear of all these events, coming to appreciate that the sulky, isolated young woman who had been vaguely troubling them had lived through profound changes over the past months, and they determined to offer her more pastoral support and space at school.

The social worker sounded relieved that the team was pulling together around Janice, realising that May was a tremendously significant person and role model to Janice and that she needed to think about including her in meetings even though she was barely an adult herself.

Reflecting processes

The importance of separating the talking position from the listening position enables people to really hear each other and to really feel heard when it is their turn to talk. This allows space to think new thoughts and to reach towards new, richer meanings. We always finish the meeting with a series of reflections from each participant about their experience of the process of the conversation. Invariably, participants express their feelings about the usefulness of meeting to talk like this, their ability to remain hopeful or not, their gratitude that they are not in this alone. For these moments, and perhaps for some time to come, this group of professionals have pulled together to act as an integrated parenting team.

Support from wider society

As I hope to have shown, parenting vulnerable children who have been through shocking and extreme early lives is complex and demanding. The care system is engaged in different aspects of the parenting function, and each aspect needs to be supported if children are to be able to recover and grow in healthy ways, either with or without further therapeutic intervention.

Civil society can and does support us in this task. The creation of dedicated looked-after children's CAMHS teams, therapeutic fostering agencies, and assessment services like ours are all able to support the care system in various ways. Providing extra resources for looked-after children in education via the pupil premium and councillors taking seriously their role as "corporate parents" are other aspects of this social endeavour (see Figure 2.5).

We know that vulnerable children will always be present in our society. These children deserve loving and devoted parenting as much as any child and there are foster carers, social workers, and support staff who wish to be able to provide this to the children they are caring for. With support and consultation offered in the right way and at the right time, we can support these colleagues to provide as much as they can to give these children the best chance of living fruitful and productive lives.

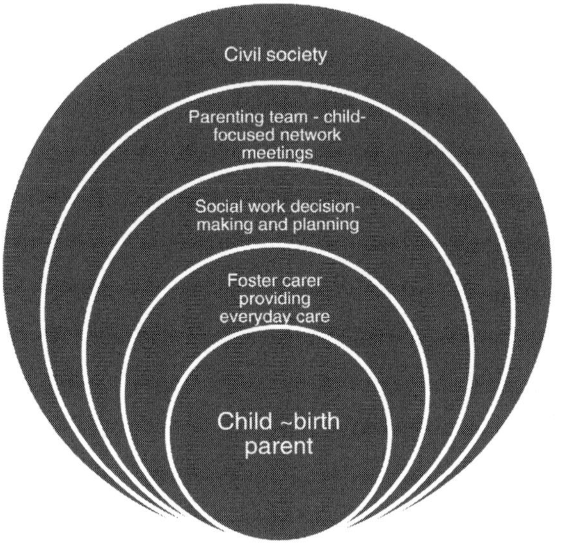

Figure 2.5. The wider society incorporated into the care system.

References

Arnkil, T., & Ericksson, E. (1995). Becoming alike and acting differently: English abstract and summary, Tutkimuksia 51. Saarijarvi: STAKES.

Bowlby, J. (1979). The *Making and Breaking of Affectional Bonds*. London: Tavistock.

Caw, J. (2014). *Team Parenting for Children in Foster Care*. London: Jessica Kingsley.

Conway, P. (2009). Falling between minds: the effects of unbearable experiences on multi-agency communication in the care system. *Adoption & Fostering, 33*: 18–29.

Department for Education and Skills (2007). *Care Matters: Time for Change*. White Paper. London: HMSO.

Emanuel, L. (2002). Deprivation x3: the contribution of organizational dynamics to the 'triple deprivation' of looked-after children. *Journal of Child Psychotherapy, 28*(2): 163–179.

Henry, G. (1974). Doubly deprived. *Journal of Child Psychotherapy, 3*: 15–28.

Kanfizer, L. (2014). Service related project. University of Essex.

Maturana, H., & Varela, F. (1980). *Autopoiesis and Cognition*. Dordrecht: Reidel.

McNamee, S. (2005). Curiosity and irreverence. Constructing therapeutic possibilities. *Human Systems, 16*: 75–84.

Munroe, E. (2011). *The Munroe Report on Child Protection: Final Report.* London: Department for Education.

Rustin, M. (1999). Multiple families in mind. *Clinical Child Psychology & Psychiatry, 4*: 51–62.

Seikkula, J. (2011). Becoming dialogical: psychotherapy of a way of life? *Australian and New Zealand Journal of Family Therapy, 32*: 179–193.

Seikkula, J., & Arnkil, T. (2006). *Dialogical Meetings in Social Networks.* London: Karnac.

Wakelyn, J. (2011). Therapeutic observation of an infant in foster care. *Journal of Child Psychotherapy, 37*: 280–310.

CHAPTER THREE

Approaches to working with foster carers and children

Sara Barratt, foster carers, and children

Introduction

Foster carers are the backbone of the care system; they provide physical and emotional care for vulnerable and troubled children and support their relationships with members of their biological families, social workers, and a range of other professionals. From a personal perspective, I spent four years in foster care and remember the way my foster families worked hard to support me in coping with all aspects of my life. I now draw on this experience in my work as a systemic psychotherapist in a Child and Adolescent Mental Health (CAMHS) team for children who are looked after, in kinship (connected persons) care, or adopted, as well as for those who are parenting them. The Fostering, Adoption and Kinship Care Team (FAKCT) offers a range of therapeutic interventions, believing that children who have suffered such profound dislocations need a responsive service and professionals on whom they can depend. These therapeutic relationships are important to children and their parents/carers. We are able to offer short and long term interventions to families and are aware that they face different challenges at different stages in their life cycle; therefore, we give careful consideration to the way we respond both at referral and re-referral.

In this chapter, foster carers describe their parenting of children and I discuss my work with carers and children. We consider the ways in which the carers and their foster children engage with different forms of therapy as well as the extent to which they see themselves as integral to the work, exploring their relationships with social workers and experiences of contact with biological families. We explore the social discourses which influence the experiences of foster carers and their children, especially those relating to traumatic early experiences and the role of the biological family, and I argue for a psychotherapy provision that is "needs based", rather than diagnosis based, and that is informed by the wishes and expectations of foster parents and foster children themselves.

A theoretical framework

Social constructionist ideas have provided a framework for my clinical work. People who have been in care or adopted can gather a range of diagnoses in their journey through life; these may include attachment disorders or autistic spectrum diagnoses, often relating to the social and professional preoccupations of the time and the particular lens through which individuals, with the power to diagnose, define different "disorders" depending on their personal and professional cultures. Thus, professionals could construct together explanations for a child's behaviour that might not have any connection to the child's reality. Gergen (2009) says: "As constructionists propose, our practices of language are bound within relationships, and our relationships are bound within a broader pattern of practice. One of the premises of social constructionism is that there are no incontrovertible truths" (p. 11). Fruggeri (1992) suggests that the practice of therapists working from a social constructionist framework is characterised by the acknowledgement of their biases. While the context for a referral to FAKCT is the wish for professional expertise, we need to acknowledge the importance of our clinical experience, questioning our professional biases and the way we might position ourselves in relation to those we work with. Allsopp (2013) describes the interrelationship between discourse and knowledge and draws on Foucault's ideas in saying, "What is simply taken for granted here is that discourses are not just sets of *knowledges* but, in their construction of subjects and their worlds, they also, carry with them relations of *power*" (p. 26). The therapist who draws on social constructionism believes that all knowledge evolves in the space between people (Hoffman, 1992) and that meaning is constructed through language (p. 116). For children in foster care who might have suffered traumatising experiences without language, the challenge is to provide a safe enough space for them to trust that we can help them make sense of those events and their effect on their current relationships. Wetherell (2012) talks about "the embodied flow of affect" (p. 38) and brings power into the discussion, asking, "Who is emotionally privileged, who is emotionally disadvantaged and what does this privilege and disadvantage look like?" (p. 17). Perhaps, as professionals, the discourse about how we believe emotions should be expressed is at odds with those whose emotional life has developed without the language to describe those emotions, or in which they have been misinterpreted (Laing & Esterton, 1964). For children to understand the reason for being in care and to develop confidence in their entitlement to be respected, we need to think carefully about the power that professionals hold in defining the "right" way to show feelings.

Speed (2014), in describing the dismantling of adult mental health services, refers to the importance of professional networks, saying that the ability of professionals to work together is crucial in decision-making. This is, indeed, the case for ensuring the best outcomes for children in care, as discussed by Wendy Lobatto in Chapter Two of this book. Aggett and colleagues (2013) also describe the way teams manage risk and the way dominant voices can silence others, recommending a framework in which different team members are able to listen to one another. Seikkula (2011, p. 181) provides a framework for a "needs adapted approach" in which multi-disciplinary teams attune their intervention to the responses of their clients. Arguing that many professionals adhere to the notion that there is a "right" approach according to a "diagnosis", he goes on to say, "In the era of evidence-based medicine all this sounds very radical, because it challenges the idea that therapists should choose the one right method of treatment after first doing an accurate diagnosis of the case". One of the strengths of our team approach is that we try to fit our interventions to the changing needs of the children and carers we work with and to make sure that the ideas of all team members are respected and taken into account. This is not easy in pressured teams and we have developed structures in which senior staff members are reminded to listen to our less experienced colleagues. As in adult mental health, looked-after children can attract diagnoses which have particular treatments attached to them and our challenge is to walk the tightrope between providing yet another assessment or, alternatively, something that might be perceived by others as "see how it goes" but is, in fact, "needs adapted" and responsive to the feedback from children, their carers, and their social workers.

Attending to the needs of looked-after children

Children are usually referred to FAKCT because they are unhappy and showing disturbing behaviour to those caring for them; there might be differences between the carers, the social workers, and the child about the "cause" of the problem and its solution. As systemic therapists, we might believe that working with the family together is a more helpful way of resolving difficulties, while a foster carer and social worker might believe that the problems originate in birth family experiences and, therefore, the child needs to be seen alone. We often need help from colleagues to monitor our biases (Fruggeri, 1992) and to recognise the times when we start to believe we "know" what should happen, thus closing our ears to different possibilities. Maintaining an awareness of my dominant stories and remaining curious is an important aspect to my work; having been in foster care as a child, I am aware that I might be too quick to ally myself with children and pay less attention to their carers. I have to remind myself that my role is to try to help them find a more helpful way of relating to one another. Children in care have been involved with many different professionals; the more worried we are, the more people we might involve and the more confusing it can be for our clients. Splits, disagreements, and rivalries could get in the way of collaborative work to develop a "team around the child". For social workers, there are conflicting discourses, including the requirement to prevent children from being taken into care *vs.* the primacy of protecting them from harm, which might lead to a failure to notice and act on concerns they might have, or could mean that children are left too long in abusive situations, which makes it harder to adjust to life in a foster family. Foster carers might privilege helping children to manage their lives day to day without violent outbursts, while CAMHS professionals might be most concerned about the importance for children of making connections between their emotional triggers and past experiences and their need to feel safe in their care environment.

What do we think we are doing to help children in care in the face of the confusion and uncertainty that is the day-to-day reality of their lives? Tarren Sweeney and Vetere (2014) say,

> To date there is remarkably little evidence that existing mental health interventions are effective for children with complex attachment and trauma related difficulties. This is, of course, not to say there are no effective interventions. Rather, the present standards with which we rate psychotherapy are disconnected from the reality of assisting children with complex difficulties in real-world settings. (p 48)

They argue that complex attachment and trauma related difficulties are both inadequately conceptualised and poorly measured and that no single intervention is likely to be as effective as employing multiple interventions for children with complex difficulties. They go on to challenge the findings of randomised control trials (RCTs), suggesting that while RCTs employed in psychotherapy research may be rigorous, their findings cannot be applied across clinical settings, especially in the treatment of complex attachment and trauma-related difficulties. This reflects our experience of children struggling with myriad complex emotions relating to past and present experiences. Developing a relationship with them and their carers is crucial for our work. This can take a long time; interventions do not make a difference unless there is a trusting relationship.

Fostering relationships

In our service, we meet looked-after children at different stages of transition; many have had so many changes of placement that they have no reason to believe that their current foster carers will commit to them any more than have previous ones. Children might be in foster care pending the outcome of court proceedings, they might be awaiting adoption, with birth siblings, or separated from siblings who are either in care or adopted, they might be struggling in school, or their relationship with their foster carers might be such that the placement is at risk. Most have suffered abuse and neglect, either through parental drug and alcohol misuse, domestic violence, mental health difficulties, or other circumstances, which are tragic for both parents and children. Of course, many return to live successfully with their birth families, but those remaining in care are still likely to be preoccupied with their biological families. This could be because their identity is strongly associated with their birth family, informed by societal discourses of family, because they hope that things can get better and their mum and/or dad will turn into the parents they dream of, or because of the fear that, when they leave care, there will be nowhere to belong other than within their birth family.

Foster carers are motivated by different cultural and lived experiences and will feel differently about different children in their care. Research undertaken by Kirton and colleagues (2006) shows that roughly three in every eight carers have considered adopting at least one foster child and that about one in eight have proceeded to adoption. They say that despite periodic attempts at clear demarcation, fostering continues to provide a significant route into adoption. In Chapter Eight of this book, Caitlin says that, after being a foster carer for eleven years, having fostered over twenty-five children, two were placed with whom she and her partner developed a special attachment and, when it was decided that they would be adopted, they applied and were accepted. Foster carers might struggle to admit, even to themselves, that they have different feelings for the children they look after. Some children cannot allow anyone close to them and others display behaviours that are hard to tolerate. It is important for us to work collegially with foster carers, inviting them to talk about the issues that arise for them in their role but being careful not to overstep the mark and convey an idea that they might need psychotherapeutic input, because they are not our clients.

Heather was taken into care with her older brother when she was seven. After a year, her brother returned to live with their mother and Heather remained with Jenny, their foster carer. The children had been differently treated by their mother and social workers thought that their mother would not be able to meet Heather's needs. For Heather, the return of her brother led her to revisit her feelings of rejection from her mother, which Jenny could not compensate for. Heather was referred to our clinic, with an assessment of complex needs, with emotional and learning difficulties. Although the referral was for individual therapy, Jenny was very clear that she and Heather needed to work together. Heather started to feel more confident and relaxed when the placement was confirmed as long term, but she started begging Jenny to be able to call her "mum". Jenny was fearful that this would be frowned on by the social worker but was also upset that Heather's wishes were not respected by the social worker, who told Jenny she should insist on Heather calling her by her first name.

Our social discourses determine that biological relatedness is more important than emotional connection and the pressure on Heather to see the love and care she receives from Jenny as less important than the relationship with her mother left her confused and needing continuing reassurance from Jenny that she would always be there for her.

Heather and Jenny raise important questions about the role of foster carers. Blythe and colleagues (2013) undertook a research project with twenty women identified as long-term carers. Participants in this Australian study saw their role as that of mothers to their children rather than "caring for" them, thus positioning themselves in a way that claims the child as family. This is very much the way Jenny sees her relationship with Heather. Below are stories of different children's experiences in foster care which support Blythe and colleagues' (2013) and Tarren-Sweeney and Vetere's (2014) views that the commitment of foster carers, sometimes with very different styles of parenting, with a consistent support system including social workers, therapists, and other professionals, is important for positive outcomes for children. This is supported by Schofield and Beek's (2009) longitudinal study of children growing up in foster care. They found that the ability of foster carers to understand and contain young people is important to their sense of stability and that many young people in care did better than predicted in adolescence: "What may be more surprising is how, against the odds, many young people from traumatic childhoods appear to be able to make good use of active and sensitive foster care when it is offered and to thrive at home and school" (Schofield & Beek, 2009, p. 257). Positive outcomes were related to the ability of carers to respond sensitively to their foster children's needs. This fits with Tarren-Sweeney and Vetere's (2014) findings that recovery for children is dependent on several years of consistent caring without a change of carer. While some carers are reluctant to attend FAKCT appointments, feeling that their children's difficulties originate in the past rather than the present, better attended to by professionals, and that it is more useful to keep the home environment separate, others are keen to attend, either in family sessions or individually, to use the space to think about how to respond to the day-to-day challenges of life with their children. While some carers want to work with children to understand and regulate their emotions, for others, staying calm and stable is more important than talking about emotional issues that could lead to an eruption. Natalie and John's attitude supports Tarren-Sweeney and Vetere's (2014) findings. They are experienced foster carers with two older birth children. Charlie and Susan were placed with them five years ago, aged nine and seven. Three years later, their younger sister, Melanie, aged four, joined the family after a foster home breakdown. The siblings had only briefly lived together before coming into care and relationships between them are often difficult. Their brother, aged seventeen, lives in residential care in another part of England. I met with Natalie and John to ask about their style as foster parents and their experience of attending CAMHS. Their strength is their steadiness; they have clear expectations of the children and, while they understand the emotional triggers for behaviour, they do not find it helpful to talk to their children about the feelings behind their different outbursts, responding to the behaviour rather than its meaning. The children understand the consequences of transgression at home, and, when they are in trouble at school, there is no question that their foster carers are determinedly behind them in sorting out the difficulties.

S.B.: And what helps you to keep going? What supports you?

NATALIE: I talk with John and talking at FAKCT helped a lot; you just plod through, don't you? With kids, things happen, there are more changes with them at the moment. Charlie has some problems, Susan's calm and, with Melanie—things will come up in a few years time.

S.B.: I'm just aware that you have to spread yourself so far to help them in so many ways. When Charlie was in trouble and was about to be expelled from school, you were cross with him but he was never in any doubt that you were going to give up on him. . . .

NATALIE: Mmm

S.B.: I wondered about love for your foster children. Do you hold back a bit of yourself?

NATALIE: Yes, I suppose you would do. I think you've got to hold back a little bit to preserve yourself—otherwise they take liberties. Training courses help. The last one was on mental health; it was too short but with the things that came up it helped me to realise that Charlie has got real problems—you have to remind yourself that, with these problems he won't ever be the same as everyone else; you've got to keep remembering. Courses on abuse remind you well, OK—I think there's a bit more to it and I think I have to remember that.

Charlie's disclosure of sexual abuse had not been pursued by social services so Natalie tried to support him and acknowledge his bravery in having the courage to tell someone and also the upset he feels at not having been believed. It is important to Charlie that Natalie believes him; she is able to manage his angry outbursts by remaining remarkably calm and sticking with her "rules", which seem to keep him safe, even though his anger can, at times, be unnerving. In working with this family it seems that, although emotions are not discussed, the children know that their carers are deeply committed to them and, importantly, that they provide a very different and safer environment than the explosive and dangerous experiences in their birth family.

The sense of belonging that Charlie feels in his foster family, and clear way in which his foster carers manage his confrontational behaviour may be at odds with social work discourses, which require carers to work at a more emotional level, but it fitted for Charlie and helped him to find a way to regulate his responses.

While the professionals and carers involved with this family were organised by different personal and professional discourses, we found a way to respect and listen to one another and our needs-led approach meant that we met and questioned whether different resources were needed at different stages in the children's lives. The children and their carers felt confident in the support we were providing. Through working closely together, airing our different views, we were able to think about what would be best for the children.

This is in contrast to Darshand and Asha's situation described below, in which the difficulties for the changing social workers in supporting the foster carers in working with us, and our different views of the children's needs, meant that we were not able to work coherently together, which might have contributed to the breakdown of their placement.

Darshand and Asha were taken into care aged ten and twelve when an older sibling disclosed sexual abuse. They had endured years of physical and sexual abuse and neglect and were referred to FAKCT because of concerns that they, who had not disclosed the abuse, needed to make sense of their experiences. They were the first children to be placed with the foster carers, who, like them, were of South Asian and white British heritage and who had successfully raised their two birth children, now adult. The children were embraced by the family and quickly settled so that, after two sessions with us, they and their carers did not feel they needed therapeutic input. They were re-referred four months later because the situation had deteriorated; they were challenging their carers and having angry outbursts at home and at school. In our initial session with the carers and social worker, we tried to make sense of what the children needed. The foster carers had applied to become long-term carers but were finding it hard to understand why Darshand and Asha did not respond like their birth children. Alongside this, Darshand was influenced by a dominant discourse about what a family should be and was very anxious that his classmates should not know that he was fostered. This meant that he struggled to make close friends, as he was afraid that they would find out that he was in care, which he found shameful.

Once the children began to feel criticised and rejected, they became angry and aggressive, and stopped conforming at home and school. After an agreement for family work, we realised that the carers did not see themselves as part of the solution to the children's difficulties, and sent the children to appointments on their own. Neither we, nor the children, were aware that the placement was in peril until, on returning from school one day, they were told to pack their bags because they were moving to another foster home. Our work suffered from our inability to provide a coherent working relationship with the foster carers and the different and changing social workers (there were four in three months) so we tended to align ourselves with the children, who were keen to continue to attend sessions on their own and to let us know how unhappy and misunderstood they felt.

The difficulties that arose in this family confirm Blythe and colleagues' findings (2013) about the importance of a supportive network. The polarised positions taken by the adults were detrimental to ensuring the best decisions were made for the children. Because of geographical distance, we did not have an ongoing relationship in which to resolve our differences. The children were relocated in a new foster family and school, and our appointments became sporadic and then stopped. Some time later, we learnt that Darshand was in a residential placement, out of school, and his sister in yet another foster family, with both children saying they wanted to return to their birth family.

Darshand and Asha, like many other "looked after" children, seem to me like invisible migrants, moving between the different cultures of birth family members, within the social care system, and in the different foster families in which they find themselves. Children have spoken about the different foods, smells, sleeping arrangements, and small matters of day-to-day life that is different in each foster family, alongside managing different parenting styles. Some families are talkative, expecting children to have the words to talk back, some hug and kiss, some expect children to manage themselves independently and children in care have to make sense of the different unspoken cultures of each family they live in. Renos Papadopoulos (2013), and Gillian Hughes and Neil Rees in Chapter Six, describe the multiple belongings for refugee and asylum seeking children, which are, in many ways similar to children in care who have to try to understand what is expected of them in different families, knowing that each family works very differently from one another and from their birth families. I have personal memories of trying to make sense of what was expected of me in different families and, as a family therapist, try to help carers learn from children what they bring from past care experiences so that they can take account of this in parenting them and understand how difficult it is to know our own unspoken family culture in order to help children make the adjustments expected of them.

Sibling relationships

The most important relationship for many children coming into care is with their siblings; nevertheless, the decision to place children together or separately is very complex. I have worked with foster families where older siblings feel stable and settled and the arrival of a younger brother or sister forcibly reminds them of their birth family, bringing forth myriad memories and emotions. Josh, whose father is African Caribbean was placed with his older, white-skinned half brother, Lucas, and his white British foster carers. Pavoa and colleagues (2007) describe the complexity of sibling relationships in which half siblings have different skin colour, sometimes exacerbated by the possibility that the parent of one was abusive to the other. Alongside talking to children about their different memories, it is challenging to develop coherent life story accounts for siblings when a parent's behaviour affects the developing identity of each child. Not only was Josh coping with the effects of abuse and neglect, but his brother resented his arrival in the foster family and the carers described walking down the street and having passers by comment on the children's different skin colour, maybe thinking that Lucas belonged to the family, and Josh was possibly adopted. This left the carers and children constrained by societal dominant discourses of family in which they felt silenced by an expectation that they had to "justify" their being a family together. These discourses also affected school life, where Josh found himself confronted with questions that paralysed him and which he could not answer. His classmates would say that he could not be Lucas's brother because he was black, Lucas did not want anything to do with him in school, and Josh was upset, angry, and silenced and it was hard for him to think that the white people caring for him could possibly understand or help him. (See Perlita Harris, Chapter Ten.) Part of our work was to help Josh and his carers develop some strategies for managing, both in school and outside, alongside working with the brothers on the difficulties that arose between them, helping them make sense of their early experiences and finding the language to create a coherent explanation.

Natalie (described above) found herself managing the difficulties between her white British foster children. Some of the most challenging behaviour has been in the sibling relationship, as Charlie's resentment of his younger siblings, especially when he was in trouble, led him to provoke them relentlessly. In family therapy, we worked on helping them to get along better, but the life experiences that these children shared, together with their difficulties in maintaining peer relationships, means the daily stress of school can lead to tensions being taken out on one another at home. I have been impressed that Natalie and John respond to this behaviour in a level-headed way and, even when they feel at the end of their tether after so much provocation, use a telephone call or a clinic appointment to talk it through and regain their equilibrium.

McCormick (2010) argues that it is usually best for siblings to be placed together, listing the circumstances that make this more complicated. These include overt hostility, competition for adult affection, one child serving as a carer to a younger child, siblings who do not have an established relationship prior to placement, and those who enter care at different times. We see most of these complications in the sibling groups we work with; some behaviour is difficult for carers to manage and decisions about separating siblings are usually taken with a great deal of soul searching. It is important to place a sibling group with carers who are able to manage their different challenges because breakdown or the departure of one child has a detrimental effect on the whole family and can lead to increasing problems with other siblings in preparation for what they see as their own departures. It is also essential to remember that the dynamics of relationships influence the way young people think about themselves. For some children, seeing a sibling praised can lead to another feeling rejected, so managing the balance between the needs of different children can be very complex.

Birth family contact

The importance of contact with birth family members is often the reason many children in foster placements are not placed for adoption. Contact can be important and disturbing for foster children, and siblings may have very different relationships with different family members; some might have been abused while others might have been favoured children, affecting their day-to-day relationships with one another. Natalie and John's foster children have regular contact with five different family members, which they are required to supervise. Contact has different emotional meaning for each of the children and often the anxiety before and the fallout after requires sensitive management and responses. Contact is more stressful for Charlie than for the other children and Natalie works hard to support the children when she believes that contact can bring back memories of abuse, which has not been disclosed or believed. Below is an extract of the interview in which she talks about contact.

NATALIE: For Melanie, times of contact are not always good. She keeps cutting up coats. She's on number five at the moment. It's just recently happened. It's not a good time of the year.

I think it's Christmas time; it's not good for any of them. I know from before when she used to have contact with the mum her behaviour was really, really naughty in school.

They still have telephone contact with their mum and dad at Christmas, and they have contact with granddad, which is good, it goes well and then there's Larry (brother aged seventeen) Charlie didn't want to go last time. He definitely decided not to go and then it went to "I'm proving a point, I'm not going, I'm digging my heels in."

S.B.: Do you think it was a mature decision?

NATALIE: No. Contact is difficult. I say, look, contact is about getting together, it's about talking. The little ones go up and give big cuddles, but for Charlie it's a real strain as it's not really for them but for their older brother, so we end up going to McDonalds and I work hard to get them talking because they don't know him. I go—I know, what's your favourite food? What's your favourite colour? . . . sort of trying to make conversation but it's difficult.

S.B.: I sometimes wonder if they had difficult times when they were together in their family. One young person told me that contact with siblings reminds him of things they suffered together—it only occurred to me when he told me that, that if they don't see one another very often, that memory could come back when they meet.

NATALIE: I can imagine it would because even as adults, if we have a bad experience and see that person, we remember.

Pavoa and colleagues (2007) describe their work to facilitate sibling contact, highlighting similar dilemmas to those confronting Natalie's foster children:

> For a child such as D, who lived in a residential facility rather than a family home, these visits seemed particularly beneficial. D's therapist noted that, ". . . it is so important for D to know he is part of a family even though he might not see them often. For the siblings, much younger when they were separated from their older brother, the visits—however sporadic—helped them to experience the reality of their birth family, to learn who their brother is and what his life is like

> in the present rather than relying on memory or fantasy to flesh out a picture of him. (Pavoa et al., 2007, p. 21)

However, if the siblings have had a more negative experience, these contact sessions can serve to trigger distress from half-remembered events in the biological family.

Part of our work with Natalie was to reflect on and understand the affect of abuse on the children's attachment patterns, and understand the relationship between the siblings without becoming overwhelmed. She and John comply with the court's decisions about contact even though they do not think it is best for the children. Decisions about contact are often taken when orders for permanency are made and might be meeting the needs of parents or older siblings rather than the children. Foster carers might struggle to manage frequent court-ordered contacts, often unsupported by social workers. It is they who live with the children, understand their distress, and manage the fallout. How responsive is the professional system to the needs of children when contact becomes too much? We are frequently invited by social workers who are trying to respect the needs of the children to support their appeals to court to amend the contact arrangements, sometimes made many years earlier, which seem to meet the stated needs of birth family members rather than the children.

Siblings have different experiences in and with their birth families; older siblings might have to "forget" some events in order to continue to be loyal to their ideas about their birth family, while younger children might be constrained to keep secrets about what really happened to them. One of the more demanding skills for foster carers is to manage the complex relationships siblings have with different family members.

One of the sources of distress for Heather (described above) is her spasmodic contact with her birth mother. She had not seen her for two years until a determined social worker listened to Jenny and decided to make it happen. It can be easy to demonise biological parents who let their children down and the foster carer has felt angry with her on Heather's behalf. We tried to find a middle ground in which Heather can maintain a relationship with her birth mother while acknowledging that she "belongs with" her foster carer. As Heather has allowed herself to become more trusting of her relationship with Jenny, she is able to be more open about her anger with her mother and has written many unsent letters telling her just how let down she feels. She is very proud to show me what she has written. This way of finding the language for feelings fits with Wetherell's (2012) ideas about finding emotional language ("emotives"), which, she says, can be a moment of crystallisation in which an utterance can allow the statement to be examined and owned or rejected. Heather is enthusiastic about her new confidence and that her feelings are valid and "allowed". She now speaks with a stronger voice and, although often seeking validation from Jenny, she is becoming more confident in deciding on the questions she would like to ask, even though she might not receive the answers.

Papadopoulos's (personal communication, 2013) term "nostalgic disorientation" applies to many looked-after children who might idealise their birth family in order to hold on to a sense of identity and belonging. While Heather's growing attachment to Jenny enables her to remember some of the very bad times in her birth family, Darshand and Asha (described above), became keener, as their foster placement disintegrated, to have regular contact with their father and brother even though they said that they were sometimes frightened of them. Even when the foster placement was going well, Asha told me that she could not give up on her relationship to her birth family because, in the end, when she left care it was better to belong somewhere, even if that place was often cruel and unhappy, than to belong nowhere. Schofield and Beek (2009) say,

> A recent national study of policy and practice for achieving permanence in foster care (Schofield et al. 2008) found that, in spite of the theoretical and research evidence support for the importance of secure, supportive family relationships and family membership in adolescence, these needs are often underestimated or minimised . . . In the complete absence of supportive family relationships, for example where young people from care are precipitately placed into "independence" or left to rely on birth families who may harm not help them, they are unlikely to thrive if they have to rely entirely on their personal resilience characteristics. (Schofield & Beek, 2009, p. 257)

This has been a concern for our team in trying to keep connected with young people we have worked with who feel unsupported by social workers, who are not able to manage "supportive lodgings", and, thus, feel very alone.

Bringing children to therapy

Referrals to FAKCT often carry a blame-laden account of a child's behaviour and, through asking questions and using a more strength based approach, we try to develop a more sympathetic description. We have to understand that the relationships we build with children and their carers can be more important than providing answers, and yet the pressure to offer solutions is very compelling. This can be a particular issue when working with looked-after children for whom the story of a traumatic past might lead professionals to look for negative attributes and ignore the children's resilience and strengths. A discourse could be constructed by those around the child based on their known lived experiences rather than their needs, often by people who do not have a close relationship with the child, whose voice is ignored. Children are frequently referred to us because the adults around them believe they need therapy to "cure" the effect of such experiences. For some children, "shutting down" may have been protective, so, in thinking about "opening up", there is a risk of not being able to cope and the strategy that has contributed to survival might be damaged. Children and adults who have suffered insecure and disrupted attachments, early abuse and neglect might "shut down" at pivotal moments; for example, when there is a chance of risking emotional connection or trusting another person.

Safiya, aged ten, had been trafficked into the UK and was rescued after police were informed that someone had seen a child huddled in the garden of a neighbouring house on a winter's night. She spoke no identifiable language, and was confused as to whether the people who brought her to the UK were her family. Professionals working with Safiya were alarmed at the level of abuse she had suffered and thought she should have therapy. Together with her foster mother, we pieced together what we knew and what she began to remember of her life. She was struggling at school, bewildered by her environment but trying hard to fit in. For her, this was more important than thinking about the past and she welcomed strategies for managing friendships and bullying. Given that she had no experience of being heard, the carer and I felt that Safiya's views should be respected; she was relieved not to take time out of school for appointments and, for the time being, the most useful way of working with her is through her foster carer, beginning to accept love, and trying to understand together some of the confusion that confronts her every day and helping her find language to describe it. In "holding steady" and being available in the long term, our team can have continuing conversations, stepping into and out of children's and carers' lives as their needs change. The service we provided for Safiya fitted with her needs at the time, although the professionals felt she needed intensive work.

In comparison, we worked with Natalie (described above) and her foster children, providing a range of different interventions, depending on the particular needs of the children over a number of years. Natalie's three foster children attended FAKCT for individual and family work and she was meticulous in ensuring that they attend, which has sometimes been a challenge when the children were reluctant. In talking to Natalie about coming to the clinic, she was not altogether sure whether therapy was helpful or whether it made the children self-indulgent; she did not feel it served any purpose for other family members to be involved. Although Charlie was challenging in school, his younger siblings were quieter and were referred because of difficulties with their peers, stealing food from them and

Figure 3.1. The hug, by Agata Morgan.

getting other children into trouble. As the children started to feel safe, they began to challenge their carers and let them know something about the abuse and neglect they had been subjected to.

In talking about coming for therapy, Natalie went on to say,

> I thought going to the Tavistock was good. It did help with Charlie talking more but I think it went on a bit too long . . . he got a bit too dependent and it was hard for him to settle in and even now he still needs a mentor—if it had been shorter he might not have needed her—but saying that it's become sort of a trend thing now. Scott came home saying he wanted therapy in school. He had it when he was young, and he's asked for it again. But he's told me that all his friends are doing it and I don't know if it's a way of releasing things from everyday life—the stresses but it's a very "in" thing at the moment—"let's have therapy".
>
> JOHN: Perhaps there are things that he wants to say or ask that he can't ask us, perhaps he thinks that he can't talk about these worries to us.
>
> S.B.: (Later.) Did it help at all for you to come to the Tavistock?
>
> NATALIE: It definitely helped, talking. You gave me different ways of talking about things. Say, for example, with Melanie and Larry (who were previously placed together), I didn't understand her behaviour because she'd been so young when she went into care, [and] you pointed out she'd been with Larry, who wouldn't allow anyone else to look after her.

It is hard for children to start to talk to therapists without being overwhelmed and they might be aware that they are conveying something adults prefer not to know. As systemic psychotherapists, asking questions to help families create new connections is one of the tools of our trade (Palazzoli et al., 1980). One of the pivotal points of change is when children start to ask questions. Curiosity, and the ability to make connections is an important aspect of our therapeutic process and, for Heather, the move from frightened silence to curiosity about her early life was the beginning of "bringing her to life". Heather was anxious to be "good"; she could not identify feelings and was not managing to learn or relate to other children in school. She had suffered extreme neglect and had been unwashed, hungry, and alone. She was barely at school until coming into care aged seven, and had lived her life in an imaginary world. Heather was scared to talk about how she felt, so we used puppets to help her name her emotions and to find the confidence to let others know how angry and upset she felt. In using the puppets, in the early sessions, Heather chose a rabbit to talk to my squirrel and Jenny became a bear. We also involved an ugly frog/snake to take the more menacing roles. Through the puppets, when not being a very bossy schoolteacher, Heather could free herself to talk about life at home that she had never spoken about before. She could ask why her mother did not feed her or send her to school, why her mother shows love to her brother, why he returned home and she did not.

They write about their experience.

JENNY: When we arrived at the Tavistock, for Heather's first appointment, I was anxious for her because she was not used to talking to people about her worries and found it difficult to express her feelings, even to me. For a number of appointments she was unable to answer questions for herself and relied on me to speak for her, choosing to play to distance herself from conversations which were about her. During one particular session, I noticed that she enjoyed using puppets and was able to make conversations with Sara (through the puppets), which related to her play theme, for example, being a school teacher. I then wondered if the use of puppets could be a way that she could feel safe to express herself at home. I decided to purchase two puppets. One I chose with a big mouth, which represented me, as I have always had to speak for Heather. The other puppet, which I chose for her, was Alice in Wonderland, because she was familiar with the character. The first time I used the puppets was the night before Heather was due to have contact with her birth mother. Contact over the last three years had been sporadic, with the mother being unreli able and quite often not turning up. I introduced the puppets and said we would be using them to talk to each other about our feelings. At first Heather seemed hesitant, so I just talked through my puppet asking what she did at school that day and talking about my day. It wasn't long before she joined in with her puppet and eventually I was able to steer the puppet talk around to the topic of contact. Heather was then able to express her feelings of anxiety and say she was worried that her mother would not turn up. This was a huge step forward.

Over a short period of time, Heather became confident in being able to talk about herself and some of the worries she had when we used the puppets at home and agreed to take the puppets with us to therapy and used them both in playing and when difficult feelings or events were being talked about. I believe that the use of puppets played a significant part in enabling Heather to be able to open up about herself and her feelings. We no longer use the puppets for therapy as she is now able to talk confidently about her worries and is beginning to feel safe enough to engage in conversations with other relevant professionals.

Heather still attends the Tavistock and has grown so much emotionally. She still needs me to talk for her on occasions, but is becoming more independent and confident.

Heather's note: When I first went to Sara I was nervous. I used puppets to help me express my feelings. When I wrote a letter to my mum to tell her how I felt, I used the puppets to help me. I can now express my feelings on my own and have written letters to my mum with lots of questions about why she treated me the way she did. Although I haven't yet sent them, it really made a difference to write them down and talk to Jenny about them. I may decide to send them one day. Seeing Sara made me feel better because I was able to trust her and practise talking which I feel much better about now.

Conclusion

The ability of professionals, carers, and birth families to keep talking, and listening to one another, and to prioritise the changing needs of children in care, is essential in order to stand up to those repeated processes of fragmentation that are so destructive. Children in foster care are making sense of many different messages about themselves and their identity. Many have had a number of changes of placement and might feel that decisions are made about them rather than with them. Attending a CAMHS clinic is similar in that it is usually adults who decide it would be helpful and children have very little choice. Our work with foster carers, children, and social workers is to create a safe enough environment for children to play and participate. We need to engage with the everyday experiences of those we work with and resist getting caught up in the dominant discourses, such as the primacy of the relationship with the biological family, or the need for therapy that might not fit for the child for whom managing day-to-day life might be hard enough without trying to identify feelings. looked-after children and their carers are continually adapting to changes in their environment and are affected by events, both within their birth families and their lives, that are often unpredictable. The services they are afforded need to adapt to these changing needs. Foster carers have different ways of parenting; while some, like Jenny, work hard to understand and respond to the emotions of their children, others, like Natalie, succeed with their steady, responsive approach, believing that too much "emotional" language can prevent children from managing their lives. In defining therapy as a separate space to talk about emotional problems with their carers, this approach offers a sense of security because of the boundary drawn between the emotional world of FAKCT sessions and the management of life in the foster family. Whatever the parenting style, children benefit from carers who convey commitment through the ups and downs of daily life, whatever their behaviour. A social constructionist framework helps therapists to listen to all involved in order to construct together a therapeutic environment, which fits and adapts to the different needs of children and their carers. Building a therapeutic environment in which children can begin to trust is a major challenge and, for some of the children described above, the feeling that their carers and therapists were willing to listen and understand what they were communicating about themselves and their worries seemed important in helping them leave behind some of the negative stories about themselves that had followed them from their early experiences.

Developing a trusting relationship with children who have been let down by adults takes time; the rapid turnover of social workers and other professionals means that many do not expect anyone to feel committed to them. It takes time to construct together a way of understanding and being understood. The current drive to suggest that a model of intervention treating a particular diagnosis is more important than a relationship will lead children in care to give up the hope that they are important enough for therapists to stick with them over time. Children who have had fragmented lives need a service that they can return to, at different times of their lives, where people are familiar, where they do not have to keep telling and re-telling their stories. They need a therapeutic service which is available over time and this is what our team hopes to continue to provide.

References

Aggett, P., Messent, P., & Staines, J. (2013). "Benign invigilation": using appreciative inquiry to reposition clinical risk in multi-disciplinary CAMH teams. *Clinical Child Psychology and Psychiatry, 18*(2): 260–269.

Allsopp, M. (2013). *Emotional Abuse and Other Psychic Harms*. Basingstoke: Palgrave Macmillan.

Blythe, S. L., Halcomb, E. J., Wilkes, L., & Jackson, D. (2013). Perceptions of long-term female foster-carers: I'm not a carer, I'm a mother. *British Journal of Social Work, 43*: 1056–1072.

Fruggeri, L. (1992). Therapeutic process as social construction. In: S. McNamee & K. Gergen (Eds.), *Therapy as Social Construction* (pp. 40–53). London: Sage.

Gergen, K. (2009). *An Invitation to Social Constructionism*. London: Sage.

Hoffman, L. (1993). *Exchanging Voices*. London: Karnac.

Kirton, D., Beecham, J., & Ogilvie, K. (2006). Adoption by foster carers: a profile of interest and outcomes. *Child and Family Social Work, 11*(2): 139–146.

Laing, R. D., & Esterton, A. (1964). *Sanity, Madness and the Family*. London: Tavistock.

McCormick, A. (2010). Siblings in foster care: an overview of research, policy, and practice. *Journal of Public Child Welfare, 4*(2): 198–218. Available at: www.tandfonline.com/doi/abs/10.1080/15548731003799662. Accessed 1 October 2014.

Palazzoli, M. S., Boscolo, L., Cecchin, G., & Prata, G. (1980). Hypothesising–circularity–neutrality: three guidelines for the conductor of the session. *Family Process, 19*: 3–12.

Papadopoulos, R. (2013). Plenary presentation. EFTA Congress, Istanbul, October.

Pavoa, J. M., St John, M., Cannole, R. F., Fischer, T., Maluccio, A., & Peining, S. (2007). Sibling kinnections: a clinical visitation program. *Child Welfare, 86*(2): 13–30.

Schofield, G., & Beek, M. (2009). Growing up in foster care: providing a secure base through adolescence. *Child & Family Social Work, 14*(3): 255–266.

Seikkula, J. (2011). Becoming dialogical: psychotherapy or a way of life? *The Australian and New Zealand Journal of Family Therapy, 32*(3): 179–193.

Speed, B. (2014). Forward. In: S. McNab & K. Partridge (Eds.), *Creative Positions in Adult Mental Health, Outside In, Inside Out* (pp. xxiii–xxviii). London Karnac.

Tarren-Sweeney, M., & Vetere, A. (2014). *Mental Health Services for Vulnerable Children and Young People*. Abingdon: Routledge.

Wetherell, M. (2012). *Affect and Emotions A New Social Science of Understanding*. London: Sage.

CHAPTER FOUR

Under our skins: developmental perspectives on trauma, abuse, neglect, and resilience

Graham Music

Introduction

These are important times for making sense of the effects of the adverse early experiences so often faced by children not living within their biological families. Disciplines and paradigms that once seemed incommensurable are now in conversation. It is clear that to help children whose lives have been affected by trauma, abuse, and neglect, we need to understand both context and individual psychology, wider systems and internal worlds, biology and culture, and how all these interlink. Neurobiology and epigenetics have shown how not just our minds, but also our brains, bodies, and even our hormonal systems are affected by our contexts and our experiences, and that genetic potentials are turned off or on by what happens in our lives. Recognising the real effects of early experiences and environments can help to change and shift patterns which otherwise can become entrenched and unhelpful.

This chapter examines how the kind of adverse early experiences suffered by children not living within their biological families can affect their psychological, emotional, and physical lives. It examines brain science and developmental psychology research and looks at how the context of the child affects the way their brains are sculpted, the autonomic nervous system develops, hormonal systems are programmed, and how children are, as a result, likely to relate to other people and the social world. I try to make some sense of why so many young people from traumatised backgrounds are at risk if they do not receive appropriate help.

Many traumatised children struggle with empathy, emotional regulation, or managing relationships. A disproportionate number of young people who have been in care end up committing crimes (Cocker & Scott, 2006). They are up to sixty times more likely to end up in prison than other children; indeed about a quarter of the prison population have been in care, and nearer half of the younger prison population. Many are excluded from schools (Viner & Taylor, 2005), struggle to find sustained employment, and others might develop psychiatric illness (Ford et al., 2007). Health outcomes for children who have been in care are, on average, worse than for other children (Viner & Taylor, 2005). We know from many longitudinal studies that adverse childhood experiences are highly predictive of long-term physical and mental health outcomes (Felitti & Anda, 2010).

While many traumatised children are resilient and have the ability to develop loving relationships, the inner worlds of others are tormented by fear, terror, and despair. Their play may be filled with scenes of aggression, cruelty, revenge, and bereft of helpful, kindly adult figures (Canham, 2004; Lanyado, 2003). Some might become violent, and show behaviours such as stealing, soiling, and substance abuse. It can be a clinical struggle to remain emotionally connected and face up to the awfulness of what some children have suffered and, at the same time, it is essential to retain a genuine hope for change.

Embedded, extended brains and neuroplasticity

We have seen major advances in our understanding of human brains in recent years. Not only is the human brain "plastic" and hugely influenced by its environment, but newer understandings of the brain have a systemic flavour, conceptualising it as embodied (Gallagher, 2013), extended, and enactive (Tikka & Kaipainen, 2014). The brain and cognition cannot be understood except as depending on our bodies acting in space, such as the importance of gestures in thinking, which depends on our external and social environment to provide thinking tools. The brain is certainly not an unchanging biological structure locked away inside individual skulls.

We can think about the brain as being like an extraordinarily complex muscle group; the parts that are used are strengthened from being exercised while others can wither from neglect (Music, 2009). Our brains are constantly adapting to their current context, especially in the early years. The human brain is born prematurely, having an overabundance of brain cells at the start but with very few connections between them. In the post-natal period there is a process of "pruning" called "use it or lose it", and cells that are not used simply die off. Schwartz and Begley (2002, p. 117) quote a figure of twenty billion synapses pruned every day between childhood and early adolescence, saying, "like bus routes with no customers, they go out of business". Once a connection is formed, it remains wired and new experience is filtered through already formed pathways, just as water will naturally flow down already formed channels, illustrating the idea that "cells that fire together wire together" (Hebb, 1949). It is in this way that a child's early context gives rise not only to particular narratives and beliefs, but also specific brain pathways which form at the expense of other potential pathways and become standard ways by which one experiences the world. Attachment styles develop in this way.

The human brain learns fast, and functions as an extraordinarily powerful predictor of the future. If the presence of adults triggers either fear or dissociative processes, as it does in many children who have suffered early trauma, these fear responses may also be triggered by other, more benign adults, such as kindly teachers or adoptive parents. The human brain, and particularly the infant brain, is very malleable, a characteristic called "neuroplasticity". The period from the last trimester of pregnancy through to the second year of life is a particularly sensitive one, although, fortunately, some plasticity remains throughout the lifespan. The parent and other carers are, in effect, growing and regulating the developing infant brain so that the parent's or carer's face is the environment that stimulates particular neuronal circuitry and hormonal baselines.

Thus, early experiences become embodied in brain architecture, cells in our bodies, hormonal programming, and posture, as well as in psychological states and narratives about life. As Perry and colleagues (1995) wrote, transitory states like fear can become traits, or, in attachment patterns, momentary responses can become behavioural patterns and expectations of relationships. This all normally happens outside conscious awareness. Therapeutic work often needs to start with making sense of reactions, which are likely to have earlier roots in bad experiences. Important adults such as foster carers and teachers are often hugely relieved when some sense is made of "bad" behaviours or attitudes. In addition, children can slowly unlearn early patterns, or, at least, learn new ones alongside old ones. Change is possible but it can be slow and painstaking and requires a lot of patience and understanding from the adults in a child's life.

Beebe and Lachmann (2013) identified patterns of interaction in infants of just four months old who would later go on to develop extremely dysregulated, disorganised behaviours. While abused or neglected infants often have already developed clear behavioural patterns and internal representations of relationships, these can shift and change, but only if adult carers develop the sensitivity to notice these patterns and take in how a child is experiencing the world. It is often hard as a caring adult, whether teacher, foster carer, or adopter, to be experienced as uncaring, untrustworthy, or even potentially abusive, while being aware of this can be the first step towards change. Early experiences build deep beliefs about people and relationships and it is these that are worked with and challenged in therapeutic work.

A whole host of research is combining to show that trauma and abuse affect a range of brain areas (Teicher et al., 2012). Victims of trauma and abuse have a smaller corpus callosum, which links left and right hemispheres, leaving less capacity for the hemispheres to communicate effectively (Teicher et al., 2004). Those subjected to trauma and violence have higher activation of the amygdala, central to processing fear and other strong emotions, leading them to be more reactive and less still and calm (Sigurdsson et al., 2007; Thomas et al., 2001). They tend to spot anger more quickly than other children, emotionally reactive brain areas such as the amygdala firing up more powerfully (McCrory et al., 2010). In children adopted from highly neglectful backgrounds, on the other hand, there is less amygdala activation when witnessing anger or other high levels of emotion, which again was presumably adaptive for children who needed to turn away from an interest in other people's thoughts and feelings to find a way to regulate their own emotions.

Childhood trauma is also linked to smaller hippocampi in adulthood (Andersen et al., 2008), and the hippocampus is central to forming and retrieving memories, among other things. We see less activation of prefrontal areas such as the ventromedial prefrontal cortex in children who have suffered maltreatment (Mehta et al., 2009). These prefrontal areas are essential for capacities such as empathy and emotional regulation, and their deactivation accounts for some of the problems maltreated children have in managing ordinary life experiences that other children take in their stride.

There is too little research as yet conclusively to show that better new experiences can shift such brain patterns. We know that areas affected by trauma can change even in adults. Amygdala and fear pathway responsiveness can be reduced through practices of mindfulness, for example (Lutz et al., 2013), while the prefrontal brain areas central to empathy and emotional regulation can become more active (Hölzel et al., 2011a; Kirk et al., 2014), and there is reason to believe that these are the areas that also respond both to therapy and good parenting.

Appropriate adaptation gets children into trouble

Many children who have been in care, and who concern professionals, might struggle to fit into social or cultural groups. We imbibe ways of acting and learn the subtle and very bodily nuances of "belonging" whether as an upper class English person, an "untouchable" in Hindu culture, a nomadic Masai warrior, or an Iranian peasant. Infant imitation (Meltzoff, 2007) is the classic template for such learning. This almost infinitely malleable capacity to fit into any culture or group does not persist as we get older. For example, our ability to recognise and learn the different sounds in languages as diverse as Japanese, English, or Xhosa diminishes greatly after about our first year (Kuhl et al., 2006). Young infants quickly learn their own cultural norms, including the emotional norms of their family, whether of a loving or violent or coldly callous one.

Recent attachment theory has been helpful here. From Bowlby and his colleagues we learnt that children with "secure" attachment styles grow up to be what most of us would think of as psychologically healthy. They form unconscious internal models which see their parents and other people as trustworthy, themselves as worthy of being loved, and generally develop good social skills and high levels of empathy. This is less often true of children who have been taken into care.

What Bowlby (1969) had not appreciated was that the different styles of attachment, including the insecure styles identified by his colleague Ainsworth (1978), are, in fact, sensible adaptations to the world the infant or child had initially inhabited. As we see more psychological issues in children with insecure attachment styles, we tend to assume that these styles are unhealthy or pathological, an assumption that runs counter to an evolutionary and a systemic understanding. If you have parents who are inconsistent and chaotic, it makes no sense to be trusting, open, and loving. Indeed, being relaxed in the face of danger can put one's very survival at risk. Children might, thus, become hyper-attuned to their attachment figures, extremely sensitive to any hint of withdrawal, aggression, or intrusion, and, consequently, tend to be both needy and defensive in later relationships and struggle to relate empathically. Becoming wary, watchful, and even clingy enhances their survival, but this has repercussions for longer-term health, such as a highly activated stress system (Schore, 2009) or a worse functioning immune response. Similarly, if a child's parents are neglectful, distant, and unresponsive, or get cross or withdraw in the face of crying or other strong emotions, then it makes sense to develop a dampened down and avoidant attachment style which is more out of touch with their own and other people's emotional needs. Such children learn to block the need for human connection and grow up determinedly self-sufficient, forming unconscious internal models which see others as unhelpful and irrelevant.

Thus, we can view most attachment strategies as successful adaptations to early contexts. In humans and most species, the character traits that give the best chance of surviving and reproducing in harsh, unpredictable, or dangerous environments are different from those that are successful in mild, stable, and benign environments. Here, a systemic perspective which takes into account the context of development meshes with an evolutionary one, in the sense of survival being enhanced by being "best fitted" (not the "fittest", as social Darwinists suggest) to one's environment. Human developmental plasticity allows for survival in a range of emotional environments, whether cold and callous, chaotic, violent, or empathic and kind. By the time maltreated children are in public care or adopted, or come to us for help, they have already adapted to their early environment. Our job, in part, is to make sense of how they are experiencing this new world they are in, and to be aware of the extent to which they might be responding to the adults in the current lives as if they were the same as previously traumatising adults. From here, we can try to help them believe in new possibilities.

Michael, ten, for example, had been profoundly neglected and had received little attuned emotional input, and, indeed, had been left alone for much of his infancy. In response, he had developed a dampened down, cut-off, almost dissociated way of being, barely able to recognise other people's emotions, or his own, and showing little interest in others and hardly any enthusiasm for life. This made him hard to relate and to warm to. Our job with children like Michael is, in large part, helping the often well-meaning adults in their lives, such as teachers, social workers, or foster carers, to realise why they respond as they do. Otherwise, they can be labelled, maybe as "surly" or "difficult", leading to the adults becoming exasperated, critical, and even rejecting. Helping the adults compassionately make sense of why Michael and others act as they do can lead to them becoming more caring and less critical, leading the children to feel differently and then respond differently, too, to others around them, and so begin to break a damaging cycle.

Jim was different to Michael. He came from a violent home with unpredictable parents. He had a hyper-vigilant state of mind that had helped him survive in such a terrifying environment, becoming able to predict when aggression was about to erupt or when a parent had been drinking. Such adaptations led to an over-awareness of others' moods and states of mind, and over-sensitivity to danger, criticism, and any hint of not being accepted. It also made him prone to over-react and be highly distrustful and aggressive, leading him often to be labelled as "bad" or "naughty" or "impossible", or worse. Again, helping the adults understand the very particular needs of children with similar experiences to Jim, and the reasons why they behave as they do, can lead to changing the way they respond, which, in turn, allows the possibility of more hopeful behavioural and interactional patterns developing. While early environments are not a life sentence, they are, nevertheless, profoundly influential and their effects are more likely to remain in place unless the busy, well-meaning adults to whom children are entrusted are helped to understand the effects of such early experiences.

We often assume that what we see develop in securely attached infants and children is "natural" and just happens, However, it is only from having good enough early experiences that four-month-old infants can know they are the object of another's benign attention (Reddy, 2000), or, at eight months old, can have sufficient understanding of other minds to be able to "tease and muck about" (Reddy, 2008), or demonstrate more sophisticated understandings of other minds, as seen when a baby and parent mutually appreciate something that they are witness to (Trevarthen & Hubley, 1978). It is consistent good interaction with kindly, sensitive carers that puts in place the building blocks of trust and faith, of being able to understand and regulate emotions, and being interested in, and caring about, another person's state of mind. Many maltreated children in the care system have missed out on these building blocks and our job, in part, is to rebuild these foundations.

Maltreatment inhibits the capacity for empathy. For example, Main and George found that ordinarily attached toddlers respond kindly to other toddlers' distress in nursery, but that the abused children in their sample showed no empathy or concern in response to other children's distress, and, indeed, could be quite aggressive to such children (Main & George, 1985). Securely attached children, who have been more sensitively attuned to, have consistently displayed more empathy (Mikulincer et al., 2005); they, for example, tend to play well with other children in pre-school, whereas there are more fights and conflicts when an insecurely attached child is involved (Sroufe, 2005). Sensitive, "security inducing" caring leads to more complex narrative capacities and language use, better emotional regulation, more pro-social behaviours and generosity (Warneken & Tomasello, 2009), and a deeper capacity for understanding other people's thoughts and feelings. The more emotionally attuned and "mind-minded" (Meins et al., 2002) input a child receives, the more fully these attributes become embedded and embodied and for such children a successful adaptation to their context leads to believing that the world is good and safe, that people are to be trusted, that when things go wrong they can be righted, and that life can be rewarding and pleasurable.

On the other hand, many children who suffer neglect or abuse lack this kind of trust and can rarely relax, gain reward from relationships, or much real pleasure in life. These are hard lessons to unlearn. Many maltreated children who end up in foster care struggle to make friends or fit into social groups. Relating to others with empathy or the desire to help another might have been absent in their families of origin. Thus, our role, in part, is to try to help adults realise that they might have adapted too successfully to their original traumatising world and struggle to re-adapt to, or even begin to believe in, an adult world that is better, safer, more kindly than the one they have come from.

Nervous systems

We use different parts of our brains when in different moods, or in different contexts, such as in a loving environment or when under threat. When in danger, we tend to become highly aroused and resort to primitive survival responses such as fight or flight, or even freeze. Our whole being and physiology, then, is geared to coming through the threat, as we tense up and prepare for trouble, while other bodily functions, such as digestion or immune responses, temporarily go into abeyance, as do higher order thought processes. Children who have suffered extreme trauma, such as many in public care, can go into such states very quickly.

Many aspects of our brain functioning are similar to those of reptiles some 250 million years ago. As well as controlling things such as heart rate, breathing, temperature, and balance, structures such as the brain stem control survival instincts for dominance and aggression. Some 100 million years later, with mammals, the limbic system came into existence. This is often seen as the seat of our emotional lives, involved in how we make judgements, learn whether an experience is likely to be pleasurable or not, and how we form emotional memories. It contains vital structures such as the amygdala and the hippocampus. The "new kid on the block" is the neocortex, a mere two or three million years old, and its most complex form is seen in humans and is responsible for human thought, language, imagination, and consciousness (Figure 4.1).

An exercise I quite often undertake with myself when working with clients is to ask whether it is the reptilian or mammalian brains or the cerebral cortex that is active at a particular moment. If one is

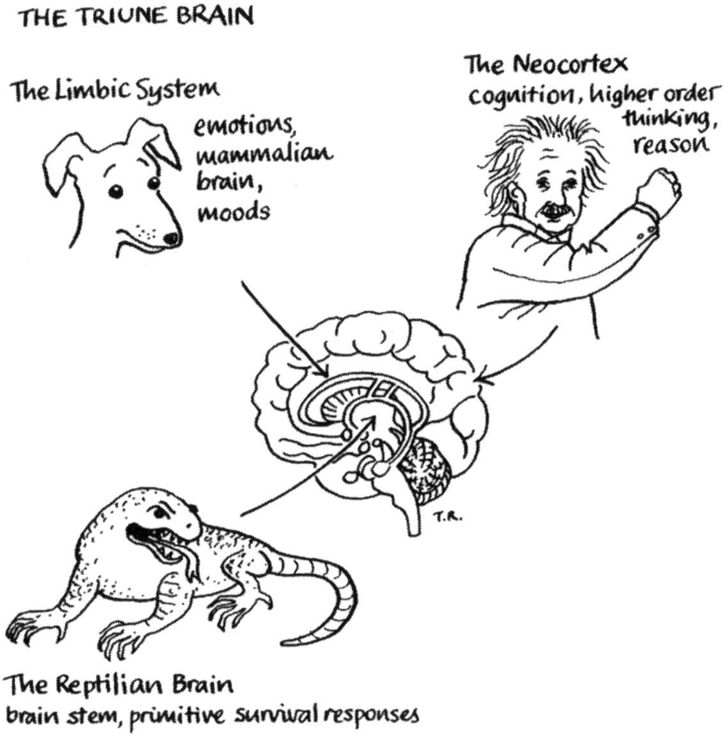

Figure 4.1. The triune brain.

confronted by massive anger or hatred in a child who at that moment has a highly active brain stem and is in "fight" mode, it is folly to make an intellectually complex comment that only the cerebral cortex could make sense of, as such complex parts of the brain are not active at such moments, but, rather, one needs to engage in a more empathic or regulatory way.

Porges (2011) has taken such an evolutionary view a step further in relation to our autonomic nervous systems. He shows that we have three very different kinds of responses to stress, each rooted in a different stage of our phylogenetic history. Our most primitive reaction is one we share with the least developed of vertebrates and its activation leads to complete immobilisation, freezing, and the closing down of our systems. Dissociation and metabolic shutdown are typical of this "rabbit in headlights" system. It is adaptive because predators are not attracted to creatures that seem lifeless. Our bodies only resort to this in the most extreme life or death situations. Many traumatised and neglected children can present like this, but their presentations might be seen as simply "withdrawn"; they might be given autistic spectrum diagnoses when what they really need is for adults to understand the developmental trauma that is affecting how they now experience the world. Only then can we help them begin to come back into a fuller, more alive emotional world.

An evolutionarily more advanced response, present in mammals, is seen when our sympathetic nervous system fires up: for example, in fight/flight responses (Figure 4.2). Under threat, this system's responses include increased heart rate, sweating, and quicker breathing, dilation of the eyes, feeling cold, and inhibited digestion. It goes into action when we feel anxiety or terror, and when attachment anxieties are triggered. We need this arousal system and all experience times when we resort to it, but children brought up in a violent environment, for example, will have a much more highly activated sympathetic nervous system; in other words, they will be easily aroused, often in a dramatic way, and will find it hard to calm down,

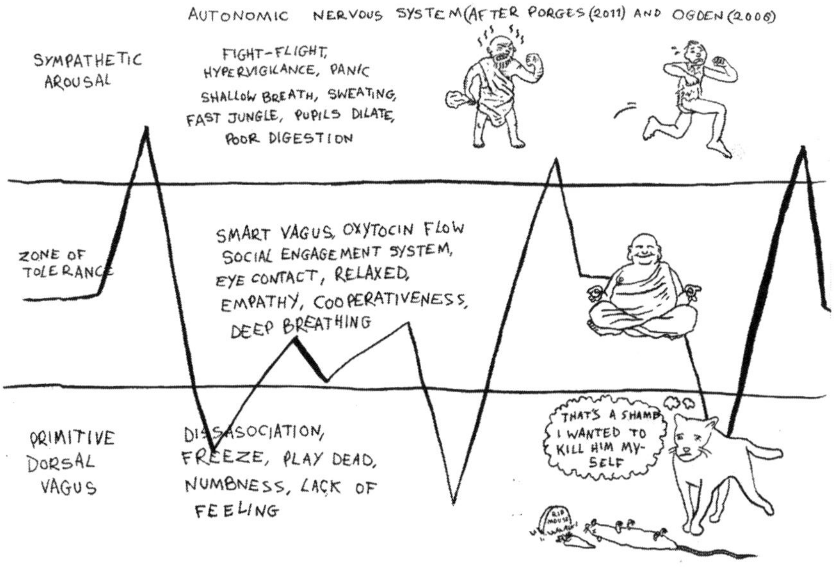

Figure 4.2. Autonomic nervous system (after Porges, 2011 and Ogden, 2006).

concentrate, or feel at ease. While we are designed to resort to sympathetic arousal states when danger looms, we are also designed to calm down quickly afterwards. Chronic bad experiences can lead to people being stuck in these anxious and fearful states. Such hypervigilance and arousal might be adaptive in a violent and abusive home, but is less helpful for the adopted child who cannot see that their new parents are benign and kindly.

An evolutionarily even more advanced element of our autonomic nervous system is seen in mammals, and especially in humans, and is central to both feeling good and being open to others. It depends on the ventral or "smart" vagus nerve, which connects our brain stem, heart, stomach, and our facial muscles. It is active in processes like bonding, attachment, social communication, language use, empathy, and care for others. This system basically turns off when we feel anxious or threatened.

This system has an opposite effect to the sympathetic nervous system's arousing mechanisms, and is part of the parasympathetic nervous system, which calms us down. Its thousands of nerve endings communicate with many of our internal organs, like the heart, which has its own neurons, and the gut, which has a whole nervous system of its own (Gershon, 1999). The "smart" vagus nerve is implicated in attachment, bonding, love, team-work, co-operation, and working together. Much therapeutic work is involved with trying to catch children and adults just before, or just as, they move out of this system into more reactive or deadened nervous system states.

People who have good vagal tone, which essentially means high heart rate variability, are more relaxed and open. This is predictive of good mental (Austin et al., 2007) and physical health. It is becoming increasingly clear that there is an important relationship between attachment style and vagal tone (Diamond et al., 2012). Children with high vagal tone are the ones who are friendly, generous, and helpful in class, generally the securely attached ones, whereas those with low vagal tone are more likely to have behavioural problems and be unhappy (Eisenberg et al., 1996).

Increasingly, therapeutic work has to take into account those bodily systems, such as how people breathe, how tension is held in the body, their stress responsiveness and emotional regulation. This requires a fine-grained awareness of one's own and others' bodily responses. With highly stressed and reactive people, we often feel on tenterhooks, maybe tightening up or breathing shallowly, and then I often find myself taking deep breaths and talking aloud about my feelings and sensations. Increasingly, trauma work is taking account of the body (Ogden, 2006; Van der Kolk, 2014). Similarly increasingly, my work with foster or adoptive parents has included trying to help them calm their children down, sometimes just by helping them be emotionally in touch, but also by subtle, manageable touch and body awareness. Measures of stress responses have become increasingly useful in showing both the effects of early trauma and also the positive effects of better new experiences. For example, Dozier's interventions with foster children have shown exciting changes in cortisol levels (Bernard et al., 2014; Dozier et al., 2006).

Hormones and opiates

Even our hormones are affected by our contexts, environments, and experiences. One study found that boys brought up in areas with more boarded-up buildings had higher testosterone levels, and were more risk-taking than boys from similar social groups living in less run-down neighbourhoods (Tarter et al., 2009). Higher testosterone is linked with increased aggression, and it makes sense that one might non-consciously become more risk-taking and aggressive when the context feels unsafe.

Thus, hormonal levels are not a given, but are affected by experiences. Children who have been subjected to high levels of trauma or suffered consistent anxiety, such as many in our clinical caseloads, will tend to have ongoing elevated cortisol rates. Cortisol has a number of pernicious effects, leading Gerhardt (2014) to dub it "corrosive cortisol", particularly in the light of how it can attack cells in the hippocampus, the part of the brain that is central to memory. Occasionally, extreme trauma can have the opposite effect and result in extremely low cortisol levels—often seen in post-traumatic stress disorder victims such as Holocaust survivors (Yehuda et al., 2005). Either way, too much or too little cortisol or stress is not what the human body was designed for.

Oxytocin is well known as the hormone central to the bonding process, whether between parents and infants or between members of a couple (Zak, 2012). Oxytocin is involved in inducing tranquillity, increasing empathy, and reducing social fear. We release it when we are being lovingly touched, and, with more oxytocin, we become more generous (Morhenn et al., 2008). Experimenters found that when shown pictures of threatening and scary faces, those given oxytocin had lower amygdala activation (Kirsch et al., 2005). Oxytocin works directly against stress reactions such as the release of adrenalin, quicker heart rates, higher blood pressure, and tense bodies. The oxytocin levels of parents rises after becoming a parent, and mothers with higher oxytocin are more sensitive to their infant's moods, emotions, and physical needs (Strathearn et al., 2012) and play more affectionately.

Biology does not rule here, but, rather, different experiences give rise to different biologies. The more good loving experiences we have early on in life, then the more oxytocin receptors we are likely to develop, while stressful or abusive childhoods lead to lower baseline levels of oxytocin (Bhandari et al., 2014).

Other hormones also play a central role in attachment and emotional well-being, not least serotonin, the hormone targeted by antidepressant drugs such as Prozac, and fundamentally linked to feeling good. We see low levels of it in depression (Carver et al., 2008) and after bad experiences (Shannon et al., 2005). Dopamine, central to the reward system and activated when we are positive, excited, or eager, is another hormone that is profoundly affected by early experiences. Depressed mothers have low dopamine levels, and so do their babies as young as a month old, and, of course, such mothers might not feel very rewarded by their infants, and their infants experience less pleasure. Mothers of securely attached children have their dopamine circuitry stimulated by seeing pictures of their infants (Strathearn et al., 2009).

The hopeful news is that change is possible, and not just in early childhood. The logical sequelae of the boarded-up homes study is that community and macro interventions will have a knock-on effect on hormones and brain states. Recent research found that even brief stressful experiences in adults, such as a ninety-minute mock job interview including difficult arithmetical questions, created an epigenetic affect whereby the stressful experience actually altered the DNA and, thus, the action of a gene central to oxytocin production (Unternaehrer et al., 2012). We know now that adverse experiences such as abuse and trauma have a significant effect on gene expression (Lesch, 2011). More hopefully, mindfulness meditation has been shown helpfully to increase melatonin, dopamine, and oxytocin levels and reduce stress hormones such as cortisol and adrenaline (Esch, 2014). It is very likely that good care from adoptive parents and foster carers, therapeutic and other support, are all ways of beginning to re-programme the brain and hormonal system so that such children can live in, and experience, a more hopeful world.

Conclusions: a developmental understanding and hope

Children's mental health services could improve their understanding of children who have suffered abuse or neglect. Many maltreated children do not meet the increasingly diagnosis-driven thresholds that enable access to services. Unfortunately, they might either fail to get a passport into services or end up with diagnoses that do not really fit them, such as ADHD, autistic spectrum disorder or conduct disorders (DeJong, 2010). A more in-depth developmental understanding could reveal alternative explanations for children's presenting behaviours.

Empathy, emotional regulation, understanding one's own and other minds, deferred gratification, symbolic play, complex narratives, autobiographical memory, and altruism are developmental capacities that tend to come on-line together, given the right early caring environment (Music, 2014). Many formerly maltreated children who are now in care might struggle to develop these capacities, which all depend on well-functioning prefrontal brain areas that are often more offline following trauma. We know that the inability to self-regulate or delay gratification can predict outcomes right into adulthood, such as the likelihood of holding down a job, managing a stable adult relationship, negotiating good friendships, to name but a few (Mischel, 2014). These are a few reasons why it is so urgent that children who have been maltreated and are referred to CAMHS and the adults in their lives are given the best chance to interrupt these trajectories and develop more hopeful ones (Figure 4.3).

How hopeful or gloomy should such research leave us? We know that patterns that are established early on can be hard to shift, and that once an experience is burnt into the circuits of the amygdala it remains there. However, we also know that new circuits can grow and form. Interestingly, this is also what research using children's play, called story-stems (Hodges et al., 2003), has shown. With positive adoption

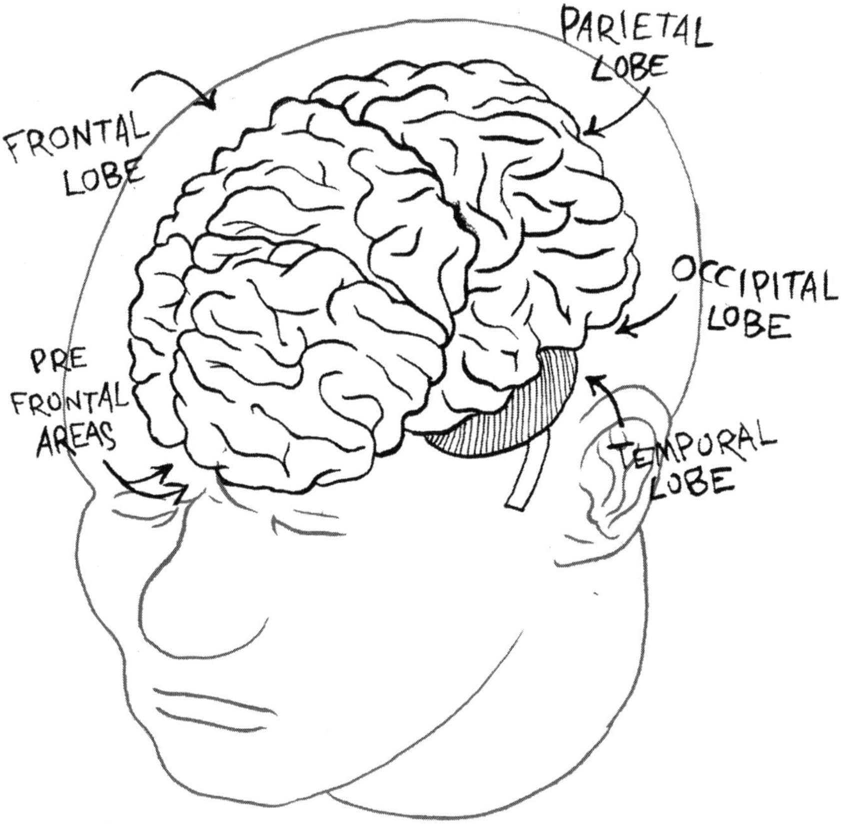

Figure 4.3. The areas of the human brain.

experiences, new expectations of parental behaviour and new views of the world can grow and become stronger. The brain can certainly change throughout the lifespan, but it is also true that there are some very sensitive periods for certain capacities, such as language development and certain emotional capacities. The best-known windows of opportunity, when there is massive brain growth and change, are the first few years of life and also adolescence, when huge changes equally occur in the brain.

We also know that change is possible throughout the lifespan. A heartening example is the fact that black-cab drivers seem to "grow" different sized and shaped hippocampi from the rest of the population (Maguire et al., 2000). There are now studies showing how professional help, such as psychotherapy (Barsaglini et al., 2014; Beauregard, 2014; Karlsson, 2011), even after serious trauma, is associated with changes in many of the brain areas pinpointed in this chapter (Thomaes et al., 2014). The research on the effects of mindfulness on the brain, immune system, hormonal functions, and much else also gives hope that serious change can take place throughout the lifespan (Davidson et al., 2003; Hölzel et al., 2011b; Schutte & Malouff, 2014). It also seems clear that other forms of caring can facilitate forms of neurobiological reprogramming (Bick et al., 2012; Fisher et al., 2011; Kroupina et al., 2012). Emotional support, such as seen in therapy or adoption, can aid the capacity to interpret the world in new and less frightening ways. The effects of such help are likely to include a better functioning prefrontal cortex, the laying down of new procedural memories, strengthened links between left and right hemispheres, enhanced reflective capacities, better understanding of other minds, greater ability to form a coherent narrative about oneself, improved capacity to tolerate difficult emotions without acting out and to sustain positive feelings, and, of course, to form and manage more secure attachment relationships.

However, there is much that we do not know. New discoveries are constantly occurring, and many are likely to turn our understanding upside down. We seem to have come a long way and have learnt a lot, but maybe more than anything we are learning how much we do not yet know. None the less, this is an exciting time for new understandings of how humans develop. Such understandings open up all manner of challenges to the ways in which we have traditionally worked, but also give hope that we can make a huge difference to the minds, bodies, brains, and attachment patterns of children who do not live within their biological families and whose lives have been affected by maltreatment.

References

Ainsworth, M. D. S. (1978). *Patterns of Attachment: A Psychological Study of the Strange Situation*. Mahwah, NJ: Lawrence Erlbaum.

Andersen, S., Tomada, A., Vincow, E., Valente, E., Polcari, A., & Teicher, M. (2008). Preliminary evidence for sensitive periods in the effect of childhood sexual abuse on regional brain development. *Journal of Neuropsychiatry and Clinical Neurosciences, 20*(3): 292–301.

Austin, M. A., Riniolo, T. C., & Porges, S. W. (2007). Borderline personality disorder and emotion regulation: insights from the polyvagal theory. *Brain and Cognition, 65*(1): 69–76.

Barsaglini, A., Sartori, G., Benetti, S., Pettersson-Yeo, W., & Mechelli, A. (2014). The effects of psychotherapy on brain function: a systematic and critical review. *Progress in Neurobiology, 114*: 1–14.

Beauregard, M. (2014). Functional neuroimaging studies of the effects of psychotherapy. *Dialogues in Clinical Neuroscience, 16*(1): 75–81.

Beebe, B., & Lachmann, F. M. (2013). *The Origins of Attachment: A Microanalysis of Four-Month Mother–Infant Interaction*. Oxford: Routledge.

Bernard, K., Dozier, M., Bick, J., & Gordon, M. K. (2014). Intervening to enhance cortisol regulation among children at risk for neglect: results of a randomized clinical trial. *Development and Psychopathology, FirstView*: 1–13.

Bhandari, R., Bakermans-Kranenburg, M. J., van der Veen, R., Parsons, C. E., Young, K. S., Grewen, K. M., Stein, A., Kringelbach, M. L., & van IJzendoorn, M. H. (2014). Salivary oxytocin mediates the association between emotional maltreatment and responses to emotional infant faces. *Physiology & Behavior, 131*: 123–128.

Bick, J., Dozier, M., Bernard, K., Grasso, D., & Simons, R. (2012). Foster mother–infant bonding: associations between foster mothers' oxytocin production, electrophysiological brain activity, feelings of commitment, and caregiving quality. *Child Development, 84*(3): 826–840.

Bowlby, J. (1969). *Attachment and Loss. Vol. 1, Attachment*. London: Hogarth.

Canham, H. (2004). Spitting, kicking and stripping: technical difficulties encountered in the treatment of deprived children. *Journal of Child Psychotherapy, 30*(2): 143–154.

Carver, C. S., Johnson, S. L., & Joormann, J. (2008). Serotonergic function, two-mode models of self-regulation, and vulnerability to depression: what depression has in common with impulsive aggression. *Psychological Bulletin, 134*(6): 912–943.

Cocker, C., & Scott, S. (2006) Improving the mental and emotional well-being of looked after children: connecting research, policy and practice. *Perspectives in Public Health, 126*(1): 10–23.

Davidson, R. J., Kabat-Zinn, J., Schumacher, J., Rosenkranz, M., Muller, D., Santorelli, S. F., Urbanowski, F., Harrington, A., Bonus, K., & Sheridan, J. F. (2003). Alterations in brain and immune function produced by mindfulness meditation. *Psychosomatic Medicine, 65*: 564–570.

DeJong, M. (2010). Some reflections on the use of psychiatric diagnosis in the looked after or 'in care' child population. *Clinical Child Psychology and Psychiatry, 15*(4): 589–599.

Diamond, L. M., Fagundes, C. P., & Butterworth, M. R. (2012). Attachment style, vagal tone, and empathy during mother–adolescent interactions. *Journal of Research on Adolescence, 22*(1): 165–184.

Dozier, M., Peloso, E., Lindhiem, O., Gordon, M. K., Manni, M., Sepulveda, S., Ackerman, J., Bernier, A., & Levine, S. (2006). Developing evidence-based interventions for foster children: an example of a randomized clinical trial with infants and toddlers. *Journal of Social Issues, 62*(4): 767–785.

Eisenberg, N., Fabes, R. A., Murphy, B., Karbon, M., Smith, M., & Maszk, P. (1996). The relations of children's dispositional empathy-related responding to their emotionality, regulation, and social functioning. *Developmental Psychology, 32*(2): 195–209.

Esch, T. (2014). The neurobiology of meditation and mindfulness. In: S. Schmidt & H. Walach (Eds.), *Meditation–Neuroscientific Approaches and Philosophical Implications* (pp. 153–173). New York: Springer.

Felitti, V. J., & Anda, R. F. (2010). The relationship of adverse childhood experiences to adult medical disease, psychiatric disorders and sexual behavior: implications for healthcare. In: R. Lanius & E. Vermetten (Eds.), *The Hidden Epidemic: The Impact of Early Life Trauma on Health and Disease* (pp. 77–87). Cambridge: Cambridge University Press.

Fisher, P. A., Van Ryzin, M. J., & Gunnar, M. R. (2011). Mitigating HPA axis dysregulation associated with placement changes in foster care. *Psychoneuroendocrinology, 36*(4): 531–539.

Ford, T., Vostanis, P., Meltzer, H., & Goodman, R. (2007). Psychiatric disorder among British children looked after by local authorities: comparison with children living in private households. *British Journal of Psychiatry, 190*(4): 319–325.

Gallagher, S. (2013). The socially extended mind. *Cognitive Systems Research, 25*: 4–12.

Gerhardt, S. (2014). *Why Love Matters: How Affection Shapes a Baby's Brain.* Oxford: Routledge.

Gershon, M. D. (1999). The enteric nervous system: a second brain. *Hospital Practice, 34*(7): 31–52.

Hebb, D. O. (1949). *The Organisation of Behaviour.* New York: Wiley.

Hodges, J., Steele, M., Hillman, S., & Henderson, K. (2003). Mental representations and defenses in severely maltreated children: a story stem battery and rating system for clinical assessment and research applications. In: R. M. Emde, D. P. Wolf, & D. Oppenheim (Eds.), *Revealing the Inner Worlds of Young Children: The MacArthur Story Stem Battery and Parent–Child Narratives* (pp. 240–267). New York: Oxford University Press.

Hölzel, B. K., Carmody, J., Vangel, M., Congleton, C., Yerramsetti, S. M., Gard, T., & Lazar, S. W. (2011a). Mindfulness practice leads to increases in regional brain gray matter density. *Psychiatry Research: Neuroimaging, 191*(1): 36–43.

Hölzel, B. K., Lazar, S. W., Gard, T., Schuman-Olivier, Z., Vago, D. R., & Ott, U. (2011b). How does mindfulness meditation work? Proposing mechanisms of action from a conceptual and neural perspective. *Perspectives on Psychological Science, 6*(6): 537–559.

Karlsson, H. (2011). How psychotherapy changes the brain. *Psychiatric Times, 28*(8): 1–5.

Kirk, U., Gu, X., Harvey, A. H., Fonagy, P., & Montague, P. R. (2014). Mindfulness training modulates value signals in ventromedial prefrontal cortex through input from insular cortex. *NeuroImage, 100*: 254–262.

Kirsch, P., Esslinger, C., Chen, Q., Mier, D., Lis, S., Siddhanti, S., Gruppe, H., Mattay, V. S., Gallhofer, B., & Meyer-Lindenberg, A. (2005). Oxytocin modulates neural circuitry for social cognition and fear in humans. *Journal of Neuroscience, 25*(49): 11489–11493.

Kroupina, M. G., Fuglestad, A. J., Iverson, S. L., Himes, J. H., Mason, P. W., Gunnar, M. R., Miller, B. S., Petryk, A. & Johnson, D. E. (2012). Adoption as an intervention for institutionally reared children: HPA functioning and developmental status. *Infant Behavior and Development, 35*(4): 829–837.

Kuhl, P. K., Stevens, E., Hayashi, A., Deguchi, T., Kiritani, S., & Iverson, P. (2006). Infants show a facilitation effect for native language phonetic perception between 6 and 12 months. *Developmental Science, 9*(2): 13–21.

Lanyado, M. (2003). *The Presence of the Therapist: Treating Childhood Trauma*. New York: Routledge.

Lesch, K. P. (2011). When the serotonin transporter gene meets adversity: the contribution of animal models to understanding epigenetic mechanisms in affective disorders and resilience. *Molecular and Functional Models in Neuropsychiatry, 7*: 251–280.

Lutz, J., Herwig, U., Opialla, S., Hittmeyer, A., Jäncke, L., Rufer, M., Holtforth, M. G., & Brühl, A. B. (2013). Mindfulness and emotion regulation—an fMRI study. *Social Cognitive and Affective Neuroscience, 9*(6): 776–785.

Maguire, E. A., Gadian, D. G., Johnsrude, I. S., Good, C. D., Ashburner, J., Frackowiak, R. S. J., & Frith, C. D. (2000). Navigation-related structural change in the hippocampi of taxi drivers. *Proceedings of the National Academy of Sciences of the United States of America, 97*(8): 4398–4403.

Main, M., & George, C. (1985). Responses of abused and disadvantaged toddlers to distress in agemates: a study in the day care setting. *Developmental Psychology, 21*(3): 407–412.

McCrory, E., De Brito, S. A., & Viding, E. (2010). Research review: the neurobiology and genetics of maltreatment and adversity. *Journal of Child Psychology and Psychiatry, 51*(10): 1079–1095.

Mehta, M. A., Golembo, N. I., Nosarti, C., Colvert, E., Mota, A., Williams, S. C. R., Rutter, M., & Sonuga-Barke, E. J. S. (2009). Amygdala, hippocampal and corpus callosum size following severe early institutional deprivation: The English and Romanian Adoptees Study Pilot. *Journal of Child Psychology and Psychiatry, 50*(8): 943–951.

Meins, E., Fernyhough, C., Wainwright, R., Gupta, M. D., Fradley, E., & Tuckey, M. (2002). Maternal mind-mindedness and attachment security as predictors of theory of mind understanding. *Child Development, 73*(6): 1715–1726.

Meltzoff, A. N. (2007). 'Like me': a foundation for social cognition. *Developmental Science, 10*(1): 126–134.

Mikulincer, M., Shaver, P. R., Gillath, O., & Nitzberg, R. A. (2005). Attachment, caregiving, and altruism: boosting attachment security increases compassion and helping. *Journal of Personality and Social Psychology, 89*(5): 817–839.

Mischel, W. (2014). *Marshmallow Test*. New York: Little, Brown.

Morhenn, V. B., Park, J. W., Piper, E., & Zak, P. J. (2008). Monetary sacrifice among strangers is mediated by endogenous oxytocin release after physical contact. *Evolution and Human Behavior, 29*(6): 375–383.

Music, G. (2009). Neglecting neglect: some thoughts about children who have lacked good input, and are 'undrawn' and 'unenjoyed'. *Journal of Child Psychotherapy, 35*(2): 142–156.

Music, G. (2014). Attachment: our brains, nervous systems and hormones. In: S. Farnfield & P. Holmes (Eds.), *The Routledge Handbook of Attachment: Theory* (pp. 127–147). Oxford: Routledge.

Ogden, P. (2006). *Trauma and the Body: A Sensorimotor Approach to Psychotherapy*. New York: W. W. Norton.

Perry, B. D., Pollard, R. A., Blakley, T. L., Baker, W. L., & Vigilante, D. (1995). Childhood trauma, the neurobiology of adaptation, and use-dependent development of the brain: how "states" become "traits". *Infant Mental Health Journal, 16*(4): 271–291.

Porges, S. W. (2011). *The Polyvagal Theory: Neurophysiological Foundations of Emotions, Attachment, Communication, and Self-regulation*. New York: Norton.

Reddy, V. (2000). Coyness in early infancy. *Developmental Science, 3*(2): 186–192.

Reddy, V. (2008). *How Infants Know Minds*. Cambridge, MA: Harvard University Press.

Schore, A. N. (2009). Relational trauma and the developing right brain. *Annals of the New York Academy of Sciences, 1159*(1): 189–203.

Schutte, N. S., & Malouff, J. M. (2014). A meta-analytic review of the effects of mindfulness meditation on telomerase activity. *Psychoneuroendocrinology, 42*: 45–48.

Schwartz, J., & Begley, S. (2002). *The Mind and the Brain: Neuroplasticity and the Power of Mental Force*. New York: Harper.

Shannon, C., Schwandt, M. L., Champoux, M., Shoaf, S. E., Suomi, S. J., Linnoila, M., & Higley, J. D. (2005). Maternal absence and stability of individual differences in CSF 5-HIAA concentrations in rhesus monkey infants. *American Journal of Psychiatry, 162*(9): 1658–1664.

Sigurdsson, T., Doyère, V., Cain, C. K., & LeDoux, J. E. (2007). Long-term potentiation in the amygdala: a cellular mechanism of fear learning and memory. *Neuropharmacology, 52*(1): 215–227.

Sroufe, L. A. (2005). *The Development of the Person: the Minnesota Study of Risk and Adaptation from Birth to Adulthood*. New York: Guilford Press.

Strathearn, L., Fonagy, P., Amico, J., & Montague, P. R. (2009). Adult attachment predicts maternal brain and oxytocin response to infant cues. *Neuropsychopharmacology, 34*(13): 2655–2666.

Strathearn, L., Iyengar, U., Fonagy, P., & Kim, S. (2012). Maternal oxytocin response during mother–infant interaction: associations with adult temperament. *Hormones and Behavior, 61*(3): 429–435.

Tarter, R. E., Kirisci, L., Gavaler, J. S., Reynolds, M., Kirillova, G., Clark, D. B., Wu, J., Moss, H. B., & Vanyukov, M. (2009). Prospective study of the association between abandoned dwellings and testosterone level on the development of behaviors leading to cannabis use disorder in boys. *Biological Psychiatry, 65*(2): 116–121.

Teicher, M. H., Anderson, C. M., & Polcari, A. (2012). Childhood maltreatment is associated with reduced volume in the hippocampal subfields CA3, dentate gyrus, and subiculum. *Proceedings of the National Academy of Sciences, 109*(9): E563–E572.

Teicher, M. H., Dumont, N. L., Ito, Y., Vaituzis, C., Giedd, J. N., & Andersen, S. L. (2004). Childhood neglect is associated with reduced corpus callosum area. *Biological Psychiatry, 56*(2): 80–85.

Thomaes, K., Dorrepaal, E., Draijer, N., Jansma, E. P., Veltman, D. J., & van Balkom, A. J. (2014). Can pharmacological and psychological treatment change brain structure and function in PTSD? A systematic review. *Journal of Psychiatric Research, 50*: 1–15.

Thomas, K. M., Drevets, W. C., Dahl, R. E., Ryan, N. D., Birmaher, B., Eccard, C. H., Axelson, D., Whalen, P. J., & Casey, B. J. (2001). Amygdala response to fearful faces in anxious and depressed children. *Archives of General Psychiatry, 58*(11): 1057–1063.

Tikka, P., & Kaipainen, M. Y. (2014). From naturalistic neuroscience to modeling radical embodiment with narrative enactive systems. *Frontiers in Human Neuroscience, 8* (online).

Trevarthen, C., & Hubley, P. (1978). Secondary intersubjectivity: confidence, confiding and acts of meaning in the first year. In: A. Lock (Ed.), *Action, Gesture and Symbol: The Emergence of Language* (pp. 183–229). London: Academic Press.

Unternaehrer, E., Luers, P., Mill, J., Dempster, E., Meyer, A. H., Staehli, S., Lieb, R., Hellhammer, D. H., & Meinlschmidt, G. (2012). Dynamic changes in DNA methylation of stress-associated genes (OXTR, BDNF) after acute psychosocial stress. *Translational Psychiatry, 2*: e150; doi:10.1038/tp.2012.77

Van der Kolk, B. A. (2014). *The Body Keeps the Score*. London: Allen Lane.

Viner, R. M., & Taylor, B. (2005). Adult health and social outcomes of children who have been in public care: population-based study. *Pediatrics, 115*(4): 894–899.

Warneken, F., & Tomasello, M. (2009). Varieties of altruism in children and chimpanzees. *Trends in Cognitive Sciences, 13*(9): 397–402.

Yehuda, R., Engel, S. M., Brand, S. R., Seckl, J., Marcus, S. M., & Berkowitz, G. S. (2005). Transgenerational effects of posttraumatic stress disorder in babies of mothers exposed to the World Trade Center attacks during pregnancy. *Journal of Clinical Endocrinology & Metabolism, 90*(7): 4115–4118.

Zak, P. J. (2012). *The Moral Molecule: The New Science of What Makes Us Good or Evil*. London: Bantam Press.

PART II

EXAMPLES OF CLINICAL WORK WITH CHILDREN AND YOUNG PEOPLE

CHAPTER FIVE

The journey to becoming a family

Adoptive parents with Sara Barratt

In this chapter, adoptive parents describe their experiences of becoming an adoptive family and of attending our Fostering, Adoption and Kinship Care Service (FAKCT). In my experience, the way foster carers and social workers facilitate and support children's transition to their adoptive family influences the way the new family is able to establish a sense of belonging together. Wendy Lobatto, in an earlier chapter, describes the importance of professional networks, which need to work together to provide a secure context for new adoptive families. It is important to be aware of what may be "hidden" stories in the transition from foster carers to adoptive families. Sometimes, adoptive parents feel that they have, in some way, "stolen" their children from a foster carer who had, for all sorts of reasons, struggled to support the children in their move to their adoptive family. Some foster carers might have hoped to keep the children, which may lead them to be disapproving or critical of adoptive parents. This initial, and sometimes subtle, message can affect adoptive parents' feeling of entitlement to parent. Gay and lesbian adoptive parents are particularly attuned to the subtleties of discrimination and often question whether professionals' or carers' reticence might also be related to homophobia or ideas about normative families.

The placing of siblings together or separately also has a bearing on how children manage the loss of their birth family. In this chapter, William and Mike talk about their attempts to find ways to talk about identity with their son, understanding the complexities of transracial adoption, alongside the impact of the trauma of his early years. Perlita Harris's chapter (Chapter Ten), which describes the challenges faced by transracially adopted children, confirms William and Mike's experiences.

Maehle and colleagues (2012) describe systemic interventions with families with troubled children when working with attachment issues. They say that the parent's sensitivity and ability to promote secure attachment in their children, is related to their narrative of their own attachment relationships and the way they are able to elaborate on them, regardless of whether or not they are positive. This is illustrated by Monica and Rebecca and William and Mike who write about their own experiences and who have worked hard to build a secure family environment for their children. Their ability to reflect on their own attachment experiences in order to understand the needs of their children has enabled the children to begin to feel safe and to trust that these parents will, indeed, work hard to understand and respond to their needs.

William and Mike's story

The beginnings

We were new to parenthood and we had had limited childcare experience when we adopted George, aged five, who had been deemed unadoptable due to his early life experience, age, and challenging behaviour. He had been placed in foster care with his younger brother when he was three and his brother eighteen months old. Both boys were moved twice during their time in care as a result of George's challenging behaviour. His level of aggression, anxiety, and attachment difficulties meant that social workers and foster carers felt that the brothers might not be able to settle together in the same family. Separate adoptive families were needed. Perhaps we were naïve, perhaps hopeful, but we believed we could make a difference and, to some extent we have. As a gay couple, we were anxious to make sure we were well prepared to meet and understand our son's needs. We were extremely well read on the issues of adoption, attachment, and child development, but no book could prepare us for what lay ahead.

There was no honeymoon period when our little boy was placed with us, it was a baptism of fire; what you saw was what you got with him and he did not care, or, rather, could not "help" who was in the firing line. Every situation was volatile. Playing games, especially board games, heightened his anxiety and lowered his self-esteem. He would become extremely upset and have tantrums if he lost a game. If he did not think he would get a drink or food, he would go into meltdown. He would take flight when out walking. He hated being last, always had to be first in the house, first in the queue, and first to get anything. This did not help the way he got on with other children when he went to school.

We were constantly questioning ourselves: are we parenting right? Did we handle that situation appropriately? Why does our child do what he does in crisis? He would be inconsolable; he did not have the skills to self-regulate his own anger, emotions, frustrations, and calm himself down. Tantrums would last for long spells. He would hit, kick, scratch, and spit. We would resort to "wrapping" him. Wrapping is like a hug from behind, gently holding his wrists to keep him safe from lashing out and keeping us safe, too. This would help regulate his emotions and make him feel safe. How does a child's memory work when his experiences are preverbal? We found no pages, no books, which answered our specific questions at that one given time, which were directly related to our experience. This is where CAMHS really came into its own.

Working with FAKCT

Helping us to understand our own feelings was one part of understanding our child's feelings. We were able to talk about our own expectations of his development, our failings as new parents and were reassured that at times it's "OK" to not feel love for a child we were getting to know and *vice versa*. Discussing our own losses, the career we had put on hold or had left behind, the loss of our identity and the unity we once had as a couple. FAKCT is not just support for the adopted child; it is also support for the carers.

George would inadvertently display a pattern of behaviour much younger than his years when attending his therapy sessions, which we saw as a clear indication that therapy was taking him back to his earlier memories and of a time when he was neglected. Therapy would open our eyes to the complexities of an abused and confused mind. He was diagnosed early on with attachment disorder, so we were always aware that part of his challenging behaviour was down to his difficulties with attachment. Family therapy sessions helped him to be less fearful of talking and being talked about through hearing his dads talk openly about him, about what we thought was on his mind, and to make it "OK" to talk about difficult subjects. During these sessions, he would do anything he could to divert the subject; playing games, being mischievous, saying random things. But it gave us tools and ideas to put into practice at home, to be freer with our thoughts, and enable him to be interested in new ways of understanding the feelings he could not articulate.

The team was also central to developing a much more cohesive environment between school and home. We were able to link George's school with the sessions we had and would invite the Deputy Head to discuss our child, help her understand her frustrations, how our son was feeling, and to open the communication between school and home. The therapists also helped us to use consistent language between school and home in a way that gave George a consistent understanding of what was expected of him and of how he would be supported and kept safe. They helped us to understand the importance of transition for an adopted child. Each year we would work with school on how best to prepare George for moving on, leaving his old teacher and classroom behind and welcoming his new teacher and classroom.

We developed a better understanding of why George always had to be first in everything he did: playing games, standing in a queue, taking pencils from a pen pot at school. It was his genuine fear of being left behind, his need for fairness, given the inequity of his earlier life, and his pure panic at not being in control. We spent a lot of time working on his low self-confidence and self-esteem, looking for ways to help him to understand why his emotions got out of control, and how, over time, he could learn ways to regulate them in a way that was not shaming to him. We would talk to him after an event, when he was calmer and somewhat removed, and he began to find the language to describe how he felt, rather than just react.

A lot of adopted children cannot talk about their past and, more importantly, their future, to their adopted parents for fear of rejection. Talking to a therapist who is not directly linked to their family helps them to off-load. However, this is clearly only possible once a secure and trusting relationship has been formed. We were amazed at how patient the FAKCT team was at building this trust when it seemed to be in very small pigeon steps. But a therapist can take it only so far. The aim eventually is to get the child to confide in his own parents and feel safe in doing so.

George did not particularly enjoy his time with FAKCT. He was more concerned about missing school. He enjoyed the play aspect of the sessions, rather than any indirect questions. We kept our reasons for him going quite basic: that he was going there to help him understand what he was thinking and put words to how he is feeling and to the experiences he has had. Ironically, when we adopted for the second time, he asked if his brother would now be going to the Tavistock and whenever his brother displayed any inappropriate behaviour he would say a visit there would probably be helpful to him. This is a good demonstration that he really did understand the reasons for his time at FAKCT.

The present

Now we have adopted for the second time, and it was agreed at the time of placement that our second child might benefit from a series of sessions at the Tavistock. The damage to him was during the first few months of his life, so it is hard to know how he will be affected as he grows and learns the full extent of his life story. With help, we are able to assess the situation while we have time and discuss how we might impart the information to him. We are able to talk about the boys as siblings and how each of them are very different in so many ways, yet alike through circumstance and stages of their adopted lives.

We have always been open about discussing George's ethnicity with him. He is of mixed race, so we felt it important to have some knowledge to the country of his birth father: showing him the map, talking about different cuisine, and explaining why his skin colour is different and why he tans very easily while we turn a deep shade of red. He is different in so many ways: having two dads, being adopted, being of mixed heritage, therefore it was important for us to talk together about our identity as a family with different identities from a very early age.

When we started our journey to parenthood, we made a conscious effort to be prepared for every possible hurdle. We were so mindful that our children might find having two Dads confusing that we bought numerous children's books on the subject. Books about having two Dads, of blue Dads, a king who falls in love with another king, two male penguins who father a chick, and a birthday picnic that has every possible family dynamic attending, and has it made any difference to our boys' outlook? No. We were given some sound advice from our therapist regarding our family makeup: do not make it an issue, unless it becomes an issue. Deal with the subject if it arises; the more of an issue we make of it the more it will make them think there is something to be concerned about. And they have been right.

Without CAMHS intervention, the first child's placement would not have survived; we would not have had the courage, determination, and hope to carry on through the difficult days. We would not be the parents we are today and certainly would not have had the crazy idea to adopt for the second time. It is also very possible that we would not be together as a couple. All our experiences and mistakes are now in practice with our second child: the adoption milestones he reaches which we have seen before, strategies we have used and are using again, and ideas and sessions that we had with FAKCT that are being used a second time round. The support we have had, and investment by, the team has been repaid in so many ways.

William and Mike have developed a network of family and friends to support their parenting of their children. They are aware that their family might need input from our team at different transitional stages and are able to let us know what they find helpful and what really does not fit for them or their children. We have worked with them for a number of years and it feels as if we have joined the network of people whom they can call on when their children are struggling: for example, at times of transition.

We worked with Monica and Rebecca (below) and their three children for a much shorter time. They were referred shortly after the children were placed with them and our team's work included an initial assessment of the family, work with the three siblings to help their relationship, family therapy, and work with the parents on the impact on their relationship of adopting three children who had suffered abuse and neglect. They describe below their experiences of assessment and the challenges of creating a new family. Both sets of adoptive parents writing in this chapter are aware of the importance for their children of having responsive parents who are able to provide clear boundaries. Many parents talk about their children's attention-seeking behaviours, sometimes thinking the best way to manage it is to withhold attention. Waters (2011) supports the idea that children seek attention for good reason and that hunger is usually best satisfied. The parents writing in this chapter feel that it is important to be responsive to their children's demands, where possible, even though it can sometimes feel impossible to provide the attention they crave. Thus, Monica and Rebecca say that they are more concerned about their eldest child, Amy, who is only just finding a way to claim attention, than their other children, who have found different ways to ensure their needs are met. Similarly, William and Mike were highly attuned to George's needs for a response, sometimes expressed in ways that lead to anger and aggression from other children and exasperation from adults. They understood that the past experience of neglect meant that, if George was not seeing a response from those around him, somehow he did not exist for them.

Monica and Rebecca's story

Two years ago, we adopted three siblings, Josie, aged two, Leon, three, and Amy, aged four. When we thought about having children we did not really consider anything other than adoption. Neither of us felt particularly strongly about having our own birth children. Monica comes from a family of four and was briefly in foster care as a child: she had always considered either fostering or adopting because it was a positive experience and she wanted to give back to other children. So, it was something that was on our minds and fitted for us both. We thought, "Why would you have your own children when there are children out there who need mothers?" It seemed like the obvious thing to do, whereas for some people it is much more important to have their own biological child. We had a bit of a debate about what we should do. We are aware that, because we are a gay couple, we could never both be a mother to biological children, so adoption was the closest we could get to having children together. We have friends who have decided to each have a child, but it was never important for us. If we had wanted a biological connection, then we might have gone a different route but, for us, adoption was the obvious choice.

In thinking about what it has been like, it was obviously mental at the start. The agency we went through was largely brilliant. We have seen a lot more frustrating situations with our friends who have adopted through different organisations. There were some difficulties at the very beginning. We had to go to an open evening, then an introductory meeting before going on the training course for prospective adopters. We had been given a date for the course but had not heard anything, and when we called we were not on their list; either there had been a mistake or they had put someone else in and did not tell us, but the worker was very defensive and repeatedly used the phrase: "people in *your* situation . . ." Then: "You're really young, you can wait", and we thought, "What, until we're really old?"

She kept repeating, "It's really important that you understand that we place really difficult children with people in *your* situation." It felt that they could not be honest with us and that perhaps they were homophobic and thought we could not do it as well as straight people. It was weird because they said "people in your situation . . ." a few too many times. Putting that aside, once we got into the process there was less of that, although they often said things such as "You'll definitely get an older child". We probably know about fifteen to twenty adoptive parents well enough to know their children and none has adopted a child older than four, so we were not sure whether the agency was saying that to manage expectations or as a way to weed out people who are not really serious. However, if they are telling everyone the same story and it is not actually true, why are they doing it?

People told us that they learnt so much about themselves and their partner during the assessment and we thought, "Really, maybe you didn't speak much to your partner or maybe we're a bit navel gazing", but I do not think we really learnt much about each other or ourselves through that at all.

The early days

Monica gave up work when the children were placed and Rebecca took the first three months off work. It was like being hit by a train and we managed because it was a sort of honeymoon period. Then Amy went to school and Rebecca went back to work and we had to adjust to the external world when we still did not really know what we were doing. Rebecca was having a difficult time at work and Monica was doing the bulk of work at home and we were under a lot of pressure. We had just adopted, we were really clueless, and aware that we were both struggling. Then everyone got sick because the germs in Sheffield (where the children came from) are different from the germs in London and we were all very unwell; as soon as the children got over one illness they were hit by another. In the first Christmas, by Boxing Day all three children had vomited on Monica; we like to think it was a sign of attachment because at least they were running towards her when they felt ill. One morning Rebecca was late for work, Leon was sick all over Monica, and Rebecca was thinking "There's me going into that lovely adult world and looking forward to a coffee" while Monica was in the shower surrounded by children washing the sick off. Then there was the distress of managing the rejection that comes when children are beginning to attach. Monica went to the doctor at the end of her tether, saying that Leon had hit her fifteen times in the week and wanting a referral to the Tavistock Fostering, Adoption and Kinship Care Team (FAKCT).

Parenting

Obviously, being a parent brings out some surprising stuff that we had not known about ourselves. We were constantly shocked by our reactions; it is really hard with three of them and finding ourselves shouting, "Just *sit* still!" I do not think we expected to be strict and maybe we would not have been strict if the social worker, whom we really trusted, had not said that the children really need strict boundaries.

We have learnt that Monica does not deal with sleep deprivation very well and that Rebecca is not as patient as we thought she would be. We are usually quite patient; we may lose our tempers, but we tend to come back ten minutes later with renewed energy. We were always the sort of people who would think a lot about the children's experiences, such as how they are managing at school, what they needed from us to help them manage it better, what sort of relationships we might have to make in order for them to develop friendships, as well as all of the day-to-day problems that occur and the triggers for them, whether that is birthdays or contact with previous foster carers or birth family members. We had conversations about other things before we had children and now we just talk about the children. They are a constant puzzle to be solved. We had some very helpful support from our wonderful social worker, who was always very thoughtful and would make suggestion about what might be going on and how to respond. Now we are much better at it and are able to get to the end much quicker and wonder, "What slightly random configuration of events has resulted in them reacting like that?"

Our social worker arranged for us to go on a really good parenting course, which went on for ten weeks on a Saturday and the children came, too. They had activities and the parents were given tasks between sessions, trying things at home and reporting back. The timing was good as it started after the children had been with us for around six months, so we knew them really well and had been with them long enough to know the sticking points. The group gave us some helpful suggestions about managing the difficulties in an intelligent way. They reminded us that children's behaviour is for a reason and not just random, particularly for Leon, who was very demanding. We began to understand the difference between him just acting up or being affected by resonances from the past. We learnt to understand the difference by the look in his eyes, a wide-eyed terror, and then he would start doing things that are quite out of character and act crazy and race around and slam doors. It is like crying "Help!"

Now he can manage to step back from hurting someone. We think he was testing us, thinking, "I'll push you away before you push me away because I'm feeling like rubbish" and we just have to let him know that that is not the reaction we are going to give, and we think he is now getting the idea that we are not going anywhere, we are staying together. It took him a long time to establish enough of a relationship with us to care about whether we were going to love and care for him. It is like falling in love and it is scary because you do not know if the other person loves you. It was precisely because he *wanted* to stay that he was pushing us away and testing. It is a counter-intuitive way to behave, but he wanted so much to love and be loved that he was scared to allow himself to go any further.

He very rarely "loses it" now; he did it a few weeks ago when Monica was away and he went over the top, but then he managed to calm himself down again, which he is now able to do. For the first eighteen months he used to smash up his room and then come in and look as if he would hurt us. Monica experienced violence and rejection in childhood and deals with it less well. Leon's anger was directed towards her because she was the one he was attaching to first, so he attacked her and often really hurt her; she might also feel more attuned to rejection and becomes more frightened, whereas Rebecca does not feel scared of him; she can recognise that he might want to hurt, but knows she is not going to let him. We had very different childhoods, Rebecca is more emotionally robust and her self-esteem and sense of self are not dented by these attacks. When we think about our friends saying they learnt about themselves in the assessment, Monica thought she had dealt with all the stuff from the past, but it became an issue. We remember the social workers saying that our children will bring out any issues we have, and that was true. Like all parents, we could have no idea how difficult it was going to be. People would say, "But they're pushing your buttons". It is amazing but they know when we are tired and crotchety and we can think, "Right, everything you do from now is just going to wind us up"; then we just have to snap out of it. They can just go on relentlessly and wind us up and then, when we snap, say, "Don't shout at me."

And we think, "I'll shout if I want to shout—just don't make me shout at you!!"

And then, "I'm so cross I can't even speak properly!!" but afterwards we can laugh at ourselves, which helps.

The process of falling in love for Leon was difficult. For Josie, it was much more natural and easy. She was younger and she used to lie on the floor and weep; she went through her grieving in an overt, public, healthy way. She said very openly, "I feel so sad and I don't know what's going on" and then she would ask for a cuddle. She would not call Monica "Mummy" because she said her foster carer was her mummy, so she called Monica her "other mama" because she had decided that Rebecca was "mama". At first she only said three words, she would just lie on the floor saying, "So, so sad", which was very upsetting, but the fact that she could voice her distress and was gradually able to allow us to comfort her meant that, in many ways, she was able to feel part of us more easily.

Amy has been the hardest, although she is easier to deal with. As the eldest, she is quite self-contained and our expectations of her have always been higher than of the others. With three siblings, one child always had to be more independent, one of them always had to walk alongside the two-child buggy and she managed her day-to-day care, such as dressing and washing, without asking for help. Leon is good at getting what he needs because he is disruptive. We have to deal with it because otherwise all hell breaks loose and Amy does not have the advantage of these skills; we celebrate when she goes crazy. She tends to storm off, which she is doing at the moment, but equally she does not have the ability that Josie and, sometimes, Leon have to be really cute. Josie has always been incredibly good at getting her needs met. She approaches things in a way that makes people want to help her and this will stand her in very good stead for the rest of her life. We are just recognising that dynamic and realising we should not do just what Josie wants and now we stop her from interrupting a conversation, remembering that she is no longer a baby. We are starting to set a few boundaries and she does not like it.

Three children

The foster carers did a great job in helping the children manage the transition to us, but they were upset when the children moved and Josie really missed the foster family. In those early months we could barely look after ourselves and could not get involved in the distress of the foster family who, at one stage seemed to need us more than we needed them. Perhaps we were slightly blasé taking on three. In some ways, it makes life easier for us because they have one another to play with, but we had not realised that three children are a lot harder than two; for example, given that most of the time there is just one of us and we have only two hands, it is hard, even on a practical basis. This was one of the irritations on the parenting course. They suggested sitting and making a collage. You cannot make a collage, or cakes, or very much with our three children because they cannot take turns. Shared activities are really stressful because there have to be three different jobs, all of equal importance, and then one child falls off the stool and one hurts herself, and if one is left out it feels like rejection. In the parenting group, we were told to spend ten minutes with each child individually each day. This was a mega guilt trip. You just cannot do it. Ten minutes a day with three children makes half an hour and then each has twenty minutes of rejection while one gets the "special time". We just had to give ourselves a break on that one and realise that you just cannot spend time on your own with one of them because they are always a group. Now, sometimes one of them gets a swimming lesson on their own and that is a special treat that gets talked about for a long time. Leon and Amy have always been very close but we have had to put some work into the relationship between the three of them. Amy had to look after Leon in their birth family and they naturally play more easily together. They were both tiny, so they had this bond, which pulls them together when they are under stress. So, any separation from one another is hard. Leon really struggled when Amy went to school. We had to work on helping Amy to be a child rather than looking after Leon. They are very tight together as a group and sometimes gang up on us. We are probably getting a glimpse of what they might be like as teenagers. Monica was in a tight band of four siblings who were very close, so she would find it weird if they were not one another's best friends. We do most things together as a family and it would be very unusual for us to do things separately. That is also a product of the children being very close in age. On the occasions that we do things separately, we are very careful about swapping between the children so that one does not spend more time with one of us than another.

Help

The parenting course gave us a bag of tools we could use; even though doing creative projects and ignoring did not really work, we got some sound advice. We also set some family rules, which made a big difference to daily life. The first sessions at the FAKCT service were quite difficult for us. There were people behind the one-way mirror and we felt we were being assessed, but we did not know who was supposed to be in charge. The children were completely out of control and we thought, "Well, they just don't behave like this at home." We just did not know what was expected; we could, perhaps, have asked, but it was all a bit unsettling. When we came away from the first session the children were chaotic and we did not want to go again because we spent most of the time out of the room. The clinicians wanted to know what we wanted and all we knew was that we needed help. The children were clearly distressed and we did not tell them off because we did not know if the clinicians wanted to see them running out of the room or not. Perhaps it was perfectly all right for them to be running up and down the corridors screaming. The team fed back an observation that we were so focused on the children that we did not look at one another. It helped to have it pointed out because that was not how we wanted it to be. It was a good punctuation point because we decided that sometimes the children would have to work around us, because if this carried on our relationship would be finished.

Without the sessions with the children at the Tavistock, we would not have realised that Josie was so astute and that she knows exactly what is going on for her siblings. Before, when she was telling us something, we tended to ignore her and concentrated on Leon and Amy as we were more worried about them because they had suffered more. We then understood that she tells us everything we need to know.

One day, after Leon had told us that he wanted to see his first family, he went absolutely out of control in the car to the extent that Monica, who was driving, stopped and sat with him on the street. While she was trying to calm Leon and herself, Rebecca asked the others if they knew what was going on. Josie said, "He doesn't want to see [birth father], he was just trying to be brave." We then asked Leon if that was right and he simply said, "Yep."

The sessions gave us a better understanding of what was happening day to day.

In the family sessions, Leon would put his hand over Monica's mouth to prevent her from speaking. He would get tools and clamp her lips shut because he did not want to be talked about. Before we went to the appointments, we would ask the children what to discuss and Josie would say, "Leon doesn't want to go because he thinks they are going to take us away", and, when we asked him if it was true, he agreed. We then realised why; he had play therapy just before he was moved from his foster carer to us, so he associated coming to the Tavistock with being moved to another family.

The parent sessions were helpful in that we had to try and think about what had been happening between us as a couple. We were also able to build trust in our therapist. We were very vulnerable at the beginning and needed to feel safe to say that we felt we were really not doing well and to be more honest. In retrospect, the different aspects of the work fitted together but at the time it did not feel as helpful as it does now. We understand more that there was logic to the process, that the therapists did not have answers, but would help us to find solutions; we were still on a fragile footing, so felt quite confused. We found the goals helpful because we felt we were working towards some sort of solution. It was helpful to be able to think about the best thing to do to achieve the goals. It was not helpful to be told it was very difficult, because we were thinking, "It's not that difficult now."

But perhaps they were telling us a raw truth that we did not want to hear. For the first six months we were running on the energy we used to have when we could sleep, and then we ran out and things started getting very hard. We benefited a lot from the help and do not think our family would be in the place we are now if we had not sought it. The help for our relationship as adults is really fundamental and it is very easy not to see that. You can lose your sense of self—which means you have got to see friends, you have got to go out, you have got to do something together.

Conclusion

Our service intervenes with adoptive families at different stages of their lives together. Lindsey and Barratt (2006) describe the adoptive family life cycle:

> The complexities that these families face and the pain and suffering of the young people is often enduring, so they are always having to rework their relationships with each other as the young people grow and develop. The evolving life cycle for families in this situation makes it particularly important that therapeutic support is available over long periods of time, so that families can return for further work or remain in touch on an occasional basis. (p. 22)

We aim to be responsive to the children's and parents' needs at different times and, as described above, we have to risk getting it wrong while helping children to develop trust and to begin to allow themselves to belong in their adoptive families. Adoptive families need positive support, which is available over time. Working in partnership with parents provides the opportunity to maintain their ability to reflect and elaborate on their own attachment experiences, which keep coming up at different stages of the journey.

The families writing in this chapter show how hard they worked to attune themselves to their children's different needs. Alongside this, as a CAMHS professional, I am aware that adoptive parents place a great deal of trust in us and that we need to provide clearer explanations for the way we work with them. They, like, us, would like to think that we have the answers, but these come from working together, developing relationship that they can trust, and finding some new ways of understanding children and responding to them with the knowledge that there is support and someone on the end of a phone if necessary. William, Mike, Monica, and Rebecca have taught me the importance of continuity in our work and of taking the risk of getting things wrong in order to support families through the ups and downs of becoming a family together.

References

Lindsey, C., & Barratt, S. A. (2006). Systemic conceptual framework. In: J. Kenrick, C. Lindsey, & L. Tollemache, L. Eds.), *Creating New Families. Therapeutic Approaches to Fostering, Adoption and Kinship Care* (pp. 13–23). London: Karnac.

Mæhle, M., Haugen, I., & Tømmerås, I. (2012). Applying child specific knowledge in reflective dialogues: presentation of an approach. *Clinical Child Psychology and Psychiatry, 17*(3), 415–432.

Waters, K. (2011). The hungry-for-attention metaphor: integrating narrative and behavioural therapy for families with attention seeking children. *Australian and New Zealand Journal of Family Therapy, 11*(323): 208–219.

CHAPTER SIX

Working with vulnerability and resilience for separated children seeking asylum: towards stories of hope

Gillian Hughes and Neil Rees

We, Gillian and Neil, are both clinical psychologists (Gillian is also a systemic psychotherapist), working with children and young people who have been separated from their families and are seeking asylum. Gillian leads the Child and Family Refugee Service at the Tavistock Centre, and Neil practises at the Newham Child & Family Consultation Service in East London. We first worked together in East London in an adult mental health team where we offered systemic consultations (Hughes et al., 2006) and have remained friends since. We have also maintained a professional relationship through the training of clinical psychologists on the doctoral programme at the University of East London, where Neil is the Programme Director (Clinical) and Gillian an honorary lecturer. We have many shared values and both of us are interested in systemic and narrative approaches, and how our practice can be grounded in communities of support. We draw on community psychology (Nelson & Prilleltensky, 2005) and liberation psychology (Afuape & Hughes, 2016), which are approaches that understand distress within social and political contexts, and relationships of power.

We begin by introducing you to the stories of two young people from Afghanistan (Afzhal and Faridun), whom we have each worked with, in order that the ideas we describe in this chapter are rooted in real practice. We ask you to picture them in their new-found situation at the point that they first came to the attention of our services.

> Afzhal sits alone in his room in the local authority hostel. The sun has gone down and he has finished his prayers, which he has managed to concentrate on despite sleeping very little the night before. His sleep is usually disturbed by a recurring nightmare through which he re-experiences the Taliban coming to his home in Afghanistan to force him to join them. Afzhal is a fifteen-year-old boy who has arrived alone in the UK. He was transported by a trafficker and left at a motorway service station. He sits, distressed, with an empty plate in front of him, as he does not know how to cook for himself. And he feels too scared to go into the busy, noisy communal kitchen.
>
> Faridun, age seventeen, sits in a classroom at college, struggling to understand what the teacher is explaining. He desperately wants to do well at school, but cannot stop thinking about his forthcoming asylum claim and whether he will be allowed to stay in the UK. He cannot imagine losing his friends, his foster carers, the adults at school who have become his family over the past four years, and he knows there is nowhere safe for him to go in Afghanistan. He feels exhausted because nightmares come to him every night now, of his father being beaten by Taliban fighters, his mother being dragged away, and of the terrifying experiences he encountered on his journey overland to the UK. Even during the day, these memories crowd into his thoughts. He has been falling far behind with his schoolwork and feels a total failure. His friends have noticed how he no longer wants to spend time with them, and that he always seems angry.

On picking up the referrals for these pieces of work, we were aware of the multiple layers of context that needed to be understood and incorporated into our interventions in order to support these young people. This idea is at the heart of practice for both of us. We both use systemic and narrative approaches in our work with young people. Within the systemic model, we particularly draw on the theory of "co-ordinated management of meaning" (CMM), developed by communication theorists, Pearce and Cronen (Cronen & Pearce, 1985; Pearce, 1994), which offers a map for understanding and working with the multiple contexts that have an impact on emotional well-being. We find narrative theory (Denborough, 2008; White, 2005a;

White & Epston, 1990) helpful as a way of understanding and working with the multiple discourses, or "stories", told about those we meet, and how these stories determine their choices about how to live their lives, and how others relate to them. These stories lived and told shape a person's identity, and to us seem to be at the heart of one of the greatest challenges for separated children seeking asylum.

A note about terminology: an asylum seeker, as defined by the 1951 United Nations' Refugee Convention, is someone who seeks the protection given to refugees. The Convention defines a refugee as someone who "owing to a well-founded fear of being persecuted for reasons of race, religion, nationality, membership of a particular social group or political opinion is outside the country of his nationality and is unable, or, owing to such fear, is unwilling to avail himself of the protection of that country" (United Nations High Commission for Refugees (UNHCR), 2007).

Refugee children and young people under the age of eighteen who arrive in a country without a parent or relative are often described as unaccompanied asylum seekers: "those who are separated from both parents and not being cared for by an adult who, by law or custom, has responsibility to do so" (UNHCR, 1994, p. 121). The term "asylum seeker" is a contentious one. Goodman and Speer (2007) suggest that it serves the political function of focusing attention on the need for asylum seekers to prove their legitimacy. The term "separated children" is preferred by some, such as the Immigration Law Practitioners' Association (ILPA). Save the Children (2004) argue that this shifts the focus away from issues of legitimacy and towards the principal problem of separation that these children are faced with, and the social and psychological needs that come with this.

Upon arrival in the UK, the vast majority of separated children are not given refugee status, and instead receive discretionary leave to remain until they turn eighteen years of age (Chase et al., 2008). They must then apply again for asylum in order to stay in the UK after their eighteenth birthday (Thomas et al., 2004). Article 22 of the United Nations Convention on the Rights of the Child (UNCRC, 1991) states that receiving countries have a responsibility to provide separated children with "the same protection as any other child permanently or temporarily deprived of his or her family environment". They will have legal status under the Children Act 1989 and the Children (Leaving Care) Act 2000 in England and Wales. Their primary need will be identified as "absent parenting" but, as Simmonds and Merredew (2010) point out, for the vast majority this only scratches the surface of the multiple needs relating to traumatic experiences in their country of origin, their journey out of that country, and their continuing separation from family and their homeland.

We will begin by examining the unique challenges that separated children seeking asylum face, before discussing how, as practitioners, we might respond in our efforts to support these young people.

The unique challenges for separated children seeking asylum

These young people have usually come from countries in various states of conflict, where they and their families have been living under constant threat. Often they have witnessed terrifying events, and all have had to deal with the loss of their entire family, community, culture, and homeland. In various states of grief and trauma, they set off alone for a safer life in the UK. For those that are trafficked overland, the journeys add further trauma, being physically and mentally gruelling, and many experience physical and sexual abuse en route.

> Faridun left Afghanistan when he was twelve, travelling with illegal traffickers for nine months, overland to the UK. He remembers walking for days over snowy mountains without food, water, or rest and witnessing one man who could not keep up being shot. At several points in the journey, he was locked for days, sometimes weeks, in bare rooms packed with people, waiting for the next transport onwards. He vividly recalls the fear every time they passed through checkpoints, and the gnawing hunger that was ever present. At one point when the group he was with had to cross a sea, they were forced at gunpoint into a boat far too small to hold them all. When they were far out to sea, the petrol ran out and they drifted for several days before a chance rescue enabled their survival. Faridun still cannot imagine how he survived this terrible ordeal.

> Afzhal tells a very similar story of the journey out of Afghanistan; one which ends with him terrifyingly hiding inches above the tyre in the wheel arch of an articulated lorry moving at speed to cross the UK border.

Once in the UK, these young people are placed in care, and many of them show an extraordinary ability to adapt and survive, learning

English and working hard at school. They often forge strong relationships with peers and the adults around them, and they learn the rules of the new culture, working out what they need to do to adapt and be accepted. However, alongside these extraordinary stories of survival are traumatic memories that separate them from their peers—memories that might be too disturbing to share, but that are with them on a daily basis.

The experience of multiple losses and dislocation presents a huge challenge to these young people's sense of identity, with the obvious negative impact this has on their emotional wellbeing. Unfortunately, this is amplified by political agendas seeking to reduce immigration, which feed public perceptions of asylum seekers as people to be feared and mistrusted. These perceptions are fuelled by racist discourses in the mass media, such as "bogus asylum seekers" or "dole scroungers", which filter down into school playgrounds. Gillian hears many accounts of racist abuse experienced by the young people she works with. The impact of racism and discrimination has a negative effect on engagement with learning (Bodkin-Andrews et al., 2013), and social stigma erodes self-esteem and psychological wellbeing through a devaluation of the self-concept (Branscombe et al., 1999; Schmitt & Branscombe, 2002). Separated children seeking asylum find ways of hiding who they are in order to avoid these negative identity definitions.

Gillian was running a group for teenage boys from Afghanistan who had travelled to the UK on their own to seek asylum. We had been talking about the stigma they felt in school associated with being in care and without their families, and they shared stories of how they manage parents' evenings. One young man said he just refuses to attend with his foster parents, another pretends to his peers that his carers are his aunt and uncle, and another said he pretends he is mixed race to explain the racial difference between him and his carers (who are black African). These accounts show not only the challenges these young people face to their identities, but also the inventiveness of their responses to this. However, the cost is that important aspects of their identities become submerged.

This assault on identity is compounded by the legal system. When young people arrive in the UK, there is an assumption of "guilty until proved innocent". When young people are unable to tell consistent accounts of their experiences, which is a common response to trauma among asylum seekers (Herlihy et al., 2002), they are assumed to be fabricating. In addition, the experience of not being believed by the state system can have a profoundly negative effect, which is particularly painful when young people have endured gross violations of their human rights. Having to give detailed accounts of traumatic experiences can further reinforce their sense of disempowerment and loss, putting them firmly in the position of damaged victim. Stories of survival and resilience can be unhelpful for the legal process, as they risk being heard as evidence that the young person is strong enough to be returned to their home country.

When Gillian was giving evidence in court for Faridun, she was asked to go into detail about his history of self-harm and risk of suicide if he were to be refused asylum in the UK. As she sat in the witness box, she could hear Faridun sobbing behind her. This ran counter to so much of the work they had done together, which had involved dismantling the negative accounts of Faridun which served to disqualify and limit him as a person, and helping him build a more enabling view of himself as resilient and a survivor.

Due to the limited pool of foster carers, young people are frequently placed with carers who do not share their culture or language, and are not able to replicate cultural and religious traditions that might connect them with their homelands. Older adolescents are often placed within residential settings that support semi-independent living, often referred to more colloquially as hostels. As well as being culturally unfamiliar, these communal environments are often noisy and boisterous and can be difficult places to live for those who are experiencing grief or reliving traumatic experiences through flashbacks and nightmares (Kohli, 2006).

Afzhal had grown up in a cultural context where, as the oldest boy in the household, he had never expected to cook for himself. As well as lacking cooking skills, he initially did not know how to shop or budget. Although there was some support to develop these skills, he initially lacked the confidence to access this support or to put the skills into practice in the busy kitchen environment. He had always been a quiet boy who had little contact with other people his age. The loud, seemingly more confident young people with whom he now shared his living space were something of a culture shock to him.

In spite of these multiple and prolonged challenges, separated children seeking asylum do usually manage to establish a network of relationships here in the UK and create a measure of stability in their lives. Unfortunately, this fragile stability is rocked when they approach the age of eighteen and have to return to court to re-state their claims for asylum. This coincides with leaving school, and the structured, safe environment this provides. It also coincides with being moved from their foster carers into semi-independent accommodation, with a new social services team, and having to move from child to adult mental health services. For many, this feels like a loss of family for the second time, at exactly the point when they are most needing support. Eighty-five per cent of referrals to the Child and Family Refugee Service for unaccompanied young people are for those aged seventeen, that is, approaching this crisis point.

However, one difference between separated children seeking asylum and their British counterparts in care are that those seeking asylum usually have positive stories of family, with memories of being raised within supportive and nurturing relationships. Their families also had the material resources and connections or knowledge to facilitate their escape, which gives them a resilience that those who have been raised with maltreatment and material disadvantage lack (Kohli & Mitchell, 2007). Our experience shows that these histories are crucial in helping young people build a solid base for themselves, as we shall explain when we describe our interventions as practitioners.

How does this have an impact on separated children seeking asylum?

It is clear that the challenges described above represent an assault at many levels on the identities of this group of young people, which erodes their wellbeing and their ability to manage trauma. The negative cultural discourses of asylum seekers generated in popular media and through the legal system permeate everyday social interactions. These dominant social narratives become internalised, and can grow into identities that limit opportunities for future action (White & Epston, 1990). As Faridun said, "It is like constantly being told you are a nobody, that you have nothing to offer, that you are not wanted." The refugee experience is accompanied by a loss of status and social capital that can have profound and far-reaching effects. Faridun expressed this when he said, "Young people will not respect me for being poor and a refugee . . . I used to come from a wealthy family and we were respected in our village. Now I am poor, I have no family. I am nothing."

Separated young people seeking asylum are, by definition, at a stage of development when the various aspects of their identities are being explored and consolidated. Adolescence is understood to be the time of life when these processes are at their height, particularly in relation to peers (Erikson, 1968). Although not inevitable, it is widely accepted that these processes can be stressful ones, even for the most well supported young people. Cultural constructions of adolescence are largely Eurocentric in their origins: adolescence is not a universal construct, as young people in many non-European cultures are understood to pass directly from childhood to adulthood. Nevertheless, all young people will have been broadening their independent experiences and forming peer social relationships, both allowing them to develop a deepening sense of who they are and who they want to be, particularly in relation to ethnic, gender, and sexual identities. Identity formation is context dependent and different contexts will support the foregrounding of varying aspects of identity. The cultural contexts in the country of origin will have been shaping the identities of separated young people, and, for many, the process of flight can arrest development as these contexts are taken away.

> In Afghanistan, Faridun was an excellent student in school and was promoted to the position of "honorary teacher", where he was sometimes put in charge of his class to lead through rote learning. In the UK, his lack of English meant he was relegated to the status of a student with special needs who required additional support. Throughout the rest of his schooling, Faridun was never able to regain his reputation as a talented student.

To state it in its simplest terms, ways of being a young man or woman in one cultural context can be very different to those in the new context of the host country. In addition, ethnic identities, when aligned with the ethnic majority of a country, have very different meanings and implications when compared to minority identities. There are challenges in the renegotiating of new aspects of identity as identity development begins again in new contexts (Sweet, 2010). Their developing identities are often subjugated by the imposed and dominant identity of asylum seeker, an identity which loses valuable information about individuals and is used by the powerful to judge others (Kebede, 2010).

Therefore, interventions to support this group of young people need to take account not only of the multiple traumatic experiences they have been subjected to, but also how this is overlaid by navigating the normal developmental challenges of adolescence within a foreign culture, and responding to the multiple contexts in which they experience disqualification of their identities. Of course, adaptation to a new culture can also bring new opportunities that did not seem possible in their countries of origin, such as a broader range of available sexual identities or ways of doing relationships. However, these choices are always made within the context of a history of cultural values that are deeply embedded and can create difficult conflicting emotions for the young person.

> Faridun had a Muslim girlfriend whom he met at school, and their relationship developed into one where they planned to make their futures together. However, with no family to legitimate this by conducting the usual cultural rituals (approaching the girl's family and offering a social contract), they felt they had to conduct this relationship in secret. Faridun did not even share this with his Muslim friends, even after they had been together for several years, because he feared their negative judgements.

This is a common story told by the young men we meet. It seems that there is a constant juggling that is necessary to fit into UK culture in order to adapt and survive, while also honouring cultural and religious expectations, and, at times, this presents insoluble dilemmas.

What role can we have as practitioners?

As practitioners faced with the complexity of the challenges that separated children seeking asylum are dealing with, it can sometimes feel hard to know where to focus an intervention most helpfully: whether to address the traumatic memories that can often be so debilitating, or to focus on helping young people develop their resources and survival skills in the present, or to facilitate the creation of a coherent story about their experiences that places distress within social and political contexts, and moving away from stories of personal failure. As therapists, we need to have at the forefront the question of when it is more helpful to think about *vulnerabilities* and trauma, and when should we be focusing on *resilience* and acts of resistance to the multiple injustices faced.

In the UK, there is an overwhelming emphasis in research and clinical practice on vulnerability. Separated children seeking asylum are often first referred to CAMHS for "treatment" for PTSD or trauma-related "symptoms". The literature on refugees and trauma is vast and specialist mental health services exist in recognition of the vulnerability this experience creates. These constructs are based on Western psychological or psychiatric models: diagnosis (using standardised classification tools such as *DSM-5* and *ICD10*), assessment, and treatment. They rely on medical and individualising constructions of vulnerability, which shape the approaches developed to address these difficulties. The NICE guidelines for PTSD recommend trauma-focused cognitive behavioural therapy (CBT) as a frontline approach, for instance. However, research suggests that separated children might have little understanding and experience of Western notions of mental health and related interventions (Lay et al., 2007). The fundamentals of Western models of psychological therapy, such as emotions, conceptualisations of the mind and body, and a focus on the individual "self" might be very unfamiliar to them (Free, 2003). Separated children become aware of the individualistic culture of the UK (Chase et al., 2008) in contrast to more familiar notions of the self as defined in relation to family or community. Non-Western cultures are more likely to define the self in this way, with less focus on independence and more focus on relationships with others (Guarnaccia & Lopez, 1998).

Bracken and colleagues (1997) offer a critique of the individualistic approaches of Western psychology, which construct distress as the result of an individual's failure to cope, and, in the case of trauma, failure to adequately process trauma memories, thereby requiring the working through of these memories for recovery to be achieved. Summerfield (2001) argues that the experiences of refugee children are the result of a broken social world and, therefore, they need social, political, and moral meaning rather than psychological meaning. Similarly, critics of post-traumatic stress disorder argue that this construct medicalises and pathologises understandable responses to experiences by labelling them as disordered (Free, 2003). It can, therefore, be challenging for professionals to respond to separated children's distress without pathologising it, and this is particularly challenging, as trauma has become a legitimised expression of distress in the west. Refugee people might, therefore, be encouraged to seek such diagnoses in order to support asylum applications (Summerfield, 2001).

To help us navigate these contexts, we (Gillian and Neil) have developed several guiding principles in our work with young people.

1. We begin by helping young people *build a secure foundation*, uncovering the stories of resilience and resources which are embedded in their social and cultural histories.
2. We guide the young people in the *re-building of coherent identities* that connect them with others, and help to bridge the cultural and religious divide between the different worlds they inhabit.
3. We adopt *a non-individualising approach* that accounts for the communitarian perspective that is congruent with their cultures of origin, and that draws on their networks of potential support.
4. When *addressing the effects of trauma and loss*, we draw on approaches that incorporate accounts of survival and acts of resistance to abuse.
5. We *work with the multiple contexts* that are contributing to the shaping of the identities of the young people, which means that interventions sometimes go beyond the therapy room and involve addressing the political and legal agendas that are so constitutive of their lives.

We shall describe how we address these considerations in our work, through different approaches.

Building a secure foundation

It is important that young people have a solid place to stand before we attempt to address traumatic memories and other difficulties they are facing, otherwise we risk increasing their vulnerability and re-experiencing their trauma.

> When Afzhal was first assessed by a colleague in the CAMHS, he was described as "not ready for therapy" as he did not have the resources needed to do the reliving work of trauma-focused interventions. His unhappiness with his accommodation, his underdeveloped life skills, his inability to focus in college, his disrupted sleep, his preoccupation with the welfare of the family he left behind, his uncertain immigration status, were all seen as potential barriers to engaging with the work of psychological therapies. It was judged that he needed to be more "stable" and supporting this was not seen as the work of CAMHS practitioners.

This view is far from unusual. Bean (2006) found that professionals refused to offer interventions to separated children, arguing that the practical circumstances of their lives would interfere with any effect of therapy. This argument becomes very circular, of course, as we can see how distress (often related to previous traumatic experiences) interferes with separated children's ability to address the difficulties in their living circumstances. We argue that addressing the practical circumstances of people's lives is very much the work of CAMHS practitioners, in collaboration with other agencies and community organisations. We believe that it is indeed this focus on helping to build a secure base that is a necessary foundation for later work and for creating a trusting therapeutic relationship. We would agree with the young people who describe the stages of resettlement as dealing with "the present first, the future next and the past last" (Kohli, 2006, p. 5). Summerfield (2002) describes recovery as the re-engagement with everyday life, which requires a focus on sociocultural, educational, religious, and economic activities.

Rebuilding coherent identities

The process of developing a coherent identity is also part of creating a safe base for young people from where they can experience a sense of agency and purpose, connecting their current lives with their personal values and ethics. The narrative therapist, Michael White (2005a) describes how preferred versions of self are often hidden in "subjugated narratives"—those that are rarely given voice. For example, dominant stories told in the UK about asylum seekers are that they are a drain on resources, and not to be trusted. Stories of people embracing British culture and of bringing something to offer are given far less space in public domains. In order to counteract these broad oppressive social discourses, it is essential to help young people develop alternative and more enabling stories about themselves.

We have drawn on narrative practices to guide us with this. White (2004) describes how to create "alternative identity projects" with people, helping them uncover alternative understandings about their life and their preferred ways of living which fit with their personal moral codes and preferred identities. These identity projects involve taking people back to their culture, community, family, and history to draw out preferred narratives of who they are, and uncover the sets of beliefs surrounding these narratives.

> In a therapy group for separated young men from Afghanistan that Gillian was facilitating, there was a conversation about how difficult it was dealing with racial taunting and verbal abuse in school from other students. As the group began to explore possible responses to this, Gillian asked how young men in Afghanistan might be expected to behave in such situations. The young men recalled a Pashto expression "barking like a dog", which was to remind people not to meet verbal aggression with an equal bark. They talked about cultural pride, and how they wanted to be able to walk away in these situations with their heads held up high, which they saw as honouring their ancestors and communities. This not only gave them a strategy that would be more likely to keep them safe, but also connected them with their communities and culture, so that they did not feel alone in their resistance to the abuse.

A non-individualising approach

Alternative identity projects involve drawing on stories told about people within nurturing and respectful relationships in the present as well as the past. The Tree of Life (Ncube, 2006) is a narrative method we have found very helpful for developing preferred identities and embedding these within the person's multiple relationships and hopes for his future. People are collectively invited to explore preferred narratives about themselves by mapping their relationships, rooted in culture and history, using a tree as a creative metaphor (Hughes, 2014). The process can be adapted to suit the group: for example, by drawing instead on sporting metaphors (Hughes & Kaur, 2014), or cooking recipes (Recipes for Life, Social Kitchen, 2015).

> Afzhal's uncovering of a narrative of himself as a sociable and confident learner was a surprise to him, as he had not accessed formal education in Afghanistan and was educated at home. His emerging narrative of himself as someone who was excited about living in and exploring one of the world's greatest capital cities is one we seldom hear associated with the narratives of asylum seekers in the public domain. Such previously subjugated identities were further strengthened for him by his involvement in a community drama group and subsequent public performances. This came with a growing pride in his developing mastery of the English language.

These alternative identity projects also involve connecting people with others, thereby creating opportunities for sharing, reinforcing, and growing into preferred identities. Identity is not seen as something that exists in isolation, but as created through multiple sets of relationships. Freedman and Combs (1996) describes this as "spreading the news", which can take the form of inviting others into meetings, or circulating the preferred story of self through tapes, letters, documents, and ceremonies.

> Towards the end of the group for separated young men from Afghanistan, Gillian took them out for a day in Richmond Park—a large green space in West London. This was in response to their request to have their last meeting in a "natural" environment. Gillian gave the young men small video cameras and they spent the day interviewing each other and filming their conversations. Their conversations were about how they had survived their experiences of coming to the UK, how they now saw themselves, and what advice they would give others in their position. The interviews were edited into a short film, which the young people agreed Gillian could show in teaching events for mental health professionals. Gillian then invited the audiences to respond to the film, following a definitional ceremony structure (White, 2007): saying what had touched them, what they thought the film showed about the values and commitments of the young people, how it resonated with their own lives, and how it might shape their practices in the future. These responses were

recorded and then later shared with the young people. (For a fuller description, see Clayton & Hughes, 2016.)

Given that identities are created within political and social contexts that serve to oppress people from refugee communities, it is also important during therapeutic conversations to witness, name, and highlight injustice (Martín-Baró, 1996) to prevent disempowering discourses from becoming internalised.

Once separated young people have developed a secure enough base, including a sense of their identity as grounded in positive values and strengths, it becomes more possible to address the troubling effects of trauma and loss directly.

Addressing the effects of trauma and loss

One of the immediate concerns relating to the present might be the seeking of information about family members left behind in the country of origin or separated from during the journey out of the country. Gaining this information and making contact can be a huge challenge, particularly if separated children have come from remote locations in the country of origin. Services such as the Red Cross international family tracing service exist to support people in this process but they can also fail if only limited information is available. Afzhal could not give a very detailed description of the location of his family home as addresses with streets and house numbers (as is typical in cities and in the west especially) did not exist in his home town. Sometimes, the work can be supporting separated children to come to terms with the not knowing and the possibility of never knowing. The grief of separation through not knowing or, indeed, the actual death of family members is often overwhelming for separated children as we begin to work with them. Narrative approaches such as Michael White's "Saying hullo again" (White, 1988) can be particularly useful in emphasising the continuing bonds with the deceased or lost person as opposed to the dominant expectations that those in grief should sever their ties with them and "move on". The continuing bonds approach can help separated children reconnect with narratives of themselves which were shared between them and the deceased or lost, and these narratives can be strengthening and hopeful and provide alternative knowledges of self.

Neil also draws on narrative exposure therapy (Onyut et al., 2005) which, although still relying on the individual reliving of traumatic memories, at least creates a lifeline with young people which situates traumatic experiences in the context of personal histories and these can be linked to social and political contexts. This approach is based on the principles of cognitive behavioural exposure therapy, where talk of the traumatic event in detail, while re-experiencing the emotions associated with the event, aims for habituation to the emotional response to the memory and a reconstruction of the traumatic memory. Thus, the "narrative" in this approach relates more to the retelling of the trauma story than to the social construction of enduring narratives of people's lives as described by narrative theory (White & Epston, 1990). However, it does also allow for stories of growth and success. The lifeline itself is usually represented by a rope that is laid out on the floor and life events that highlight growth and success are represented by real or artificial flowers placed along the lifeline. These accompany stones, which are placed along the lifeline to represent traumatic events. The young person and therapist will take each stone in turn and the young person will be invited to give a detailed account of the event. The approach allows for the construction of a narrative of the person's whole life in order to situate the trauma experiences and to accommodate multiple traumas. This approach was developed specifically for refugee people as multiple and lifelong traumas can be addressed. The dominant trauma-focused therapies are designed to address isolated trauma incidents, and, therefore, they fall short in addressing lives lived in areas of constant conflict and the multiple trauma experiences that separated children have usually encountered.

> Afzhal was keen to do some work to address his reliving of trauma memories as this was causing him so much distress. The lifeline approach made sense to him, especially as his very first memory was of hiding from artillery fire and so we completed narrative exposure therapy. While focusing on an area of vulnerability for him, the approach also allowed for stories of survival and strength to be brought forth and celebrated.

In response to the concern that contemporary accounts of trauma often support the construction of a vulnerable and fragile sense of self, Michael White (2005b) refers to the therapist's responsibility in shaping conversations that can support constructions of a robust sense of self. He describes ways in which therapists can be honouring of people's lives, thus enabling greater possibilities for how to go on. One way of doing this is to view pain as testimony. "Ongoing psychological pain in response to trauma in the history of people's lives might be considered a testimony to the significance of what it was that the person held precious that was violated through the experience of trauma" (White, 2005b, p. 19). This can include people's understandings about treasured aspirations and moral visions about how things might be in the world. In our work, we aim to create safe places in which young people can stand, helping them to reclaim aspects of their identity, rooted in their cultural heritage, which can sustain them. In this way, young people can begin to voice the unspoken and start to accommodate memories of trauma into the storylines of their lives, to reassociate dissociated memories and link them to their personal histories so that beginnings and endings are assigned to traumatic experiences.

When inviting people to give accounts of trauma and abuse in an attempt to make sense of their experiences, we find that Allan Wade's (1997) idea of "small acts of living" can be extremely helpful. Wade makes the observation that whenever people are treated badly, they resist. He proposes that alongside every story of oppression is another parallel story of determined resistance, even if this is made up of small and sometimes quite subtle acts. This can have a profound impact on people when they understand that they were not passive recipients of abuse; that through small but significant actions (and sometimes more dramatic actions) they have been able to hold on to their personal values and self-worth, and resist the effects of degradation that comes with abuse.

> Faridun talked about how it took him two hours to walk to school every day. The Taliban did not want children attending any schools other than the madrassas, so it was dangerous to attend, and necessary to take a route over fields and away from the main routes to avoid being caught. His father, who opposed the Taliban and was murdered for it, put great emphasis on his son's education. Once in the UK, Faridun continued to work hard at school in spite of his difficulties with concentrating and the intrusive memories that made it so difficult to focus. His studying became a symbol of his ongoing resistance, and an honouring of his father's

> memory, which helped him combat the moments when he felt like giving up. He realised that the value he himself had come to place on education was part of a wider commitment in life to gain the skills and means to help others. He wanted to be someone who gave something back to society, unlike the Taliban, who had taken so much away.

Therapeutic conversations, which help draw out the parallel stories of trauma and oppression can free people from the burden of memories that have no hope attached to them. They enable people to identify their resources and commitments to life, and give people a reason to go on.

Working with multiple contexts

In the Tavistock Refugee Service where Gillian works, we see our role as not just helping people to cope with a disempowering world, but we also offer interventions that challenge this status quo. For example, we represent people in court, we offer community workshops to tackle mental health stigma or begin the debate about cultural beliefs that maintain domestic violence, we talk to journalists, and we contribute to parliamentary select committees to influence government policy on immigration. Many practitioners view their role as existing only in the therapy room, but we argue that this does not account for the fact that we, as practitioners, occupy a potentially powerful and privileged position, and that we have a social responsibility to use our voice in ways that will benefit those we are attempting to help.

Conclusion

Separated children seeking asylum present with a very complex set of needs: dealing with the effects of multiple losses and trauma, living with the ever-present anxiety about the safety of family members back home with whom they have lost touch, managing uncertainty about their ongoing physical safety with the threat of deportation and the requirement that they revisit accounts of their traumatic past in court, living with the effects of racism and disqualifying messages about who they are, voiced within public discourses such as in national newspapers, having to navigate a new culture and language without the support of family, and, within all these challenges, holding on to some sense of their identity and direction in life.

As a practitioner, it can feel overwhelming at times knowing where to begin to support these young people. The majority of literature that might help us with this focuses on the first challenge only—managing the effects of trauma, where asylum seekers are viewed almost exclusively as vulnerable people. We argue here that it is important to also focus on resilience and stories of hope, helping young people to develop a solid base from where they will be more able to deal with the multiple challenges they face.

We need to work with people to develop identities that connect them with their heritage and culture, and with relationships, which sustain them from the past as well as in the present and into the future. These ideas are reflected in Kohli's (2006) research with social workers, which found that the relationships separated children made with professionals

> . . . appeared to form the foundation for the young people to "re-member" their lives, in two important ways—first, by reclamation of "whole" life stories, which, over time, displaced their thinner accounts of suffering as refugees; and second, through the establishment of networks of protection and care that would be steady and lasting. (p. 8)

If we neglect these aspects in our work, we risk perpetuating the unhelpful discourses circulating in society of separated children as being vulnerable and a burden. The individualising nature of many psychotherapeutic approaches ignores contexts of power and oppression and the structural injustices, which are very real in the lives of separated children seeking asylum. We need to find ways of addressing these contexts in our work with young people if we are to practise ethically.

References

Afuape, T., & Hughes, G. (2016). *Liberation Psychology: Towards Emotional Wellbeing Through Dialogue*. Abingdon: Routledge.

Bean, T. M. (2006). *Assessing the Psychological Distress and Mental Health Care Needs of Unaccompanied Refugee Minors in the Netherlands.* Rotterdam: Optima.

Bodkin-Andrews, G. H., Denson, N., & Bansel, P. (2013). Teacher racism, academic self-concept, and multiculturation: investigating adaptive and maladaptive relations with academic disengagement and self-sabotage for indigenous and non-indigenous Australian students. *Australian Psychologist, 48*(3): 226–237.

Bracken, P., Giller, J. E., & Summerfield, D. (1999). Rethinking mental health work with survivors of wartime violence and refugees. *Journal of Refugee Studies, 10*(4): 431–442.

Branscombe, N. R., Schmitt, M. T., & Harvey, R. D. (1999). Perceiving pervasive discrimination among African Americans: implications for group identification and well-being. *Journal of Personality and Social Psychology, 77*(1): 135–149.

Chase, E., Knight, A., & Statham, J. (2008). *Promoting the Emotional Well-being and Mental Health of Unaccompanied Young People Seeking Asylum in the UK.* London: British Association of Adoption and Fostering.

Clayton, S., & Hughes, G. (2016). The use of film and creative media to liberate young refugee and asylum seeking people from disempowering identities—a dialogical approach. In: T. Afuape & G. Hughes (Eds.), *Liberation Practices: Towards Emotional Wellbeing Through Dialogue* (pp. 89–99). Abingdon: Routledge.

Cronen, V., & Pearce, W. B. (1985). Towards an explanation of how the Milan Method works: an invitation to a systemic epistemology and the evolution of family systems. In: D. Campbell & R. Draper (Eds.), *Applications of Systemic Family Therapy. The Milan Approach* (pp. 69–86). London: Grune & Stratton.

Denborough, D. (2008). *Collective Narrative Practice: Responding to Individuals, Groups and Communities Who Have Experienced Trauma.* Adelaide, Australia: Dulwich Centre.

Erikson, E. H. (1968). *Identity: Youth and Crisis.* New York: Norton.

Free, E. (2003). *Young Refugees: Providing Emotional Support to Young Separated Refugees in the UK.* London: Save the Children.

Freedman, J., & Combs, G. (1996). *Narrative Therapy. The Social Construction of Preferred Realities.* New York: Norton.

Goodman, S., & Speer, S. A. (2007). Category use in the construction of asylum seekers. *Critical Discourse Studies, 4*: 165–185.

Guarnaccia, P. J., & Lopez, S. (1998). The mental health and adjustment of immigrant and refugee children. *Child Psychiatrist in the Community, 7*(3): 537–553.

Herlihy, J., Scragg, P., & Turner, S. (2002). Discrepancies in autobiographical memories – implications of asylum seekers: repeated interviews study. *British Medical Journal, 324*: 324–327.

Hughes, G. (2014). Finding a voice through 'The Tree of Life': a strength-based approach to mental health for refugee children and families in schools. *Clinical Child Psychology and Psychiatry, 19*(1): 139–153.

Hughes, G., & Kaur, P. (2014). Young men from refugee communities score goals for their future using the Team of Life. *Context, 134*: 25–31.

Hughes, G., Williams, N., & Coecup, J. (2006). The experience of service users receiving systemic consultations in an adult mental health psychology team. *Human Systems, 17*: 15–28.

Kebede, S. (2010). *The Struggle for Belonging: Forming and Reforming Identities among 1.5-generation Asylum Seekers and Refugees*. Working Paper Series no. 70. Oxford: Refugee Studies Centre.

Kohli, R. (2006). The comfort of strangers: social work practice with unaccompanied asylum seeking children and young people in the UK. *Child and Family Social Work, 11*: 1–10.

Kohli, R., & Mitchell, F. (Eds.) (2007). Introduction. In: *Working with Unaccompanied Asylum Seeking Children: Issues for Policy and Practice* (pp. xii–xviii). Basingstoke: Palgrave Macmillan.

Lay, M., Papadopoulos, I., & Gebrehiwot, A. (2007). *Safer UK: Preventing Sexual Maltreatment of Unaccompanied Asylum Seeking Minors and Improving Services for them*. London: Middlesex UniversityResearch Repository. Available at: eprints.mdx.ac.uk/6329/1/PreventingSexual Maltreatment.pdf

Martín Baró, I. (1994). *Writings for a Liberation Psychology: Essays, 1985–1989*, A. Aron & S. Corne (Eds.). Cambridge, MA: Harvard University Press.

Ncube, N. (2006). The Tree of Life project: using narrative ideas in work with vulnerable children in Southern Africa. *International Journal of Narrative Therapy and Community Work, 1*: 3–16.

Nelson, G., & Prilleltensky, I. (Eds.) (2005). *Community Psychology. In Pursuit of Liberation and Well-Being* (2nd edn). Basingstoke: Palgrave Macmillan.

Onyut, L. P., Neuner, F., Schauer, E., Ertl, V., Odenwald, M., Schauer, M., & Elbert, T. (2005). Narrative exposure therapy as a treatment for child war survivors with posttraumatic stress disorder: two case reports and a pilot study in an African refugee settlement. *BMC Psychiatry, 5*(7): 1–9.

Pearce, W. B. (1994). *Interpersonal Communication. Making Social Worlds*. New York: HarperCollins.

Save the Children (2004). *Separated Children in Europe Programme: Statement of Good Practice* (3rd edn). Accessed 7 November 2009 at: www.separated-children-europe-programme.org

Schmitt, M. T., & Branscombe, N. R. (2002). The meaning and consequences of perceived discrimination in disadvantaged and privileged groups. *European Review of Social Psychology, 12*(1): 167–199.

Simmonds, J., & Merredew, F. (2010). *Expert Paper 23: The Health Needs of Unaccompanied Asylum Seeking Children and Young People*. London: British Association for Adoption and Fostering.

Social Kitchen, London (2015). Recipes for Life project. Accessed 18 March 2015 at www.socialkitchen.org.uk/training-/

Summerfield, D. (2001). Asylum-seekers, refugees and mental health services in the UK. *Psychiatric Bulletin, 25*: 161–163.

Summerfield, D. (2002). Effects of war: moral knowledge, revenge, reconciliation and medicalised concepts of "recovery". *British Journal of Medicine, 325*: 1105–1107.

Sweet, R. (2010). Transition to adulthood: experiences of unaccompanied asylum seekers in the UK. Unpublished doctoral thesis, University of East London.

Thomas, S., Thomas, S., Nafees, B., & Bhugra, D. (2004). 'I was running away from death'—the pre-flight experiences of unaccompanied asylum seeking children in the UK. *Child: Care, Health and Development, 30*(2): 113–122.

United Nations (1991). *United Nations Convention on the Rights of the Child*. London: UNCRC.

United Nations High Commissioner for Refugees (UNHCR) (1994). *Refugee Children: Guidelines for Protection and Care*. Geneva: UNHCR.

United Nations High Commissioner for Refugees (UNHCR) (2007). *Convention and Protocol Relating to the Status of Refugees*. Accessed 17 February 2012 at www.unhcr.org/3b66c2aa10.html.

Wade, A. (1997). Small acts of living: everyday resistance to violence and other forms of oppression. *Contemporary Family Therapy, 19*(1): 23–39.

White, M. (1988). Saying hullo again: the incorporation of the lost relationship in the resolution of grief. *Dulwich Centre Newsletter, Spring*: 17–29.

White, M. (2005a). Children, trauma and subordinate storyline development. *International Journal of Narrative Therapy and Community Work, 3/4*: 10–22.

White, M. (2005b). *Michael White Workshop Notes*. Accessed at www.dulwichcentre.com.au.

White, M. (2007). *Maps of Narrative Practice*. New York: W. W. Norton.

White, M., & Epston, D. (1990). *Narrative Means to Therapeutic Ends*. New York: W. W. Norton.

CHAPTER SEVEN

The best thing is the lunch! My friends! Being with other people in the same situation! Oh, and the slow walking! The Fostering, Adoption and Kinship Care Team Children's Group

Julia Granville

Once or twice a year for a week during the school holidays, our team has run a group for 7–11-year-old children who are fostered, adopted, or living in kinship care. It is named simply after the season in which it takes place: the "summer group", the "spring" or "autumn" group.

We make films, take photos, play, eat a lot, make and draw things together; we try out new skills, we role-play with puppets, we become mindful and talk. This chapter describes how we developed the group, how it works, and the benefits and, indeed, joys of running it, being in it, and for the parents and carers seeing their children participate in it. I draw on examples from the groups, which are composite and real cases, and names and identifying details have been changed to preserve confidentiality.

The team is a specialist service, the Fostering, Adoption and Kinship Care Team (FAKCT), for children who are fostered, adopted, or living in kinship care and their families that is part of CAMHS at the Tavistock and Portman NHS Foundation Trust. The team offers a range of assessments and therapeutic interventions drawing on systemic, psychoanalytic, developmental, and neurological perspectives. We are a multi-disciplinary team and the complexity of the situations we work with calls for a collaborative approach, working together across disciplines and modalities and engaging with the networks around the children and families who come to the service. Many of the children have been, or could be, given a range of diagnoses and, as is common with many children who have experienced early trauma and substitute care, their needs, presentation, and difficulties are complex (Meltzer et al., 2002). They may show many aspects of a number of diagnosable conditions. Sometimes, these are just below thresholds for diagnosis, but, in combination, mean that the children and those who care for them are struggling—occasionally to breaking point (Tarren-Sweeney, 2008).

The client group is varied socially and ethnically, reflecting our location in London. We see increasing numbers of children in kinship care as well as adoptive and foster families. Children are generally past toddler stage and have often been in placement for some time. The exception to this is the number of secondary school aged children in foster care, who might have had a series of moves and where professionals are looking for help in stabilising their situations.

The children and families we see, following initial assessment, may be offered brief or longer-term interventions, including working with the network around a child, family therapy, individual or sibling group psychotherapy, psycho-active medication, parent work, and support groups.

Origins of the children's group

The children in their social contexts

Many of the children we work with struggle with their social relationships. Some are cripplingly shy or withdrawn. Some seem to be in their own worlds and do not engage with classmates, hovering around the edges of groups, playing on their own, without any particular friends. They might not be actively rejected or excluded and appear to be coping, but are often on the edge. Others seem somehow just to get it wrong socially, being over keen, over-close, or over-physical, perhaps problematically controlling, wanting exclusive friendships, falling out, and suffering terribly when a friend moves on a bit. Some get angry and aggressive, seemingly out of the blue. Other children might become wary of them, even when they are attracted by their liveliness, humour, or, indeed, naughtiness. The children we see might be well-known clowns or troublemakers in the school. They are often the ones who do not get invited to parties or for play dates, or for a return visit. This is unbearably painful not just for the children, who might sometimes have a veneer of not being bothered, but excruciatingly so for their parents and carers and, indeed, for us, their psychotherapists.

Many of the children and young people have serious difficulties with managing emotions. They escalate dramatically on the anger scale without apparent warning. Those around them feel shocked, because they had not seen it coming. It feels unpredictable, disproportionate, and incomprehensible. The children connect readily to the metaphor of volcanoes, but often find it hard to recognise emotions in themselves or others, especially in the here and now. They are often the ones who take a great deal of teachers' energy, can be hard for them to "manage" and still work with the rest of the class. Puzzled and frustrated teachers might wonder if they have ADHD, or ASD. In any case, these children slowly but surely pick up "sad", "bad", or "mad" labels, which can enter corrosively into their identities and their sense of who they are.

On top of all this they are children who are also making sense, or not, of their experiences of danger, trauma, abuse, and/or disruptions in their most significant relationships. Some talk easily of adoption, of being in care, or of their birth families. Stories might have become repeated so often that they are almost formulaic. Others never mention these histories, "disappearing", literally or psychologically, if these sensitive topics are mentioned, even tangentially.

Both at home and in the therapeutic work, we and the families we work with face dilemmas about what to address and what to leave unvoiced; we think about how much is helpful to speak about, facing feelings of fear about making things worse, and addressing the most difficult emotions of loss, rejection, and shame. Conversations about these dilemmas are often helpful and sometimes they produce real change in families' communication with each other, which can be a relief for everyone.

Groups as an added benefit

So, we would sit and talk about all this as clinicians and with some of the parents and carers, feeling the hurt, distress, isolation, and shame that can be around despite so much good intention and hard work by those who love and care for the children. We kept coming back to the idea of a group, to share common experiences, to have a place where, for once, children's experiences might not be so different from their peers, where everyone would be in some way "in the same boat". A group would be a place to work together on social skills with a lot of support to facilitate making relationships and connections. Here, children could experiment in a safe space with how to talk, listen, show interest, and respond to others in ways that would help them build friendships and enhance the relationships within their families. Could this be a space where perhaps they could strengthen, develop, and enrich their identities through relationships with each other and through finding ways to talk, communicate, and create meaning together and individually about their experiences?

Alan Cooklin, in his Kidstime workshops over many years, created groups where children with parents with mental health difficulties, often young carers, could talk, play, understand more about mental illness, and get support. The value of these groups is powerfully communicated in the films made with participants in the workshop and in Cooklin's writing (Cooklin, 2006a,b).

Target and Fonagy (2005), in their useful summary of evidence for treatments in children and adolescents, report findings that group delivery of CBT, treatments for anxiety, training in social skills and in relation to specific difficulties such as conduct problems and ADHD, can be effective. Another account of group work for anxious children argued that alongside being time efficient and cost effective, it offered an opportunity for normalisation and exposure to social situations within a protective setting (Rapee et al., 2000).

Group analytic approaches point to some of the particular gains a group offers in therapeutic work (Bion, 1961; Dalal, 1998; Foulkes, 1990). A group provides a context to experience what is shared with others and what is not shared, and what are the norms and expectations, the feelings of belonging and not belonging. Groups can offer a chance for what a person may perceive as their own isolated experience to be transformed into something that is understood, spoken about, and, indeed, experienced by others. What might be felt as pathological can become more ordinary and benign.

For the children we work with, in their complicated situations of living, being in a group with others who are in a range of similar situations is not an experience they have generally had. It gives them a new chance to experience their circumstances and the emotional meanings attached to them and for these to become less defining of their identities, less exclusively attributed to them individually. Differences and similarities between children might become thought about more expansively, building richer, thicker descriptions of themselves and each other. Being able to think about experiences at a slight remove, such as through the use of puppets, role-play, advice giving to someone else in a similar situation, can make such exploration more manageable and safer. An example of this is in the work of DeGangi and Nemiroff (2010), who describe their narrative based use of advice-seeking letters to their children's group and the therapeutic value of the discussions that ensue, enabling comfortable ways to talk about uncomfortable things.

Within this group context as a systemic practitioner, I draw much inspiration from the work of Jim Wilson to foster engagement with children. The combination of use of toys, play and art materials, play acting, and story telling is a potent, engaging, and child focused way to explore themes and emotions with children with a systemic frame, drawing on improvisation and creative aspects of workers and children alike (Wilson, 1998, 2005).

In developing our programme, we thought about what elements might need to be included. For a start, it needed to be fun, so we included playful elements; games, activities, puppet play, a comfortable colourful environment, warmth, food, outside space, and treats. Additionally, we wanted to create space for talking, listening, exploring feelings, mindfulness, CBT, EMDR, Tree of Life (these are described later in the chapter). A clinical psychologist colleague and I had both run parents' and children's programmes. We had enjoyed and valued the children's programme from an American parenting intervention, "Strengthening Families" that we had run jointly (Kumpfer et al., 1989). We sat together and devised a five-day programme, drawing on elements of this programme and adapting it for children no longer living with birth parents. We developed additional sections on talking about different kinds of families, and exercises to work on self-esteem and children's own stories, and added a sprinkling of playful mindfulness practices adapted for children and some group EMDR exercises.

The evolving programme

The group runs for four hours each day for a week, including lunch. It is highly staffed with around one staff member to two children. This high staffing level ensures that we are able to include children who need close support in group contexts. Each child is allocated a key-worker who supports and connects with the child and their parents and carers at the beginning and end of each day. This is a therapeutic group and to truly support children in engaging with others in positive and challengingly different ways requires the adults to be present, observing, naming what seems to be happening, making suggestions, modelling, and setting some boundaries when needed. This work is high input and high intensity. It can perhaps be seen as more like a residential or inpatient context. There is no lunch break for the workers; we are in there with the children for the duration. As, of course, are their parents, carers, and teachers in their daily lives. What we do and how it feels is rather different from the hour or two a week or fortnight with a client, which is the shape of most of our usual work.

When recruiting workers for the next group, the requirements are to be willing to muck in, muck about, make a bit of an idiot of ourselves, and to step outside our usual theoretical frames and ways of working. The boundaries around use of self are different. There are usually one or two core members of our team, family therapists, psychologists, psychiatrists to date, and a wonderful group of trainees—assistant and clinical psychologists and child psychotherapists. We have also been assisted by our great team administrators and our Trust's Chief Executive, who have joined at times for play, activities, and celebrations. In these days of "austerity", we have had to call on help from a local charitable trust to fund materials and a local supermarket, which donated lunches and made us one of its local projects voted for by customers.

Lunch

It is a timely knock to any possibly overblown egos that the children almost always say the best thing about the group is the lunch! They are, of course, delicious, if pretty simple. The most important aspect has been our decision to set up a well-laid table with cloth and platters of food, to sit with the children, and to model and encourage talking and discussion as a group; we encourage rather formal manners, with lots of use of "please" and "thank you" and "may I have". We sit together, interspersing adults and children, offering, asking, and passing food. The conversation rolls around as it does with a good shared meal: likes, dislikes, favourite dishes, things enjoyed, places people have been, pets, languages we speak, jokes, plans, shared interests (Minecraft has recently figured substantially).

Tanya, aged eleven, was very reluctant to eat anything, both at home and at school. There was some concern about her body mass index (BMI) and she looked rather pale and waif-like. We hypothesised, as a staff team and talking with her carer, about what it would mean in terms of loyalties to her birth family for her to accept the food of her foster carer. On the first day, all she ate was a crisp or two and a few strawberries, protesting that she could not eat any of the food on offer. No one made a fuss and she brought something of her own the next day from home, but this time tried the bread sticks and hummus. By the end of the week she was sitting and chatting happily while trying a small selection of sandwiches and pizza without comment. Our hypothesis around this tentative change was that having the feeling of being torn between loyalties to birth families and current families talked about in general non-threatening ways had loosened the bind in which she found herself. Being with other children similarly situated who were able to eat and take pleasure seemed to enable her to allow a little of that for herself.

Games and play

Throughout the day we play. We have a range of warm-up games, small and large group games. The children seem to "get hooked" on something particular each time and, like much smaller children, want to repeat it. "Wizards, dragons, and trolls", a variant of "tic-tac-toe" is a perennial favourite. These games provide lots of opportunities for interaction and fun, for trying out winning, losing, leading, following, intuiting, taking turns, getting close to all the different children. There is space for quiet games such as Connect Four, skilful fine motor games such as Jenga, and uproarious games like run-outs. For us as adults, we connect to our playful child selves as well as our teacher selves, our therapist selves, and our parental selves.

Different families

We make a point in the first session of introducing ourselves and the team we work in. We do not want to put children "on the spot". We do not ask them to say anything about their circumstances. Yet, by our "coming out" as working with families where children are not able to live with their birth parents, families where children might be adopted, living with foster families, or with kin such as grandparents or family friends, it is clear that all those in the group are indeed in this situation. We hope to make this as comfortable as possible, making inclusive comments about families coming in all different shapes and sizes. Just as a starter, we hope for this to be a different experience from the one where children, at the beginning of most school years, are asked to do a drawing or piece of writing about their family and are straight away thrown into a dilemma about how to manage disclosing or concealing their circumstances. Many parents and children have talked about this to us and the distress, anxiety, and even school phobia it causes.

In the group, some children are desperate to tell everyone about their situation, perhaps with an idea that this is what they are here for, perhaps with a more habitual disinhibited way of handling the anxiety of it. Others, we can see, are listening with a dawning realisation that they are not alone. When Dawn, aged ten, was going to be absent the next morning because she was having contact with her dad, Mikey, aged nine, did a "double take" and, eyes wide, said, "Oh, do you go to contact too? I go to contact!" This may be a small moment, but it was so important for Mikey, whose discomfort and shame at school about living with his grandma led to him "kicking off" with her at the beginning and end of school days.

There is much surprising sharing; "Do you go to contact?" "Oh I live with my Nan too." "My mum died/took drugs . . .", "So did mine." "I've got a brother but I don't see him now, I don't know him." These might seem quite small moments but the effect can be considerable. It could be the first time a child has been able to talk about his situation with another child. This was the case for Ben, adopted as a toddler, when he was able to say in his keywork group, while doing his tree of life, that his birth mum had not been able to look after him. Ben was a child who had recently been suspended from school for punching another child who had asked him something, perhaps innocently, about how old his mum was.

An "All about Me" poster and the "Tree of Life" (Figure 7.1) exercise both provide opportunities for the normalisation and acknowledgement of the circumstances of the children's lives. They provide opportunities for identifying stories and influences on the children, for finding interests, strengths, and exploring a child's inner and outer resources. As the poster or tree develops and is filled out and peopled,

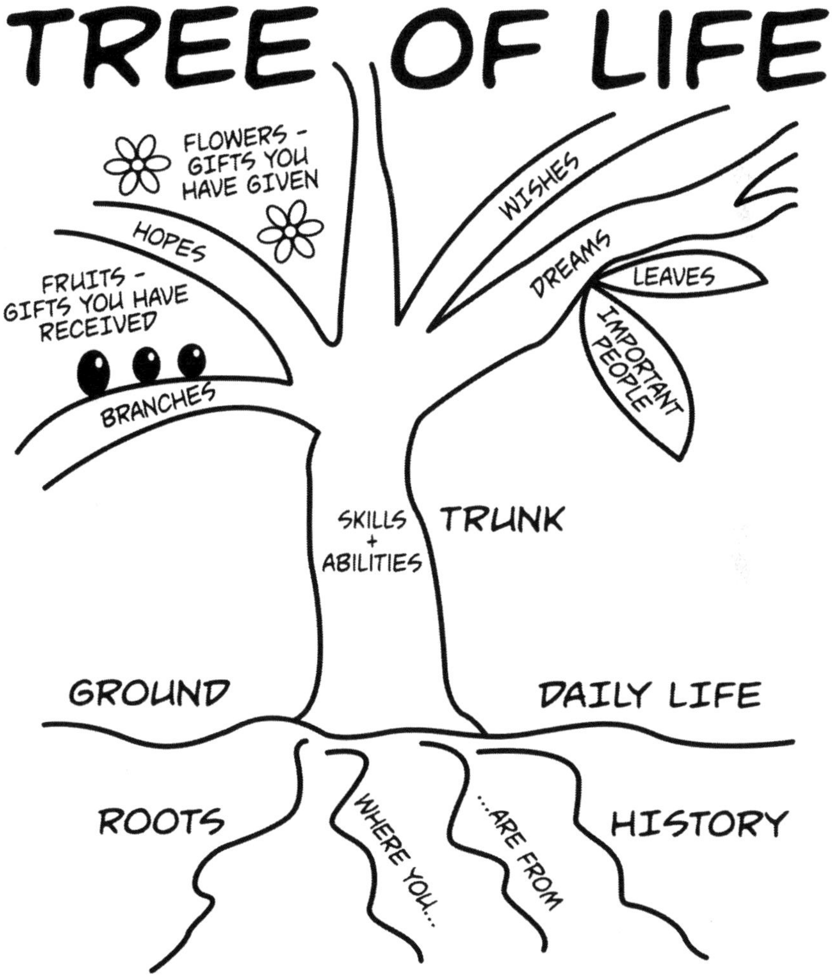

Figure 7.1. A "Tree of Life" poster.

it can seem as if the child's sense of self grows. The possibility of a fuller, richer view of themselves is invited, not ignoring or denying the reality of the difficult things they have lived through, but neither seeing that as the only, or even the most important, part of who they are. The audience for these tentative, sometimes entirely new ideas about selfhood is the workers and the other children. Having others witness and endorse their skills and strengths helps to thicken and embed these new descriptions.

Working with puppets

We have a collection of large hand puppets, boys and girls and a wise old bird known as Professor Qwaarrk (Image 7.1). They are from different ethnicities and develop personalities as the group progresses. In fact, these personalities, though they develop and change, weirdly seem to have some continuity from group to group, perhaps holding some rather archetypal characteristics that serve a helpful function for the group; shy, extrovert, embarrassed, sad,

Image 7.1. Some of the puppets we use.

cheeky, needy, angry, kind, boastful. It is much less persecutory for the children to give the puppets help, advice, and practice on how to handle common dilemmas than to talk about these directly and having to own or own up to the issues themselves. In a kind of side-by-side way, they are able to talk about some of the most sensitive topics that they have to deal with in their social interactions. We have a series of scenarios that the puppets encounter. These can be interspersed with periods of didactic learning of specific social and communication skills. The puppets are enacted by the children or advised by them on how to practise these skills and tackle dilemmas.

For example, puppets Jasmine and Tom are in the playground on the first day of term. Tom asks Jasmine, "Who's that brings you to school, that's not your Mum?" The children are asked, "What could Jasmine say to Tom?" Lots of answers come: "It's my Aunty/Nan" "None of your business!" "Just ignore it and change the subject!" "Yeah, say hey let's play dodge ball." After some lively debate, the team psychiatrist (who is working in the group this time) asks, "Jasmine, do you think it's private that you live with your aunty?" The child psychotherapy trainee (on his third round of the group) replies as Jasmine, "Yeah it can be, I don't have to tell people if I don't want to, but sometimes I do want to, it's a bit confusing."

The psychiatrist asks the group, "Do any of you have that at school?" and Amy responds, "I told my friend Ruby that I was adopted and Toby was sneaking behind and he heard. Then later he came over and said what does adoption mean and I explained it but he still didn't understand it." I respond, "Wow! So how did you explain, what did you say?" Amy, "I said something like adoption means when you're with your first Mum and Dad and they can't look after you and you go to foster parents and they try to get other mums and dads to look after you properly."

Social and communication skills

We have a didactic and experiential component in the group where children practise talking and listening skills, they get ideas for how to interrupt well, how to keep a conversation going; they go through worksheets and exercises in pairs and small groups. They have a folder containing sheets of tips and suggested home activities. These get highly decorated and are taken home each day. The walls are festooned with flip charts and children take turns contributing to these, reading things out, quizzing each other, and role-playing. Children interview each other and practise listening so that they can feedback to the group.

We work to develop a culture within the group of supporting each child to contribute to the group conversations and learning activities. The keyworker–child relationship is particularly important in this. The children do many of the activities with their particular keyworker, who will be looking out for them across the day and who is usually best placed to have an idea about how a child is doing and how best to enable them to participate. Tracking our own inner dialogues about what we are observing and the relationships we are developing in the group with the children and, indeed, with each other is our tool for this. We draw on our embodied experience in interaction with a child or within the group to help us get a tentative sense of what might be happening for individual children and in the group process. Having explicit conversations about this supports the developing relationship (Burnham 2005; Rober, 1999).

Inevitably, sometimes the exercises are a struggle. Noticing our own responses to these moments of difficulty, using our observational skills and our ability to enquire with a gentle curiosity about a child's experience, allows us to develop tentative ideas about what is happening. We notice how we are feeling and think about how we might then use that to inform our interventions, what we say, do, think about. We might comment on, or ask tentatively about, the difficulty of speaking, of feeling that your thoughts and ideas are worth sharing, remembering stuff, how it feels if someone comments or laughs about what you say or about a difficulty, how it feels if you feel you know something and want to have that acknowledged, what it might be like to find your voice in a group where some people seem to have big confident voices. We might use ourselves; "I'm feeling a bit worried . . .", "I think if that happened to me, I might feel . . .", or ask specifically "How do you think it is when . . .?" Speaking to these dynamics in a gentle way can interrupt the flow of the programme and create pressure on us in getting through the material, but it is fundamental to creating a helpful group process and supporting the emotional development of the participants. I write about this further in the following section.

From a more behavioural perspective, we also sparingly use rewards, stars, and stickers to support children in fitting in with the group rules, such as they are. They help each other at times as well as getting competitive about these. We have to keep it going or we risk the children seeing it as unfair or pointless. We have to remind ourselves, as parents and carers often have to, that consistency is important and targets need to be achievable in order for reward systems to be effective.

Recognising feelings, working on emotional expression: relational and self-reflexivity as an essential tool

Although many warm, moving, and enjoyable interactions and experiences happen in the groups, it would be unrealistic to suggest that it does not get difficult. There have been moments when we felt we were losing our grip on the whole process, where we felt exhausted, or pushed to a limit by a particular child, when we get in touch with some highly uncomfortable feelings. Having a team to debrief with at the end of the day, to think with about how to engage helpfully with specific challenges, has been invaluable. So, time before and after each group to do a "what's on top?" round, to think about the group process for us and the children, to think about the day from the perspective of each child as well as to write a few brief notes, has been essential. This adds to the time requirement for running the group but it cannot be skimped. In order to do all of this for the week of the group means not doing much else and taking seriously the need to prioritise the space for the group. If only all our work could receive that amount of time for reflection! As I write, I find myself internally arguing for the other side of the coin, which is the joyful creativity that can occasionally emerge from the necessity to "wing it", but happily that is also inevitable in a boisterous group of children.

A familiar challenge in the group is when children "kick off", will not join in, get angry with us or with each other, start to "gang-up", say mean things, or provoke each other. All those familiar with working or living with children who are unable to live with birth parents and those who have experienced abuse of many kinds will know that many have developed ways to protect themselves and survive, which can result in them showing angry, withdrawn, destructive, controlling, hostile, aggressive, and, indeed, belittling and cruel actions and words to others and/or to themselves at times. We are invited into many ways of responding to this when it manifests in the group, which, of course, it does. Sometimes, I find myself wanting to pretend it did not happen, to "pretty it up", make it better by putting a nicer or "didn't mean it" gloss on the harsh or cruel encounter. At other times, my own harsh and punitive self is evoked and I find myself wanting to put down or retaliate. At yet other times, I want to comfort, console, and make amends. At these moments, awareness of one's own processes is essential. If, individually and together, we can hold on to those responses and then get alongside the children and speak about whatever is going on in a way that can make it more manageable, more digestible. Sometimes, this is simply naming what has occurred, sometimes saying how it is making us feel or what we think we might have been feeling if it had been us, being left out, getting worried, not being able to answer, thinking about not being with our mum.

We will often pair up and reflect like this when something difficult is happening. This is spontaneous, depending on eye contact and keeping an observant eye and heart open to the dynamics happening in the group and for each other. We save each other and often the children from angry acting out in this way and it can help regulate the emotional temperature. We draw on our different systemic, psychoanalytic, attachment, and mentalization based frameworks and understandings in this. Ogden explores the relationship between Winnicott's ideas about holding; a process enabling a developing infant to hold together, to "go on being" and Bion's notion of the container–contained, which Ogden describes as "centrally concerned with the processing (dreaming) of thoughts derived from lived emotional experience" (Ogden, 2004, p. 1362). It seems to me that this activity, this process, inserts some space and thinking into an explosive or upsetting moment. It cools things down, gives the children and us an experience of having someone thinking about what this feels like. It makes a bit of space for the possibility of choice and, in more Bionic terms, might be seen as containing the unwanted or unbearable emotions that arise from lived experience from the past resonating in the present (Bion, 1985).

Mindfulness and self-regulation

Having trained in mindfulness based stress reduction and the Mindfulness in Schools programme and learnt of the increasing research evidence for their effectiveness (Baer, 2006; Kabat-Zinn, 1990, Kuyken et al., 2013; Mindfulness in Schools programme, 2015), as well as experiencing both the personal and professional value in practice of mindfulness, it seemed to me a helpful idea to experiment with bringing this into the group. Offering mindfulness to children in group contexts has a number of advantages. It can be time and cost effective and offers children the chance to learn with, and from, each other and to provide mutual support in managing stressful situations (Semple et al., 2006) We decided to do this by offering some short playful practices to the children. Being present in experience, connecting to sensations in the body, slowing things down seemed intuitively to be a potentially helpful idea. We use a simple brief body scan, particularly encouraging children to feel their feet on floor and their bottoms on the chairs or cushions. This practice, called FOFBOC (from Mindfulness in Schools programme), becomes a first line "place to go" when things are hotting up or feeling a bit manic.

We do some mindful eating exercises, taking something as ordinary as a raisin and something surprising like chilli chocolate and exploring it as if we are aliens from Mars and have never seen this before. We focus on all our senses, noticing in close detail the look of the raisin, the feel, the smell, the taste. Each child has a different response to this, and some are really surprised by their experience. During the chocolate eating, Ben initially says, "Err yuk, I hate it, chilli! Spicy!! Quick, I need to spit it out!" then later, "but then I kind of liked it, you know, the soft chocolaty stuff with spiciness in your mouth, I can still sort of taste it. I kind of liked and didn't like it; do you know what I mean?" He was able to notice both the pleasant and unpleasant aspects of his taste experience and the change in this over the time of the exercise and after. He managed to stay with his experience. Although eating chilli chocolate is not a life skill in itself, the ability to slow down reactivity, to notice the shifts in experience, to hold both pleasant and unpleasant sensations at the same time can be most valuable for any child but, perhaps, especially those who struggle with impulsivity.

At lunch, following the mindful eating exercise, we all pause and take our first mouthful of food in the same way, taking time to experience our senses fully. It is amazing how much more we appreciate what we are eating. We do this intermittently throughout the programme. Some of the children struggle with regulating appetite:

stuffing, hoarding, feeling desperate around food or rejecting it, feeling wary of it. The mindfulness is a helpful way to begin to shift some of this, to notice responses, to really be there while eating, to notice the physical sensations of hunger, taste, fullness.

We have long moments of quietness and (relative) stillness, listening to the long reverberations of a singing bowl, eyes closed, facing outwards from the circle, seeing who can hear the bell for the longest. We count breaths, we breathe together, watching and following the expanding and contracting of a large colourful sphere of interlocking plastic pieces (Hoberman's sphere, an isokinetic structure that expands and contracts thanks to its jointed structure. Fun as a toy and also as a rather mesmeric aid to breathing practices. Can be purchased online).

This scaffolding of the mindfulness practices is essential for young children and makes the exercises fun and do-able. We have all been amazed at the capacity of the children to do these things, to take them home and do them there, and, indeed, to teach their parents and carers about them. Even the most hyperactive children have engaged with some of these practices. The children might not always sit still on a cushion, many prefer to keep their eyes open, they might giggle and, on occasion, chant "Om" and dissolve into hilarity, but they do like it. They like to do the walking meditation round the room, slowly feeling their feet on the floor, and out into the garden like a slow-motion conga line.

In a brief session with the parents and carers on the second day of the group, it often turns out that they like it, too. Some children start to use it for sleep preparation at night. Jean, Rosie's Nan, tells us she noticed Rosie doing something funny the other day. She asked her what she was doing and it turned out she was counting her breath on her fingers when she was feeling cross with her Nan before bedtime. Jean was particularly pleased because Rosie often raged at bedtime, sometimes hitting and kicking Jean.

Dealing with difficult memories; drawing on eye movement desensitisation and reprocessing (EMDR) and CBT

Throughout the week, difficult memories or stories might arise for children. This can happen at the very beginning with a child telling immediately that he is here because his Mum died because she used to take drugs. For another child, a memory surfaces in a quiet patch that seems to connect to his time in an orphanage in Eastern Europe. These difficult memories are around for many of the children we work with. They may be conscious and accessible or nudging at the edge of consciousness, colouring their moods without clarity. They might be deeply buried and inaccessible to conscious memory or language. Recognising the limitations of a one-week group, none the less we wanted to give some attention to this in the group. Two members of our team had training in eye movement desensitisation and reprocessing (EMDR), a trauma therapy that has shown some positive results in research. Some had used CBT for trauma. We now incorporate some exercises from both these modalities in the group. We do "special exercises" from CBT for trauma, which are aimed at calming the arousal system and helping children to manage in the face of fear and anxiety or flashbacks. The simple exercise combines physical movement, focus on breathing, and positive self-talk and goes as follows, "Stretch, stretch, stretch . . . shake shake, shake . . . breathe, breathe, breathe . . . (then saying in your mind) I am calm, I am calm". We do this a few times each day of the group. We do it big, standing tall and stretching right up, and small, sitting as we are and flexing and shaking out fingers and hands. On the final day, all the children lead the practice with their families.

From EMDR, we draw some guided visualisations. Children imagine a special safe place for them and practise going to that place in their minds. They then bring a mildly difficult thought or memory to mind and use a butterfly hug and tapping on their upper arms to produce the bilateral stimulation that is the EMDR method of producing desensitisation to the distress of the memory. Children are prompted with examples, such as having to turn off the television, having an argument with a friend, to pick something quite ordinary here. The adults join in with the exercises while also keeping an eye on how children are responding. (For a brief resumé of EMDR see EMDR Association, 2015.)

Tree of Life

Alongside the activities, as described previously, children may talk a bit about their histories. On the third day of the programme, we introduce the Tree of Life, which specifically includes opportunities for this. This is an approach that has been developed in work with indigenous peoples and communities and groups who have experienced hardship and adversity. It has been used in many contexts around the world, with individuals and with groups (Tree of Life, 2015). The approach uses the metaphor of a tree. The children draw a tree outline, with help if needed, although we emphasise this is not about being a good artist. I do an example that demonstrates this amply. We talk about the different kinds of trees the children know, the different parts of trees. In this activity, the roots represent a person's history, where they come from, the things, ideas, and values from the past that influence them, their personal roots. For the children in the group, how they respond to this varies considerably. For example, for Tanya, the roots were her family, meaning her birth family, her Granddad, her old school, and the hospital where she was born. She also put in the word love. For Jamie, it was the city he lived in before he was adopted, and its football team.

The ground represents daily life, what you do, where you live, what you like and enjoy. Children often put their schools, their friends, their house or bedroom, their favourite band, sport, game, or football club here. The trunk of the tree stands for skills and abilities. Some of the children can find these relatively easy to identify, but for many others this is a complex and difficult process, which needs to be supported by their key worker. Using gentle circular questions and much influenced by narrative ideas about identities (Freedman & Combs, 1996), we can explore children's ideas about themselves here, thickening their stories of their identities. Moving between what White and other narrative therapists refer to as the landscape of action and the landscape of identity, we can gently scaffold an exploration of their lived experience and what this means for them in their ideas and feelings about themselves (Morgan, 2000). This is not an activity of persuasion that they are all right really, but, rather, an emergence of pools of warmth and even beauty in an often bleak internal landscape that has long been a place of feelings of worthlessness and fragmentation, walled off in not caring, shut down or attacked when there are any glimmers of vulnerability. We have found much value in engaging in "re-membering" conversations here, talking with children about people who might be present in their lives now or no longer around, but who have been special in their lives in the past. We explore the ways that figure has been important to them and how they have been important to that person. What does this say about them and who they are? For children who have lost a lot, through early trauma and disruptions, in terms of the actual people in their lives and/or a view of themselves as worthy of love and care, this can be a very powerful conversation, though needing to be entered into with care and sensitivity to the child's feedback. White describes such conversations as helping someone to imagine themselves into the valued figure's position and that figure's view of the person. This conversation is then "initiating a rich description of the ways in which this connection shaped/had the potential to shape the person's sense of who they are and what their life is about (person's identity through the eyes of the figure)" (White, 2005).

With Tanya, for example, a question was: "What would her [beloved, late] Granddad say was special about her?" We identified a special friend at school and explored what kind of friend she was and what she enjoyed about her as a friend? What did that tell her about herself as a person and what was important to her in her relationships? Out of this conversation began to emerge some tentative ideas of her positive attributes, being caring as when she used to rub her Granddad's sore feet and make him a cup of tea, funny, making her friends laugh, loyalty. So, the bleak spaces begin to fill, peopled by more benign and appreciative words, images, and qualities.

All aspects of this exercise can yield equally rich material; the leaves as the important people, the branches, the children's hopes and dreams, the fruits the gifts, material and emotional, received from others, the flowers the gifts of whatever kind the child has given to others.

When the trees are finished, we put them up on the wall to create the children's "Group Forest of Life". Each child shows their tree and looks at those of the others. We take photos and think a little about how trees can weather the storms that might come.

Endings and celebration

We spend some time with children and puppets thinking about goodbyes and ways to do that and how it feels. Some of the children say how sad the ending is, some make plans for next time, some say they are looking forward to not having to get up in the morning. As an ending ritual, they make coloured card cut-outs of their hands and each child and adult writes something on every other child's hand. They can get help with the writing if they need it. The idea is to write something they appreciate about each other. There are sometimes moments of temptation for some children to say something teasing or a bit mean, but with help they all manage to be positive and to find something they liked and enjoyed in each other. So everyone has something special to take away. We have one for the workers, too, and we get some great comments..

During the groups, we and the children take photos, do some video recording, and interview each other about the group. For each group, we have made either a short film or a slideshow with sound. The film is just for the group and we talk this through with parents and carers in order to be clear about confidentiality. The children are involved on both sides of the camera, in the making and in being filmed and interviewed. There is great fun involved as well as quite a lot of work in editing the final version. This is shown first to the children and then again to all the parents, carers, and siblings who come to the celebration party on the last day. The film, in all its amateurishness, still captures much of the joy and fun as well as some profound moments. It encapsulates something and is another ritual for acknowledging the relationships that have built over the week of the group and opening that up to the families. Parents and carers are often delighted and moved by witnessing their child in the group, hearing them talk, seeing them engaged, interacting, and surrounded by other children.

The celebration is a chance for the parents and carers to meet, for their child to show them what they have been doing in a formal way. There are certificates, presented by our Chief Executive or another senior manager. It feels important that someone "high up" from outside the group comes and, in a brief but formal way, acknowledges all our collective—children's and adults'—hard work. Each child gets a small memento of the group; recently, this has been a special children's group mug. The posters, trees, and folders are collected up, carefully wrapped to be taken home, a final handover takes place, and the group ends.

Parents and carers

Each day we receive and hand over the children to their parents and carers. This is done by the keyworker with the child. At the end of day, we talk a bit about the day, and how the child has been, getting the child's eye view throughout. In the mornings, we hear how it was overnight, what it was like coming this morning, if they tried anything out at home, and so on. Sometimes, the children are busy playing and we talk a bit about issues that might be coming up. There's a rhythm of relationship building, as we think together about each child.

In the parents and carers session, held on the second day, those who can stay hear about the shape of the week, the different areas we are working on, and have a chance to try some of the mindfulness exercises. Most importantly, it is an opportunity to meet each other.

In the group, parents get to see their child mixing with others, sometimes succeeding in making social connections when this is something they have struggled with a great deal. They know that, for their child, this is a place where their context is neither unusual nor unmentionable. Some have talked about children feeling different about therapy as well, feeling less worried about what coming to the clinic means. One child was reported telling another at school that "It's good to talk about things and coming to the Tavistock is all right even if it's a bit weird at first."

Amy's mother tells us that Amy has been talking about how she misses her birth family and would like to see her siblings. Mikey's Nan is smiling when I see her in the corridor a few weeks later. She tells me Mikey really enjoyed the group, although she had not thought she would be able to get him there. He had been adamant on the first day that he was not coming. He is already asking about the next one. Tanya's foster carer talked in the parents and carers session about Tanya's worries about her siblings and that she cannot let go of feeling responsible for them being in care. She is keen to put the Tree of Life up on the wall, to help them talk a bit more about this. Ben's parents talk about how helpful it has been at the beginning of their work with our team to feel that we have really been able to get to know Ben, that even though he is very active and can get into lots of difficulties, he was able to stay in the group. They hope that this really could be a service that understands what it is like for adopted children.

We hope that parents and carers also gain from having other adults really thinking about their child, knowing, from this albeit brief experience, what caring for their child is like, being honest about that from a position of care and concern and a heartfelt desire to understand and make sense together.

Conclusions

I think we have found a good balance between the emotional and skills learning aspects of the group. Both are important and seem to be useful. We have done some evaluation that seems to indicate positive responses, but more systematic evaluation over time would be helpful.

One of the positives of the group is that we see a different side of children, their social selves, over time and in a much more intense way. This gives us a fuller experience of them and is helpful, not only in building our relationships with them, but also in informing our ongoing work. We can draw on detailed experience and observation of interactions with adults and children, including our experience of the transference relationship, to help develop our understanding of their internal world and external relationships, their struggles as well as their strengths and resiliencies. This is shared with therapists working with children. Keyworkers will, perhaps, join a subsequent family session or meet with parents, carers, social worker, and therapist to share thinking. Assessment is fuller with the addition of this experience and detailed observation of a child, though that is not the primary purpose of the group.

For many of the children, the group gives them a rather different experience of the clinic. It becomes a more relaxed kind of a place, one where they feel more at home and can have more confident interactions with staff and also with other children, for instance, in the waiting rooms. After all, they know the CEO by name, they greet us on the stairs, ask when the next group is, or when we will do one for older kids. Some friendships have formed that have been continued outside the group between children and their grown-ups.

For staff, it is a rare opportunity to work as a team together. We also see different sides of each other. There is a liveliness that comes with the group and it enters the institution as a whole, making it a bit more chaotic but also more creative, more homely, perhaps, while the group is running. The potential, too, for the clinic to have a less institutional, more human and accessible feel is increased while the group is on.

My experience of the group, and I do not wish to make overblown claims for it, is that much therapeutic value for the children has come from the experience of being with others in the same situation, listening and sharing together, feeling a part of something and being loved, seen, thought about, and given to, fed, both literally and metaphorically, by a group of very available clinicians, not doing therapy as such, but listening, talking, gently approaching, and responsively moving in and out, in relation to profound issues around who they are, where they belong, and who they can be.

References

Baer, R. (Ed.) (2006). *Mindfulness-Based Treatment Approaches: Clinician's Guide to Evidence Base and Applications*. London: Academic Press.

Bion, W. R. (1961). *Experiences in Groups*. London: Tavistock.

Bion, W. R. (1985). Container and contained In: A. Colman & M. Geller (Eds.), *Group Relations Reader 2* (Chapter 8). London: AK Rice Institute.

Burnham, J. (2005). Relational reflexivity: a tool for socially constructing therapeutic relationships. In: C. Flaskas, B. Mason, & A. Perlesz (Eds.), *The Space Between* (pp. 1–17). London: Karnac.

Cooklin, A. (2006a). *Being Seen and Heard: The Needs of Children of Parents with Mental Illness* (DVD). London: Royal College of Psychiatrists.

Cooklin, A. (2006b). Children as carers of parents with mental illness. *Psychiatry, 1*(5): 32–35.

Dalal, F. (1998). *Taking the Group Seriously*. London: Jessica Kingsley.

DeGangi, G. A., & Nemiroff, M. A. (2010). *Kids' Club Letters: Narrative Tools for Stimulating Process and Dialogue in Therapy Groups for Children and Adolescents*. New York: Routledge.

EMDR Association (2015). www.emdrassociation.org.uk/home/about_EMDR_therapy.htm. Accessed 1 October 2015.

Foulkes, S. H. (1990). *Selected Papers*. London: Karnac.

Freedman, J., & Combs, G. (1996). Story development. In: *Narrative Therapy* (pp. 77–112). New York: W. W. Norton.

Kabat-Zinn, J. (1990). *Full Catastrophe Living*. New York: Delta.

Kumpfer, K. L., DeMarsh, J. P., & Child, W. (1989). Strengthening Families Program: Children's Skills Training Curriculum Manual, Parent Training Manual, Children's Skill Training Manual, and Family Skills Training Manual (Prevention Services to Children of Substance-abusing Parents). Salt Lake City, UT: Social Research Institute, Graduate School of Social Work, University of Utah.

Kuyken, W., Weare, K., Obioha, C., Ukoumunne, R., Vicary, R., Motton, N., Burnett, R., Cullen, C., Hennelly, S., & Huppert, F. (2013). Effectiveness of the Mindfulness in Schools Programme: non-randomised controlled feasibility study. *British Journal of Psychiatry, 203*: 126–131.

Meltzer, H., Gatward, R., Corbin, T., Goodman, R., & Ford, T. (2002). *The Mental Health of Young People Looked After by Local Authorities in England*. Newport: Office of National Statistics.

Mindfulness in Schools (2015). Available at: http://mindfulnessinschools.org. Accessed 3 March 2015.

Morgan, A. (2000). Tracing the history and meaning of the unique outcome and naming an alternative story. In: *What is Narrative Therapy? An Easy-to-Read Introduction* (pp. 59–72). Adelaide, Australia: Dulwich Centre.

Ogden, T. (2004). On holding and containing, being and dreaming. *International Journal of Psychoanalysis, 85*: 1349–1364.

Rapee, R., Wignall, A., Hudson, J., & Schniering, C. (2000). *Treating Anxious Children and Adolescents: An Evidence-based Approach*. Oakland, CA: New Harbinger.

Rober, P. (1999). The therapist's inner conversation in family therapy practice: some ideas about the self of the therapist, therapeutic impasse, and the process of reflection. *Family Process, 38*: 209–228.

Semple, R., Lee, J., & Miller, L. (2006). Mindfulness-based cognitive therapy for children. In: R. Baer (Ed.), *Mindfulness-Based Treatment Approaches Clinician's Guide to Evidence Base and Applications* (pp. 143–166). London: Academic Press.

Target, M., & Fonagy, P. (2005). The psychological treatment of child and adolescent psychiatric disorders. In: A. Roth & P. Fonagy (Eds.), *What Works for Whom? A Critical Review of Psychotherapy Research* (pp. 385–424). New York: Guilford Press.

Tarren-Sweeney, M. (2008). The mental health of children in out-of-home care. *Current Opinion in Psychiatry, 21*: 345–349.

Tree of Life (2015). www.dulwichcentre.com.au/tree-of-life.html. Accessed 4 March 2015.

White, M. (2005). Workshop notes *Re-membering Practices*. Dulwich Centre. www.dulwichcentre.com.au/michael-white-workshop-notes.pdf. Accessed 24 February 2015.

Wilson, J. (1998). *Child-Focused Practice: A Collaborative Systemic Approach*. London: Karnac.

Wilson, J. (2005). Engaging children and young people: a theatre of possibilities. In: A. Vetere, & E. Dowling (Eds.), *Narrative Therapies with Children and their Families* (pp. 90–106). London: Routledge.

CHAPTER EIGHT

The strength to smile behind my mask

Chloe Charles

My poems were written as a form of anger management. I was an extremely angry foster child who was torn between the loyalty and love for my biological mother and learning how to accept the love and care from my foster mother. I had to leave a mother who was young, troubled, and struggling and felt forced into a situation I was not happy with. I lived with my younger brother's aunt, which was difficult for me to accept, especially coming from parents who made it very clear that they were my parents and were not going to be replaced. I acted out and pushed away all forms of kindness, even though deep down all I wanted to be was loved. I did not want to be happy knowing that my mother was all alone and probably unhappy.

In secondary school, I became keen on English, especially poetry. One day when I was having one of my many rage-fuelled strops, my aunt wrote me a poem and I decided to write one back expressing how I felt. This became a way of communication and a big sign of relief for both of us.

After living my childhood and most of my adolescence feeling uncomfortable and alone, as many young women do, I fell in love! Even though I was, and still am, young, I know I am very much in love. At times I struggle to accept love and appreciate the strength it takes this young man to love me and I know I can make it hard, but I am happy to say that I will never stop learning how to accept love and loving him back with all of my being. Love is a blissful thing.

I felt that falling in love at this young age was perfect because it helped me understand something I was finding difficult: how to accept love. Not only does he love me, but he encourages me to forgive and be open-hearted to forgiveness.

I would like to dedicate my poetry to my family for their inspiration and to my boyfriend, Otis Best, for making me so happy and loving me despite my flaws. I will always love you past my mind, beyond my heart; I love you from my soul. To my mother, Judy Charles, you made me in our image and gave me the best parts of you . . . I forgive you for my downfalls, but I love because, above all things, you are you! To my aunty Celia, I thought you were a replacement, but you are a driving force, someone to pick up any pieces that everyone leaves behind, a guardian angel to push me in the right direction. Thank you, and I mean that from the bottom of my heart.

My mask

I try to hide behind this mask but,
Honestly it's got a few hairline fractures
I'm scared to cover them because I know it's
Just a matter of time before a new one will appear

The smiles I hide behind really must mislead you
Because you claim to understand but,
I know that's not possible.
Because hurt faces me around the next corner, too.
But my mask hides it all well away.

When I laugh you see me laugh, you see a happy child
When I laugh I feel a cover up.
When I hold my head high you see an amazing character
When I hold my head high my neck feels defeated

My mask is a visible disguise
My mask is like a spy because it goes unnoticed
My mask tightens every time I cry
My mask is what protects me from you but never ever from me.

(Chloe Charles, age fifteen)

This was one of the first poems I had ever written when I was torn between both my aunt and my mother. I was finding it hard to cope, especially feeling so distant from the family I was raised in. I felt it was necessary to hide my feelings from my aunt as I did not want to seem unappreciative of all her hard work, but, even at fifteen, living with her for over ten years, I still missed my mum and wished she was with me. The mask was the happiness I hid behind when around other people; I just felt no one understood.

You want to know why

You want to know why I don't cry,
You want to know why I'm strong,
You want to know why I'm so stable
And you want to know why I lie.
You want to know why I never let anyone in.

I never cry because I'm never heard
Don't ask me why because I just don't know.
Tears are not worth shedding over something that you can't resolve.
So don't ask me why because it's hard to explain.

Strong, who says I'm strong, Should I laugh?
I only appear strong. Because that's what I'm trained to do,
It's taken me years to develop this mask so you only see
  who I'm trying to be.
So don't ask me why because it's hard to explain.

As for stable, to you maybe but in my head,
I'm a prisoner to a firework display. Confused indefinitely.
You unload your problems like I don't own any
So don't ask me why because it's just too hard to explain.

Lie. I don't mean to lie but it comes so naturally.
The truth hurts, I know because at times I'm a victim of it.
So don't ask me why because it's hard to explain.

I never let anyone in because a problem
Shared will never be a problem halved
You're trying to bring me into this great spotlight
where I don't ever want to be.
You say you want to know why but trust me you really don't.

You really don't know that I secretly cry
You really don't know that I'm secretly weak

You really don't know that I'm secretly unstable
You really don't know that that lie was really the truth
And you will never know why I won't let you in.

Because I know you will never understand.

(Chloe Charles, age fifteen)

This was an attempt for me to express that I am trying to not be emotional, in order to save myself from being hurt. I was unhappy in the situation I was living in, although I was loved and had a lot of material things. I was surrounded by friends from two parent households, who did not understand the pressure I was under in sharing my affections between my maternal figures. I was, and still am, the friend you run to for advice and sometimes it is hard to stay tough, when, in reality, you are finding it hard to cope.

Broken Machine

I'm a broken machine that never gets to the menders.
I'm something that feels like it can never be fixed.
I'm a rusted door hinge that never gets oiled.

I feel broken, dismantled.
I feel that what ever I do is wrong
Even when I try to please people - You,
I don't know whether it's my approach or my general facial expression.

I'm a broken machine that never gets to the menders.
I'm something that feels like it can never be fixed.
I'm a rusted door hinge that never gets oiled.

I'm a block of clay needing to be moulded.
But every time you my non-visible creator begins
I rebel, why? I wonder, I think, Why?
Well, guess what? I want to and I'm willing to be moulded.
So my creator now visible I'm truly sorry for my rebellion.

I'm a broken machine that's just got to the menders.
I'm something that feels it can be fixed.
I'm a rusted door hinge that's just got oiled.

(Chloe Charles, age fifteen)

By far one of my favourites! This poem was written in an emotional state, like many before and after. I spent many years watching my dysfunctional biological family not being able to communicate about important things like emotion, and had become so accustomed to being emotionless. I began to feel broken, as if I was not normal and began to really throw myself into my ongoing therapy. I did not want to continue to find it hard to communicate or be dragged down by the emotional weight I was carrying. Thank you to my therapist, who was great listener and a special push when needed.

Foster Mother

You are a very special woman
That needs to be recognised

You are a very special woman
Close to my heart

You are a very special woman
That means so much

You are a very special woman
That is needed and wanted

You are a very special woman
That is cherished

You are a very special woman
Loved unconditionally

You are a very special woman
Beautiful in every way

You are a very special woman
Divided in many ways new mother, friend and enemy

You are a very special woman
Always around

You are a very special woman
Always in the back of my mind

You are a very special woman
Who is now my mother and the best at that.

(Chloe Charles, age sixteen)

At sixteen, I began to feel that it was very important to show my aunt that I appreciated everything that she had done. As a budding wordsmith, I expressed this through words. My aunt has been a big part of my life; she has cared for me as if I were her own. I think she appreciated my words, but could sense I was still very conflicted.

A letter to my human incubator

For you, my human incubator
Words are insufficient:
Mother, carer, joker,
None of those apply.
Tell me, my human incubator, how you wear that mask so well.

For you, my human incubator:
Are you worth my love, only time will tell?
Foul, pathetic, misunderstood
Three words that describe you oh so well
Tell me, my human incubator,
Of all the possible eggs why me?

For you, my human incubator:
How do you obtain that motherly mask
Cracked, broken, chipped,
And even scarred
Tell me, my human incubator
How did you manage to deceive us?

For you, my human incubator:
The one who ruined us all
Emotionless, heartbroken, bruised
Three words our hearts now feel
Tell me, my human incubator
Why emotionally tear us apart?

For you, my human incubator:
Money, games, loveless
What mother tries to buy her children . . . you
Tell me, my human incubator
What possessed you because love was all we needed?

For you, my human incubator:
Trust, love, happiness
Three things I can never achieve
Tell me, my human incubator
Why you never gave me a single foundation for any.

For you, my human incubator:
Time, breath and struggling emotions

All things I've wasted on you
Tell me, my human incubator
How you feel now I've stopped?

For you my human incubator:
Time wasting, unnecessary, a failure
A description of our relationship from my first breath.
Tell me my human incubator
Why did you always push me away?

For you my human incubator:
Puff, puff, puff
The way you smoked away the last 16 years
Tell me my human incubator
Do you even know me?

For you my human incubator:
Secrets, lies, mistrust
An inheritance unwanted
Tell me my human incubator
How do I get away?

For you my human incubator
Tears, weeping, tears
There's not a tear left because I've already shed too many
Just know my human incubator
That this apple fell far from the tree.

The girl you incubated.

(Chloe Charles, age seventeen)

This poem was written in my rebellious stage. I became very emotional, at a time when I resented my mother. I poured all my pain and hurt into this poem, all the downfalls my mother had at being just that, my mother. I left all of those feelings in every letter that created every stanza in this poem. This allowed me to see my mum for who she was. She is funny, kind-hearted, and full of good intentions. Just like me, my mum has layers of emotions and a sad past, but even though she might not believe it, she is a survivor, a champion of her circumstance. Everyone has their lows and she may have had many, but what she fails to realise is that she has five children who love her, just because she is not only the person who gave us life, but because we know that she loves us! Mummy, I forgive you and I love you above all, xx.

Finally Loved

There's a man I love
A man who shelters me from the storms of life,
A man who puts me first
A man who loves me for me!

There's a man I love
A man who makes my heart beat double time
A man who has wisdom he doesn't even know
A man who sees my deepest secrets & doesn't judge me
A man willing to put up with me

There's a man I love
A man with a body that sends electricity through mine
A man whose lips are softer then any flower petal
A man with emotions I have unlocked
A man who works on all my fears

There's a man I love
A man who I was made for
A man who was made for me
A man who completes me
A man who thank god I don't have to fear

There's a man I love
A man who holds my heart in his hands
A man that with one look has me weak in da knees
A man who I'll love till the end of time
That man I love, that man is you

There's a Man I love . . . who loves me too!

(Chloe Charles, age twenty)

Falling in love is a milestone that, I hope, every individual comes to in his or her life. Luckily for me, I got there earlier then most and hope to hold on tighter than most. I found love in the form of a young man named Otis Best; I think we both bring a lot of stuff to each other's life. He shows me that love does exist and that whatever pits life throws us in, the love of another human being can really brighten our own darkness. I am not going to lie and portray love to be all fairy tales and happy endings; love is the hardest journey you will ever take, but also the most fulfilling. He builds me up and I give the quiet man in the corner the best kind of crazy . . . ME!! And he accepts me and loves me, which is all I have ever needed.

CHAPTER NINE

Helping children through working with their adoptive parents

Sara Barratt

In this chapter, the parents in three adoptive families who have used our specialist CAMHS Fostering, Adoption and Kinship Care Team, (referred to as FAKCT) describe their experiences of professional involvement and of work with our team. Their children were referred because of concerns about their emotional problems and, for two of the families, following our initial meeting, we decided together that we would work, at least initially, with the adults. Their children were either in the process of being adopted or recently placed and, as professionals, we are mindful that children who have been in care are very attuned to rejection. As Monica and Rebecca describe in Chapter Five, children feel very anxious about clinic appointments as it signifies that things are going wrong and, therefore, they might be rejected again. Thus, some parents find it helpful to work separately to unpack their difficulties in understanding and responding to their children, alongside describing the challenges from working with different agencies. We initially met Simon and James with their adopted daughter, now aged seventeen; her brother aged fourteen did not want to attend. Following a family crisis, their daughter stopped attending; we offered to meet her individually but she did not take this up. Simon continued to welcome individual appointments; he writes about his experience as an adoptive parent below. Other contributions are from Caitlin and Brian, who adopted Elizabeth and Rosa, now aged eleven and four, and Beatrice and Martin, who adopted Lorcus, now aged three and a half.

With each of these families we agreed to work with the parents to think with them about their children's difficulties and to find ways of responding to signs of distress while enabling the children to feel safe and contained. Although we had anticipated meeting the children at some stage in the work (and, indeed, we had met Simon's daughter), their parents felt that our conversations with them, as adults, helped them to feel more confident and supported in managing their children's distress. For us, it was important to respect the way they felt we could be most helpful and, indeed, at the end of our work, they all said that life was better and that their relationships with their children had benefited from the work we had undertaken as adults. This needs-adapted approach is described in Chapter Three of this book. The families contributing to this chapter come from diverse white European backgrounds and, as you will see, have very different ways of talking about the challenges they faced and the help they received. Although Caitlin and Beatrice had difficulties with professionals, they were able to reach a collaborative way of working with them; however, Simon describes a more problematic experience of professional input.

I would like to offer my sincere thanks to them all for so generously contributing to this chapter.

Simon's story

Experiences of "help" as adopted parents.

It has been approximately nine years since James and I were first introduced to the children we came to adopt. At that time, our daughter was nine years old and our son six. I knew at the time that the odds of making a "success" of this, defined conventionally as a "happy ever after forever family", were against us. But then, I had always liked a challenge and, as a therapeutic professional, I believed in the possibility of change and that I had what it took to make a positive difference to someone's life. Over the course of this journey I have come into contact with all sorts of professionals whose role it is to offer help and support to our children and ourselves. Some of that help has been exceptional, some adequate, and some has been distressing, adding unnecessary stress to a system already under duress.

Few people understand the specific needs of adopted children and their parents. This makes getting help really difficult. Many of the professionals I have worked with are so keen to "normalise" my adoptive family that they fail to appreciate its unique and specific challenges and so fail to offer relevant help. I have often found myself educating professionals about the specific needs of adopted children before I can get the help that is needed. This doubles the burden of getting help because I cannot trust that professionals have the requisite knowledge to deal with the problem we are seeking help for and then am perceived as "defensive" or "controlling" when I question their understanding or the solutions offered. Most often, we have been told to "trust the process" and when the validity of this is questioned, we become the object of scrutiny as the "cause" of the problem.

I do not necessarily blame professionals for not understanding the specific needs of adopted families, although I do not think that many practitioners understand what it is like to try to develop an emotional attachment with a child whose internal model of relationships are skewed. I also object strongly to professionals who do not listen or are not sufficiently aware of the limitations of their own expertise. One such example is when our daughter was referred for psychotherapy offered by a charitable organisation, which puts trainee psychotherapists in schools. When we asked what the focus of this work would be we were told that "When she moved in with you, your child suffered a tremendous loss of a mother figure. The foster carer was one of the best mothers that this school has seen and it's important that we offer your daughter space to really understand and grieve what she has lost." When I suggested that this communicated a profound lack of understanding of the nature of adoption and raised the potential harm that such a focus might have on the process of our daughter developing an attachment to us, these concerns were dismissed by the trainee psychotherapist as irrelevant.

The phrase to which I keep returning is "parenting in wonderland". The moment the child walks through the door, families pass through an invisible barrier into another world where the normal rules of human relationships do not apply, rules based on the values that, to date, we had lived our lives by, such as what it is to love and be loved, to be a good person, and to live a good life. Suddenly, these rules do not work and the values are not important to the child with whom you now share your life. So, you begin the long and exhausting process of trying to enter the child's world. This is a world where expressions of love and affection are threatening, where feelings of safety are scary and can only be dealt with through aggression, where simple things such as combing hair are trigger points for re-experiencing earlier traumatic experiences, where you must monitor the basic building blocks of affection for signs of inappropriate sexualisation. Adoptive parents must do this on their own, because no one else can do this work. The impact of living with this is immense, and wonderland is a scary and exhausting place. One part of your brain is always "on" and attuned to working out the unique and specific details that govern your child's inner life and, thus, their outward behaviour. The work is visceral and physical. For much of the time it does feel like "work", with long periods where you have to look really hard for any sense of pleasure or mastery. There is a constant sense of threat, partly emotional from living and caring for someone who is unpredictable, and some physical, from the very real and sustained episodes of verbal and physical aggression that must be endured, and somehow understood. However, you plough on because you have no choice—this is the commitment that you made and the stakes are unbelievably high, both for yourself and the child to whom you have yoked your current and future happiness.

Understandably, parents become exhausted. There are few opportunities for real breaks because family and friends cannot cope with your children and even when you have no choice but to allow others to look after them, their behaviour on their return is usually worse because they experience the separation as rejection So, while there can be periods of respite, they often come at too high a price. The same can be said of seeking help. Our children were resistant to any formal therapeutic help. They experienced it as distressing and would behave in extreme ways to get out of it. Understandably, they did not want to talk about their past and the very act of being referred to a therapist was experienced as reinforcing the fact that their behaviour was unmanageable and they were in danger of being moved on. Both of our children have said to us on numerous occasions, "I don't want to go to therapy. You are my parents—it's your job to help me with my feelings." This was a sentiment that I largely shared.

Adopted parents are resourceful people and have been selected for precisely this quality. When we ask for help, professionals must realise that we have tried lots of things and that seeking help is a time of extreme vulnerability for adoptive parents, Many of us have been living with extreme behaviours for so long and have been pushed to the very limits of our endurance. Some of us behave in ways that are difficult to reconcile with the person we believed ourselves to be before adoption. And so we are burdened with an extreme sense of failure on all counts; that we have failed our children, that we have failed ourselves, and we are in the process of losing faith that we are good people, and that the world is a fair and just place. We have been sucked into wonderland, and entered the world of our children, losing our grip on reality. We are stuck, and contracted, and inflexible, clawing desperately for someone to be on our side, for someone to recognise the absurdity of our situation and to throw a rope and anchor us to reality before we get totally lost.

When help has worked, it used the tools that work well with situations characterised by lack of control and extreme duress. It has positioned itself alongside us, listened to us, and accepted the difficulty of the situation without judgement or attempts to explain it all away, or to prematurely fix it with "tools", "techniques", or "courses". But, importantly, it has remained hopeful. This is not the "hopefulness" of the positive thinking variety, but, rather, of the determined rolling-up-of-the-sleeves-and-getting-down-to-business variety. The best therapists for us have been "stoics", not "saviours".

Many professionals we have worked with have looked so horrified by our experience that we were left feeling totally abandoned. The last thing you need to see before your head sinks under the swamp is someone standing helplessly on the shore looking on, aghast, while you drown. What you need to see is the strong and grim face of someone determined to pull you out of the shit. Some therapists we consulted looked plain disinterested and others seemed more concerned with finding something clever to say than actually listening to our experience.

Too often, the needs of the child take precedence over considering the needs of the parents. Over one particular period of eighteen months, our family was in regular contact with at least three different mental health services, two social work teams, and a variety of education professionals. These involved lengthy meetings with plenty of talk about "coping" and "not coping" and "stress". Although unaware of it at the time, I was clinically depressed for much of this period and it is only through being a mental health professional myself that I was able to spot the signs and seek medication from my GP. It is notable that not one professional thought to enquire or make a suggestion that I might be depressed. Even though the signs were obvious from comments such as, "You look/sound terrible today! Are you OK in yourself?"

Experienced adoption professionals understand only too well the extreme nature of the challenges faced by adoptive parents. When parents break down, family breakdown is almost inevitable. However, it is difficult for parents to recognise that they might need help for themselves. It felt as if I could not articulate my needs, since this would detract from the needs of the children, as if my mental health was not a legitimate target of intervention within a children's service. The truth is that my depression was directly related to ongoing stress associated with living for nine years with two children with extremely challenging behaviour. I needed a therapist who understood the specific burdens that comes with this and who was sufficiently experienced to help me navigate my way out of this very specific kind of swamp. There are so many other things I could reference:

- inappropriate referrals: for example, being sent to a parenting course designed for younger children when encountering extreme physical aggression from my teenage daughter;
- various professionals explaining to me that by pushing us to the limits, my child was only seeking to replay earlier instances of rejection and not feeling good enough (as if I didn't already know this);
- social workers who attempt to make us feel better about our own situation by telling us about parents who have got it so much worse, or by explaining that "If you think this is bad, just wait until your son starts going through it".

Professionals need to accept that they do not have the answers about adoption, especially late adoption. It seems to me that there is no happy endpoint and no clear, consistent, and reliable guidance as to how to help children who have experienced extreme neglect and/or abuse to negotiate their way through to a happy adult life. There are very few long-term outcome studies on late-adopted children and those that exist have no accounts or research into parents' experiences. It is, therefore, unfair to fob us off with false hopes or crass explanations, or refer us to inappropriate interventions just for the sake of doing "something". We come for help when we lose our way in wonderland. Perhaps the best thing professionals can do is to sit with us, listen to our experience, accept and validate the craziness of our situations, and be our anchor to reality. It is not just about the children. We eventually found this with FAKCT, and while the input we got did not mean the end of the difficulties or prevent some really awful things from happening, the support of the team meant that we were able to emerge considerably less scathed than would otherwise be the case. And for that we are very thankful.

I do not believe that there could have been a different outcome for our daughter and ourselves. The help that was offered was important in

- acknowledging the enormity of our experience, listening to us, and believing us;
- not offering false hopes or over-promising what could be achieved;
- being a consistent presence throughout the journey;
- working from a position of expertise in this area—albeit in a non-expert way.

It seems to me that adopted parents often suffer from a similar problem as their children when it comes to receiving help. In the same way that our children cannot often trust their adopted parents to help, support, and love them because of bad experiences in the past, adopted parents might struggle to accept help because of previous experiences of being manhandled by a system that does not fully understand their needs.

Caitlin and Brian's story

I was asked to contribute to this chapter giving an account of my family's experience of receiving support from FAKCT at the Tavistock Clinic and how it helped us in supporting and parenting our adopted children. I hope to link some of our personal experiences to research, particularly in relation to the therapeutic support needs of adopted children and their (adoptive) parents.

The current government "agenda" regarding adoption support is largely a response to the consequences of a previous situation of either none or sporadic and inconsistent support for adoptive families (Rushton & Monck, 2009; Social Services Inspectorate, 2000). This inadequate support for adoptive families was seen to contribute to poor outcomes for many adoptive children, including increased risk of mental ill health and an increased risk of adoption disruptions (Rushton & Monck, 2009).

Our family's adoption journey began in 2011, when two children arrived at my home one winter's night. I had been a foster carer for eleven years and had fostered over twenty-five children and young people. These particular children were placed as a "short-term placement" while work was done with their mother to make it safe for them to return home. The children continued to see their separated birth parents regularly, and sometimes there were eight contact sessions in any given week. Care proceedings were protracted for many reasons and within a few months it was the view of the local authority that the children could not return home and that a permanent placement should be sought for them. It still feels difficult to put into words the bond and attachment I felt towards them at a very early stage—almost immediately, which I had not had with any of my other fostered children. Previously, I had grown to love and feel strong bonds towards the children I fostered, but this had grown over time, rather than being immediate. I remember, within the first days of the girls arriving with me, watching them "play" together, and feeling really strongly that if they could not return home, then I would want them to stay with me. We immediately asked to be considered to be their permanent or adoptive parents and the necessary assessments began. We finally adopted the children, Elizabeth and Rosa, at the end of 2013, almost three years after they had first come into our lives.

During the care proceedings for the children, assessments were made of their emotional and psychological health, their attachment styles and needs. Separate assessments were undertaken involving an independent child psychiatrist, independent child psychologist, and independent child psychotherapist. These assessments considered that Elizabeth, aged nine at the time, was in need of therapeutic support regarding her previous maltreatment and associated attachment needs, the loss of her birth family, and her determined resistance to the plans for her adoption. As a result of these assessments, the local authority made a referral to FAKCT and we received a service from them for a year.

While we felt confident that we would be able to rise to the challenge of parenting our two children, we were hugely thankful for the referral and the support we received in helping us in that task. I felt reasonably equipped to negotiate the road ahead; however, although we had fostered many children, we had never been parents before, let alone adoptive parents, with all the added dimensions which adoption brings. Our children had birth siblings who were to be adopted by another family. The local authority was concerned that the needs, wishes, and feelings of our eldest child, Elizabeth, conflicted with those of our younger child, Rosa (whose birth father was the main perpetrator of the serious physical abuse). They were also concerned that Elizabeth, who was resistant to being adopted and had consistently stated that her wish was to return home to her birth mother, might jeopardise Rosa's place in our family. There were times when they were considering placing Rosa in a separate adoptive family, which caused us much distress. Fortunately, it was agreed that both children could remain with us, but that careful thought should be given to how we would balance their current and future needs.

Lowe and colleagues (1999, p. 436) state, "The primary task of adoption support should be defined as enabling adopters to learn as rapidly as possible the skills of parenting children who have experienced extraordinary and turbulent childhoods" (cited in Gilkes & Klimes, 2003).

This "definition", albeit somewhat simplistic, probably summed up our initial expectations of the kind of support we felt we needed. I had expected that we would be seen together as a family, certainly with Elizabeth, if not Rosa (who was under two at the time of the referral). My previous experience of attending CAMHS with looked-after children was that the child was present for most, if not all, of the (post assessment) sessions. The psychological assessments of Elizabeth (conducted during the care proceedings) concluded that she was "highly defended", "parentified", and had "significant attachment needs". One of the recommendations included individual psychotherapy for her.

Prior to us attending for our initial meeting, we had a telephone consultation with one of the therapists. Elizabeth had become very distressed at home the previous evening, saying she was afraid she was going to harm people at her school and that she did not know why, but she felt she wanted to really hurt people, even though they were her teachers and friends. She had no history of violence and aggression and was only a small and slight nine-year-old, so I did not have immediate concerns for anyone's safety. However, my daughter was clearly distressed and frightened by the thoughts she was having. I contacted her social worker, who said they would immediately contact the FAKC Team to ask if Elizabeth could be seen sooner than our planned initial appointment in a few weeks.

One of the therapists from the team telephoned me straightaway to talk through what had happened and what my worries were. We had not, at this point, had any contact with anyone at the Tavistock Clinic and so this was our first experience of having a "service" from them. The telephone consultation was helpful on a number of levels. First, it was a prompt response to what felt like an urgent issue. I had taken on some of the panic and distress Elizabeth was feeling. Speaking to the therapist soon reassured me that I *did* have the skills and knowledge to help Elizabeth and that I was the best person to do this. He pointed out that she had voluntarily told *me* about the scary thoughts and feelings she was having, which was itself an indicator that I was the person she wanted help and support from. Looking back, all of this seems so obvious, but, at the time, I felt as if this was something way bigger and more complex than I could manage on my own.

During our initial meeting, the therapists introduced the idea of working directly with us, at least initially, but not actually seeing our children. While I had theoretical knowledge of this way of working, I had never experienced it before and was not expecting it to be the model that would be used for Elizabeth, given the recommendations of the independent psychological reports. However, as soon as we started to think about and discuss the benefit of working in this way, it made perfect sense and seemed entirely appropriate and preferable. Hart and Thomas (2000) suggest that direct interventions or sessions with children can compromise significant attachments, in cases where the child already has attachment needs, but that indirect therapy (with parents and carers) actually promotes these attachment relationships.

Furthermore, parents and carers feel empowered to provide the required support and nurturing to their child rather than feeling that only therapists are able to do this. We certainly felt, at every stage, that working in this way had huge benefits for us. We felt supported to parent our children and provide them with the therapeutic care they needed without them needing to see a therapist. Indeed, Elizabeth had little or no knowledge of the fact that we were attending FAKCT. We talked to her in very general terms about meetings with people who help us to think about how to be good adoptive parents, but this would almost always be responded to with a "but you *are* good adoptive parents". While we feel that we would still have been good enough, attending the sessions helped us to think in more detail about the best way to support our children and to challenge previous assumptions we had around this.

Following our initial meeting, Brian and I attended sessions at 3–6 weekly intervals over twelve months. Golding and colleagues (2006), writing about the psychological needs of children who are looked after or adopted, emphasise the importance of having a reflective team in a room when discussing the best ways to support children and their parents. They also stress the need for any interventions to be focused on the parents' or carers' views rather than those presented by other professionals. For us, it was helpful to meet with two therapists, which enabled us to think things through more. We tended to derive different benefits from each of them and it was really positive to have that level of reflexivity in the sessions. We also felt we were able to "lead" the sessions in terms of what we wanted to bring or discuss, rather than simply receiving the views or assessments of other professionals. This meant we felt heard and listened to as though we were, in fact, "the experts" on *our* children and their needs, something which we had not felt in many of our dealings with the local authority.

Probably our most immediate concern was Elizabeth's emotional wellbeing. She had experienced and witnessed extremely frightening situations within her family, including serious physical abuse and domestic violence. As the eldest of four children, she felt a big sense of responsibility and guilt at not having been able to protect her younger siblings. She was also fiercely loyal to her mother, despite the serious concerns about her parenting and protection of her children.

The local authority was concerned that Rosa's father posed a serious risk of violence to our family and his imminent release from prison meant that we were required to move to a different area and change all our names. This meant that Elizabeth had to move to a new school. We knew all of these things would be very difficult for her, particularly alongside being adopted and no longer having direct contact with her birth family. We predicted that she would really struggle with all of this given that she found any small change difficult, for example, a new front door, me having my hair cut, me tidying her bedroom or changing her bed linen. The therapists helped us think through the impact of these changes and, while we had done a lot of thinking about the impact this would have on the children, we had probably minimised or "parked" the significant way in which it affected us as adults.

During our sessions, we explored how *we* were feeling and what our anxieties and fears were for ourselves. I recall that I felt a huge sense of sadness about leaving my previous home and street and neighbours to move to my partner's home in an area where I knew only him and one other person. I was also struggling with the prospect of changing my surname, as I really identified with my name, which I had kept, despite being previously married. As a couple, we had never lived together; rather, we spent weekends at each other's houses, with the children, and lived separately during the week. We both knew that living together would have its challenges, but we were in no doubt about wanting to do it. I recall we had a tendency to minimise the impact on *us* and concentrated on the needs of the children. Having the opportunity, time, and space to think about and talk about *ourselves* was really helpful, and probably would not have happened otherwise.

Our children seemed to adjust to the changes amazingly well. Dance and Rushton (2005) cite a number of issues that can cause difficulties for children adopted in mid-childhood. For Elizabeth, they included starting a new school and what to tell new friends about being adopted. With the therapists, we thought about ways to help Elizabeth negotiate those conversations and we spent a fair amount of time talking with her about what *she* wanted to say to people if they asked and what *she* wanted her story to be. She decided on the information she wanted to share and now feels confident in managing what she tells different people about her history. Both children seem to have settled well into our new home and community and both have new local friends.

Despite the huge adjustments both children have had to make, Elizabeth still struggles with the loss of her birth family. She no longer has direct contact with her birth mother but often speaks of "finding her" when she is older. She is particularly saddened by the loss of her other siblings. The plan for all the children was that there would be regular and ongoing face-to-face sibling contact, but the other adoptive family do not want to continue this and letterbox contact has been disappointingly sporadic. This has been really tricky for us, as a family, to negotiate sensitively. I struggled with the decision of the other adoptive parents not to maintain contact with our children. This was largely due to seeing Elizabeth's distress and feeling powerless to do anything. While I continue to feel saddened, angry, and frustrated by the lack of sibling contact, thanks to the sessions I am able to pull back from this unhelpful position and concentrate instead on helping our children to manage the situation as it is. I was particularly conscious of the overlap and blurring of Elizabeth's feelings about the lack of contact with my own, and I wanted to ensure I focused on her feelings rather than on mine.

For us, both as foster carers and adoptive parents, our focus has always been to build positive and nurturing relationships with the children we care for. Rosa has lived with us since she was a few weeks old and appears to have little or no memory of her birth family. Elizabeth remains fiercely loyal to her birth family and always resisted becoming part of another "family". She has found her own ways of making this all right for her: for example, by being clear she was not actively consenting to her adoption, by never calling us Mum or Dad, and by talking frequently about her birth family. Our sessions were helpful in reminding and supporting us to maintain what Hart and Thomas (2000) call a "therapeutic role" in our parenting. Key elements of this included totally accepting Elizabeth where she was "at" with her feelings around adoption, her birth family, and what we signified in her life. We are fortunate that she feels able to tell us what she is feeling and what might be troubling her, knowing that we will accept and support her with whatever she brings (Figure 9.1).

Hart and Luckock (2006) also state that many adoptive parents can feel reluctant and uneasy about attending therapy sessions, as they are anxious that their discussions, anxieties, and feelings might be shared with the social workers. They explain that "In fostering and adoption, the adults who bring their children to therapy find their parenting

Figure 9.1. Alone, by Agata Morgan.

under the spotlight of the very authorities they had persuaded to let them try" (Hart & Luckock, 2006, p. 30). It was important to us that FAKCT was independent of the local authority and we felt we benefited hugely from the service we received. Our first contact over the phone, at a time of high anxiety, was very reassuring and "containing" and our direct sessions with the therapists were appropriately challenging, empathic, and reflexive. One of the therapists attended two professionals' meetings, and made helpful contributions about the impact of the threat posed by the birth family on our day-to-day family life. We, as a couple, had possibly played down the realities of that threat and the impact it had on us and it was, therefore, useful to have this issue kept on the professional agenda.

Hart and Luckock (2006) cite a number of "core principles and therapeutic objectives" (p. 29), which are key to working with adoptive and foster families. These include "offering prompt attention", which we certainly experienced, and "continuity of agency and therapist", which again we were lucky enough to experience over the course of a year. The model of supporting our child "indirectly" via our sessions with the therapists certainly worked well for our family. The therapists felt that it was important that Elizabeth, who had seen and been visited by a huge number of professionals since coming into care, should be supported by *us* as her carers and prospective parents. The team felt that it would be more therapeutic for Elizabeth for us to help her manage her feelings and anxieties rather than attending therapy sessions herself. While this was not the model we were expecting, we were really pleased that this is the way in which we all agreed to work and we feel it has benefited our child much more than had she herself been "seen" at the Tavistock Clinic. It is now almost a year since our final session and we are continuing to use what we learnt there in caring for and parenting our children. We certainly do not get it "right" all the time, but, overall, both our daughters are settled, happy, and healthy children and family life feels good.

Beatrice's story

We adopted our son through an agency, which provides excellent continued support and it was our social worker there who referred us to FAKCT and I am very grateful that I worked with a family therapist who was able to understand and whom I could trust.

Lorcus was placed with us at eleven months and two weeks old. He presented as a happy and stable child. The chief medical officer of the council we adopted from had warned us that he would "undoubtedly suffer from learning difficulties". We could find no medical evidence for this and trusted our instinct that this was wrong. He is now three and a half and shows no signs of such difficulties. However, he was very scared.

From the start, Lorcus seemed to have no idea how to give or accept a cuddle. He would not sit on our laps and he pushed away when in our arms. He woke up screaming, sometimes twelve times a night. He played completely independently. He did make good eye contact and he was clearly "advanced". He was toddling and had been for months and he learnt to speak very soon after we became a family. The lack of sleep was poleaxing for us all. We now realise it was sleeplessness that our social worker wanted us to get help with. By the time this help was needed there was a far more overwhelming problem, and it was this that we wanted help for. The second problem was violence, or what we learnt very quickly to identify as Lorcus's fear manifesting itself as violence. Some days it was impossible to set him down in the park without him rushing at the nearest (usually younger) child and really hurting that child if we did not get there first to stop him. He grabbed handfuls of hair, he would bite, hit, and kick, and used anything that came to hand as a weapon. There were scary and well-aimed blows. He also attacked Martin and me. I did keep an occasional diary and, on one average day, he attacked me eighteen times, sometimes drawing blood with his bites and scratches to the eyes. By the time we were referred to the Tavistock, Lorcus was two and three quarters, this had been going on for a year and a half, and he still sometimes took hours to get to sleep and often woke up five or six times a night.

Martin and I had no idea what form the help would take and we were not sure if we should all be going or just me. We decided that the last thing Lorcus wanted was a visit to another place that felt like social services. He must have spent so many hours in those kinds of places as a baby and I could not begin to imagine how I would describe what was going on and what we needed in his presence. I knew enough to know that the change had to come from us, and that magic was what was needed. We had to become parents who knew how to give him what he needed and then give it. As I type this, I am recalling how extraordinary it was to feel heard. On that very first session the family therapist was clear that this was work that needed to happen between the adults and the thing that struck me, profoundly, was that her support seemed to be tailor-made for me, as if I was the first person she has seen in this way. It sounds pathetic, but I so needed to feel unique. I needed to feel validated and, far more urgently, I needed practical help.

On that practical level I was able to spill out all the horrible realities of daily life. Just "telling", in what felt like an endless stream, although scary in a "Pandora's box is now open" kind of way, was also vital. I had to tell and have her tell me back that "yes, this is very bad and there is no point in blaming yourself" before I could actually allow myself to admit the worst, which was that in my darkest moments I had reached the end of my resources. I knew I would not kill myself because I could not leave Lorcus with that horror, but the therapist did enable me to admit that I was imagining how to die as if by accident. She also embarked on what felt like a fast-forward psychotherapeutic analysis of my own childhood and the vagaries of how I had been parented. She released years of anger, but constructively, so that I was able to move on and start to see how I could do things differently.

I have had a lot of psychotherapy over the years and what was offered was very different. This therapist talked back. She gave a lot of advice, which was unconventional, but it was constructed to the individual needs of our family. The most instantly useful thing was a reward system, which is not usually recommended for an adopted child. This was suggested with the proviso that if it worked it would also stop working, but it gave us six weeks with controlled and transformed violence. This came over Christmas and it opened the floodgates of hope because we saw that Lorcus could stop hurting. It also gave us breathing space for empathy, which was much easier to give when the abhorrent behaviour stopped.

The psychotherapist also freed me from idealising the foster carer; I began to form my own opinions about how adopted children should be supported through the beginning of placement and developed confidence to stop slavishly following rules which clearly were not working for the kind of parents we are or the kind of child Lorcus is. The things I wish I had decided for myself during those first few months and which differ from current thinking on adoption are the following.

- I wish we had observed Lorcus in a neutral environment, like play group, before placement, and that we would have been allowed to do this five to six times if this was what we felt we needed.
- I wish we had changed his name and that the foster carers had introduced that name and called him by it.
- I wish we had let other members of our family cuddle him rather than following the advice to be the only ones to touch him. We did this for over six months, creating such neurosis around him and a barrier between him and our loving family.
- I wish we had sent our clothes to dress him, and items with our smell on them before we saw him, as well as introducing items from the foster carers' house to ours so that their smell was within our home.
- I wish we had insisted the foster carers visited for weeks after placement rather than worrying that it was too painful for them.

While I was able to admit these wishes, I was also able to move on from the regrets. I left every week with an action plan, often a "script" that I had requested and phrases that I could use to speak constructively with Lorcus. Once it was a remarkable tapping exercise from EMDR. I needed these practical exercises like a lifeline to start off with, and was aware that the week I stopped scribbling everything down was the week I really begin to use the ideas. As I write, I realise that I began to feel empowered in my parenting choices, consequently enabling me to love my brilliant boy on a completely different level. No mean feat.

Lorcus is now three years and eight months old. He can still hurt Martin and me, but we often have days where this does not happen and, if it does, we contain it and can understand why it is happening. He still attacks other children in the park but this is only about once a week rather than every child that comes near him. He still, occasionally grabs his cousin's hair, but it is no longer a frenzied, ongoing attack. There have been whole play dates where it has all been shrieks of delight and rough and tumble. Lorcus now sometimes sleeps through until five in the morning and recently bedtime has started to resemble a "normal" routine with no door slamming or screaming (from any of us!). We now use humour and patience, wherever possible, for the seemingly endless frustrations around all forms of transition. I have been known to sit silently waiting in the loo for up to half an hour for Lorcus to come and have the pee he is clearly bursting to have. We use descriptive praise slavishly.

Lorcus has started nursery, although he weeps and clings like a baby monkey when I leave him. He has been there for six months for four mornings a week; he is coping and he has never hurt any of the other children there. Martin and I hold hands again and I have started to go out and about on public transport with Lorcus again. He is often rude to strangers and sometimes spits at them, but he hits out rarely. I have learnt that ignoring my deep-seated desire to be seen as a golden parent and blank out Lorcus's behaviour, no matter how offensive, helps him through it quicker than telling him to say sorry and getting off the bus. Lorcus has learnt to hug. It is just for a second or two, but it is magic.

Conclusion

Simon, Caitlin, and Beatrice's stories are both as differing and unique as the children they have adopted. While there are often common themes in parenting adopted children, adoptive families are by no means a homogenous group, as these three stories show.

What is clear from these three accounts is that every adoptive parent, adopted child, and adoptive family is different. There is no cure-all model of working with children and parents which works for every adoptive family. However, what seems to have been crucial for all three parents in this chapter is the need to be heard and listened to by professionals and for someone to acknowledge the immense challenges and difficulties that can arise for adoptive parents.

References

Dance, C., & Rushton, A. (2005). Joining a new family: the views and experiences of young people placed with permanent families during middle childhood. *Adoption and Fostering, 29*: 18–28.

Gilkes, L., & Klimes, I. (2003). Parenting skills for adoptive parents. *Adoption and Fostering, 27*: 19–25.

Golding, K., Dent, H., Nissim, R., & Stott, L. (Eds.) (2006). *Thinking Psychologically about Children Who Are Looked After or Adopted*. Chichester: Wiley Blackwell.

Hart, A., & Luckock, B. (2006). Core principles and therapeutic objectives for therapy with adoptive and permanent foster families. *Adoption & Fostering, 30*: 29–42.

Hart, A., & Thomas, H. (2000). Controversial attachments: the indirect treatment of fostered and adopted children via parent co-therapy. *Attachment and Human Development, 2*: 306–327.

Lowe, N., Murch, M., Borkowski, M., Weaver, A., Beckford, V., & Thomas, C. (1999). *Supporting Adoption: Reforming the Approach*. London: British Agencies for Adoption and Fostering.

Rushton, A., & Monck, E. (2009). *Enhancing Adoptive Parenting: A Test of Effectiveness*. London: British Association of Adoption and Fostering.

Social Services Inspectorate (2000). *Adopting Changes: Survey and Inspection of Local Councils' Adoption Services*. London: Stationery Office.

PART III

THE VOICES OF ADULTS WHO HAVE BEEN ADOPTED OR EXPERIENCED THE CARE SYSTEM EITHER AS CHILDREN OR AS THOSE WHO ARE CURRENTLY PARENTING CHILDREN

Extracts from two poems by Jackie Kay

Jackie Kay's poems describe her adoption by a white Scottish couple and her search for her birth parents. In two poems she offers the mother's and the daughter's feelings about belonging to one another and the struggle with identity.

The poem "Black Bottom" opens with the mother's voice:

> Maybe that's why I don't like
> all this talk about her being black,
> I brought her up as my own
> as I would any other child
> colour matters to the nutters;
> but she says my daughter says
> it matters to her.
>
> (Kay, 1991a)

In the poem "Generations", the daughter writes,

> I have my parents who are not of the same tree
> and you keep trying to make it matter,
> the blood, the tie, the passing down
> generations.

We all have our contradictions,
the ones with the mother's nose and the father's eyes
have them;
the blood does not bind confusion,
yet I confess to my contradiction
I want to know my blood.

(Kay, 1991b)

References

Kay, J. (1991a). Black Bottom. In: *The Adoption Papers*. Newcastle upon Tyne: Bloodaxe Books, reprinted in *Darling: New and Selected Poems*. Newcastle upon Tyne: Bloodaxe Books, 2007.

Kay, J. (1991b). Generations. In: *The Adoption Papers*. Newcastle upon Tyne: Bloodaxe Books, reprinted in *Darling: New and Selected Poems*. Newcastle upon Tyne: Bloodaxe Books, 2007.

CHAPTER TEN

The lived experience of transracial adoption

Perlita Harris

> "Adoption is dislocating and confusing. Loss is distressing and disorientating. Racism is devastating; it claims lives . . ."
>
> (Dewan, 2003, p. 125)

Introduction

This chapter centralises the experiences of adopted adults who have been placed domestically and transracially in the UK, in order to examine the lifelong effect of transracial adoption. I begin with the historical and socio-political context that gave rise to the practice of transracial adoption, followed by the current socio-political context which ensures that transracial adoption continues as a permanency placement option for looked-after children in England. Following an overview of UK and USA research on the experience of transracially adopted children and adults, I draw upon service user knowledge to explore the lifelong impact of transracial adoption.

Historical context

No figures exist regarding the number of domestic transracial adoptions that have taken place in England (Selwyn et al., 2010). Over the past sixty-five years, there has been a shift from UK adoption practice viewing black children as "unadoptable" or "hard to place" (Rowe, 1991; Small, 1982), to adoption agencies demonstrating that black children are adoptable. Historically, there has been a correlation between social factors and an increase in domestic transracial adoption. With the decline in white babies available for adoption from the late 1960s onwards (from 14,000 in 1968 to 1,400 in 1988) (Prevatt Goldstein & Spencer, 2000), transracial adoption became an established practice. Further, targeted recruitment initiatives in the 1970s and 1980s showed unequivocally that black adoptive families can be found for black children (Brunton & Welch, 1983; James, 1986; Small, 1986; Soul Kids, 1977) and agency failure and institutional racism became viewed as the reasons for the shortfall in black adoptive families (Kirton, 2000).

In the 1980s, the Association of Black Social Workers and Allied Professions placed the practice of transracial placements on the agenda (ABSWAP, 1983). A number of challenges were made against transracial adoption: that white families are ill-equipped to prepare black children (including mixed ethnicity children) for the racism they will experience in society, as they have not experienced racism themselves and are, therefore, unable to provide children with coping skills for confronting racism or to enable children to develop a positive black racial identity, and that a positive black identity is vital for self-esteem. On the other side of the debate, social services departments have been charged with "political correctness" for trying to place children with families of a similar "race", culture, religion, and language, with the crucial matter being seen as love, which many white families can provide. It is against the backdrop of this discourse that transracial adoptions have taken place.

In line with practice in the 1990s and 2000s of taking account of race and ethnicity among a range of important considerations when matching children and prospective adoptive parents, transracial adoption has continued as a placement option for black and minority ethnic children, particularly disabled children (Ivaldi, 2000). The Adoption Register for England and Wales reported that of 335 children matched with adoptive parents through the Register in 2010–2011, 16% (52)

were "outside the child's ethnicity" (Adoption Register for England, 2011, p. 10). While most social workers view a "same race" placement as best able to meet a child's needs (Selwyn et al., 2010), not all view ethnic matching as essential (Dance et al., 2010) and there is little evidence of delay due to ethnic matching (Ofsted, 2012).

About a quarter of looked-after children in England are black or minority ethnic (Department for Education, 2014). Compared to white children, they are slightly more likely to have a Special Guardianship Order or Residence Order than adoption and more likely to be adopted by their foster carers (Selwyn et al., 2014). Five per cent of looked-after children were placed for adoption in the year 01.04.2013–31.03.2014 in England, 17% of whom were black and minority ethnic, including mixed ethnicity. The majority (76%) were aged one to four years (Department for Education, 2014). Neither the child's gender nor ethnicity is associated with a greater risk of adoption disruption (Selwyn et al., 2014).

Current socio-political-legal context

Despite the historically high rates of adoption (Barn & Kirton, 2012), the government "wants to see more children being adopted by loving families without delay" (Department for Education and Skills, 2013, p. 9). It views the weight attached to race and ethnicity in matching as causing delay in the adoptive placement of Black and minority ethnic children (Department for Education, 2012, 2013). A more nuanced understanding is put forward by Barn and Kirton (2012). They state that Pakistani, Bangladeshi, and African children are "least likely to be adopted" (p. 26), while mixed ethnicity children are more likely to be adopted, often by white families, having the highest adoption rate of any ethnic group (Selwyn et al., 2010; Owen & Statham, 2009; Thoburn et al., 2000). Rates are lower for Black Caribbean children and lower still for African children, with black children taking significantly longer to place (Barn & Kirton, 2012). Selwyn and colleagues argue this delay is due to entering care at an older age, a lack of black and minority ethnic adopters, poor social work practice, the age structure of communities, poverty, low income, and housing (Parliament UK, 2013; Frazer & Selwyn, 2005; Selwyn et al., 2004). Others highlight that adoption is lowest among communities where religious or cultural objections to legal adoption might exist (Barn & Kirton, 2012). Significantly, there has been a shortage of adoptive parents from all ethnic groups, including white British (Adoption Register for England and Wales, 2014), particularly for older children, disabled children, and sibling groups, with government concern about the delay all children experience waiting for an adoptive family (Department for Education, 2012; Department for Education and Skills, 2013), including due to court proceedings (Ministry of Justice, 2011; Ofsted, 2012). For a small minority of children where adoption is the plan, an adoptive family is never found (Ofsted, 2012; Selwyn et al., 2010).

The absence of recruitment strategies to increase numbers of black and minority ethnic adoptive families among some adoption agencies, alongside the government's position, suggests that transracial adoption could become the government's preferred placement option for black and minority ethnic children. The coalition government's "An Action Plan on Adoption" did not mention recruiting black and minority ethnic adoptive parents, espousing instead a "colour blind" and "love is enough" rhetoric:

> . . . it is not in the best interests of children for social workers to introduce any delay at all into the adoption process in the search for a perfect or even partial ethnic match when parents who are otherwise suitable are available and able to provide a loving and caring home for the child. (Department for Education, 2012, p. 22)

Yet, the notion of a "perfect match" is a fallacy and an over-simplification, given the evolving and "fluid" nature of ethnicity and culture. Significantly, section 3, Children and Families Act, 2014, has removed race, culture, religion, and language from the list of factors to which adoption agencies must give "due consideration" when making an adoptive placement (Department for Education and Skills, 2014). This risks these significant elements of identity being overlooked in matching decisions (Barn, 2013), and the provision of adoption support services (British Association for Adoption and Fostering, 2013). This repeal could be viewed as an attack on ethnicity and matching (Barn, 2013). On the other hand, writers on ethnic mixing and mixedness highlight the diversity among mixed families and argue that "family difference may be important or it may not" (Caballero et al., 2012, p. 22). It "occurs against the backdrop of a broader debate over the continuing significance of 'race' in society" (Trenka et al., 2006, p. 5) and the alleged failure of multiculturalism due to "segregation" and "threatening national values" (Phoenix & Simmonds, 2012, p. 4).

Research

There is a dearth of literature concerning the experiences of domestic transracially adopted children and adults in the UK. What research there is has been dominated by a tendency to "whitewash" any difficulties in such placements and a concern to defend transracial adoption against the challenges made against it, including minimising the significance of race and racism (Kirton, 2000) and failing to view race and culture as central to outcomes (Samuels, 2010, p. 27). Outcomes have been found to be positive in the UK (Rushton & Minnis, 1997) and the USA (Evan B. Donaldson Institute, 2008; Feigelman, 2000). These tend to allow children's perspectives to be mediated through their adoptive parents or assume children will speak about race and racism with a virtual stranger (Kirton, 2000). Further, research has tended to conflate race with culture (Samuels, 2010). Although disruptions are no higher than in "same race" placements in the UK and the USA (Feigelman, 2000; Quinton, 2012), some question as to whether all placements are successful when outcome measures include satisfaction or racial and cultural pride (Moffat & Thoburn, 2001) or argue that multiple measures are needed (Burrow & Finley, 2004). Crucially, research is only beginning to explore domestic transracial adoptees' experience of childhood into adulthood.

Transracial adoption is more common for younger children and black children with one white parent in the UK and the USA (Samuels, 2009; Selwyn et al., 2010; Thoburn et al., 2000). In historic placements, these children tended to see themselves as "'white' in all but skin colour" (Gill & Jackson, 1983, p. 81), as culturally white (Samuels, 2010), and were less likely to identify as black (Quinton, 2012), with adopters taking a colour-blind approach to parenting (Kirton, 2000; Kirton et al., 2000; Samuels, 2009). Many of these children had little or no contact with other black people, growing up in predominantly or exclusively white communities in the 1960s, 1970s, and 1980s (Gill & Jackson, 1983; Samuels, 2009) and had engaged in attempts at "whitening" themselves (Kirton, 2000; Kirton et al., 2000, p. 9). Less is known about the experience of children adopted transracially more recently, although research has highlighted racial discrimination, experienced particularly by African American males (Evan B. Donaldson Institute, 2008).

Looking back at their childhoods, UK and USA transracial domestic adoptees have reported significant experiences of racism, sometimes within the immediate and extended family and school, including widespread racist bullying, verbal abuse, and violence, with school the most frequent location (Harris, 2014a; Kirton, 2000; Kirton et al., 2000; Patel, 2009; Samuels, 2010; Shekleton, 1990). Kirton's (2000) study with ten UK transracially adopted adults found they had "an uneasy . . . relationship with 'whiteness' and an equally ambivalent one with 'community of origin', characterised by a powerful gravitational pull but also by distance and discomfort" (p. 90). They felt unsupported and had protected their parents from learning about their experiences of racism. Patel's (2009) study of six UK transracially adopted adults found they had developed a "positive mixed racial identity" (p. 103), although the process had been difficult.

Significantly, UK transracially adopted adults search for information at a younger age than their white counterparts (25.8 years compared to 31.2 years), with "racial" and ethnic identity issues featuring strongly in their reasons for searching (Howe & Feast, 2000). More UK transracial adoptees search for their (black) birth father, both initially and subsequently, than white adoptees (Kirton et al., 2000). Some feel anxious or ambivalent about searching for their white birth family for fear of being rejected because they are black (Greenwood & Forster, undated). Further, they are more likely to feel different from their adoptive families, less likely to feel they "belonged", or "at home" with their birth relatives than their white counterparts, or to have had their "racial" and ethnic identity needs met following reunion (Howe & Feast, 2000; Kirton et al., 2000; Triseliotis et al., 2005). Significantly, a small minority of UK transracially adopted adults of historical placements have reported experiencing child abuse and neglect within their immediate or extended adoptive family, and unmet adoption support needs as both children and adults (Harris, 2014a,b).

The lived experience of transracial adoption

In this section, I explore the childhood and adulthood experiences of UK domestic transracial adoptees. My starting point is valuing transracial adoptees' first-hand experience as a basis for knowledge. Of course, service user knowledge is not new (Beresford, 1999). What makes it different from other knowledge is that "They alone are based on direct experience of such policy and provision from the receiving end. Service users' knowledges grow out of their personal and collective experience of policy, practice and services" (Beresford, 1999, p. 3).

I draw upon writing by UK transracial adoptees of both historical (Harris, 2003, 2006, 2012) and contemporary adoptions (Harris, 2008), making "collective sense of individual stories" (Wilkins, 2000, p. 147), plus research, to provide insight into the lived experience of transracial adoption. This material is drawn primarily from adoptees who joined their respective adoptive families in the 1950s, 1960s, and 1970s. We, therefore, need to recognise that significant changes have taken place in adoption policy and practice since then, as has our understanding of the impact of racism and discrimination in the lives of black children.

Children from a young age, including adopted children, are able to give their views about a wide range of topics and want more say in their lives (Thomas et al., 1999). Indeed, adopted children "are likely to have their own concerns or questions" (Thomas & O'Kane, 2000, p. 341). Transracially adopted children are active participants in creating their adoption story, in creating meaning, and seeking to understand their respective adoption narrative. Many adopted children ask themselves four key questions: Who am I? Where do I belong? How did I get here? What is going to happen to me? These concerns are multi-faceted for transracial adoptees.

Children joining an adoptive family may feel mixed emotions: excitement and anticipation, fear, and sadness due to leaving a foster family (Harris 2008; Thomas et al., 1999). They might also worry about being the only black child in their adoptive family, demonstrating an acute awareness of "race".

> "When I came here, I was a bit scared at first but, then, when I actually got to know mum and Renee, I felt they wouldn't do anything like smacking and hitting because they don't believe in that. Renee's brown too. It's nice being with someone else who's brown. When I first met her I was like, 'Oh thank God, I'm not the only one who's brown . . .' In foster care, I was worried I'd go somewhere where I was the only brown person". (Rachel (age 10), in Harris, 2006, pp. 51–52)

Looking back, many adult transracial adoptees describe their parents taking a "colour blind" approach to parenting and say they did not (and do not) understand what it is like to experience daily racism and gendered racism.

> "My parents believe that everyone is equal and that colour doesn't matter . . . but the moment I stepped outside the warmth of my family, colour seemed to matter terribly" (Laura Fish, in Harris, 2006, p. 203)

> "When I moved schools and my history teacher abused me for being 'ethnic', I didn't really understand. When my friends started to call me 'Paki', I began to understand. When two men in a van stopped me on the way home from school and spat in my face, I understood more. When I saw graffiti abusing me for being 'a disgusting Paki', I understood. I was different, not white. But who could I turn to? Not my parents . . . I didn't think they'd understand". (Nick Pendry, in Harris, 2006, p. 191)

As a result, they struggled alone to make sense of their experience of racism and discrimination.

> "As a child, I accepted racism quite calmly. I had known it from day one and nobody explained what was happening or why it happened . . . [I] resolved never to show the pain, no matter how severe. So I rarely reacted when attacked or abused". (Fish, in Harris, 2006, p. 204).

As well as overt racism, many report being subjected to unwanted interest and intrusive questioning due to their visibility as an adopted child. This unwanted attention could result in irritation, discomfort, and distress.

> "When people ask who my parents are, I just have to say, 'I don't know my real mum'. . . . I just tell them, 'I don't know who my dad is' . . . And then I just make up something". (Rachel (age 10), in Harris, 2006, pp. 54–55)

> "People used to (and still do!) pat my head, feel my hair, and comment on how well I speak English. I was continually the object of curiosity and interrogation. 'Do you love your parents? They're not your *real* family? Do you want to find your *real* mother?' (Laura Fish, in Harris, 2012, p. 204)

Even as adults, people's questions and assumptions can cause frustration and pain.

> "A simple question, 'Where do you come from?', is loaded for me. I never know whether to respond with my life history or to say, 'I live in Bristol. Where are you from?' (Jade, in Harris, 2006, p. 44)

> "All my life people have asked questions about where I am from, and when I say I'm half Iranian they assume I can speak Farsi and that I know something about the culture". (Jade, in Harris, 2006, p. 41)

One of the key issues transracial adoptees have spoken about in research is the lack of resemblance to their adoptive family. This, in turn, compounds their sense of "racial" difference (Kirton et al., 2000; Patel, 2009; Samuels, 2009), as can living in a predominantly white community. Others growing up in multi-racial London or Manchester also report feeling uncomfortable around black and minority ethnic people, due to a lack of shared experience, social class, culture, and language (Harris, 2006). However, seeing a photograph or meeting someone they resembled could help to strengthen their self-identity:

> "We share a father, we are family, and at last I know who I am". (Liz Sibthorpe, in Harris, 2006, p. 235)

> "For the first time I could see someone I resembled. By hugging her or holding her hand like a young child, I could touch some tangible evidence of my mother: a mother I had never known; a mother I had only dreamt about; a mother who had been absent . . .". (David Gilbert, in Harris, 2006, p. 123)

As with all adopted children, transracially adopted children and adults may have continued thoughts and worries about birth parents, siblings, and other family members. This can be exacerbated where there is a lack of information about the current welfare of birth family members or no ongoing contact.

> "I don't have any contact with my birth mum; I don't have a clue where she is. I think she's in heaven. My nan said she might be in Canada, but I don't know. I've just got a feeling . . .". (Rachel (age 10), in Harris, 2006, p. 53)

Adoption-related losses may be triggered by seemingly innocuous events and family occasions. For children and adults, birthdays, religious celebrations, Mother's Day, and Father's Day might be a reminder of the loss of one's birth parents.

> "I feel a bit sad when it's Mother's Day because I never made my mum a card but this year I did and I put it in my small garden so she could see it, from heaven". (Jade (age 10), in Harris, 2008, p. 13)

Some adults report feelings of embarrassment, shame, and the stigma of transracial adoption.

> "I grew up feeling embarrassed about our unusual family. I didn't want to be part of my adoptive parents' family, but I didn't know where else I belonged". (Liz Sibthorpe, in Harris, 2006, p. 233)

The impact of racism, racial stereotypes, and discrimination could exacerbate these feelings.

> "If I accidentally brushed past them in class, they would act like I was contaminated with a deadly disease as it repulsed them that a black person had come into contact with them . . . they would say I resembled a gorilla and tell me to go back to the jungle where I belonged. I had absolutely no ammunition to defend myself with; I could only hang my head in shame". (Kym Cooper, in Harris, 2006, p. 257)

Some have spoken about racism at school and bullying by their peers, often violent, with ineffectual responses by teachers, including viewing the adoptee as the trouble-maker (Harris, 2006, 2014b). Others have spoken about racism within the immediate or extended adoptive family (Harris, 2006; Sawbridge, 1998). In addition to self-blame for being on the receiving end of racism and immense, but often unspoken, pain, many transracial adoptees report wishing they were white, as children and, sometimes, as adults.

> "No, I just kept it [racism] to myself, and just wished I was white". (Nick Pendry, in Harris, 2006, p. 191)

> "I would wrap a towel around my head and pretend that I had long blonde hair like the girl in the *Timotei* advert. I would pray to God every night that I could be white and fit in with my family. I quite literally used to avoid looking in the mirror because I could not stand what I saw looking back at me". (Kym Cooper, in Harris, 2006, p. 256)

Little attention has focused on the impact of class on the development of identity among transracial adoptees, yet USA research suggests "Class is also key to shaping black identity" among transracial adoptees (Butler-Sweet, 2014, p. 219). The "racialised gender and class politics" (Patton, 2000, p. 17) in transracial adoption is reflected in Darshan's reflection on his childhood:

> "I felt I belonged in my immediate adoptive family but, in my head, I felt that I was not living how I should be living, as I was living in a privileged and not working class family". (Darshan Davies, in Harris, 2006, p. 308)

Research in the USA has reported that domestic transracial adoptees speak about their adoptive families in ways that reveal gratitude and feeling lucky, coupled with an awareness of what their lives might have been like had they not been adopted (Butler-Sweet, 2014). In the UK, feelings of gratitude, of being "rescued" and "lucky" are similarly not uncommon (Harris, 2006, 2014b).

> "I would hate anyone to think that I am not grateful for my upbringing in white, middle-class society . . ." (Nicole McKenzie, in Harris, 2006, p. 69)

Many transracially adopted adults are able to articulate the multiple losses that they have experienced and continue to experience, plus express their pain and grief.

> "Do you know how I still ache with the pain of my adoption? Do you have any idea how much I yearn to piece together the jigsaw of my life?" (David Gilbert, in Harris, 2006, p. 176)

These losses include the loss of family, culture, language, and ancestry (Harris, 2006).

> "I can't be alone in thinking that being transracially adopted, we have lost something: lost our languages, traditions, cultures, and most importantly the subtleties and nuances of those cultures. We have lost something we never had . . . and yet, we continue to mourn. Am I alone in this grief?" (Michelle Anderson, in Harris, 2006, p. 97)

> ". . . the loss of my birth mother through adoption has meant the loss of my birthright; of a way of life within the Indian community; of a

> rich and beautiful culture; of knowledge of my maternal history and ancestry; and of my ability to speak my mother-tongue with birth maternal and paternal relatives". (Shobha, in Harris, 2003, p. 129)

Pain, sadness, and, often, anger at the loss of lived cultural experience and connection to birth family and community could be expressed. Transracial adoptees might articulate a sense of dislocation, of not feeling they fully belong in the white British community or their community of origin. Many will distance themself temporarily from their adoptive family while immersing themselves in their birth culture and seeking to find their place in the world.

While many desire to connect with their community of origin, this is not necessarily an easy process, leading to a range of emotions, and exposing the adoptee to accusations of being "too white". It can accentuate the loss of shared culture and language, confirming to the adoptee that she does not "fit in" here either.

> "The questioning continued at university. People would ask why my culture did not match my Asian appearance. The Asian and African-Caribbean students would ask why, if I knew I was Pakistani, I hadn't done anything about this . . . I was dumbstruck. I did join the African-Caribbean and Asian society . . . I remember being called 'a coconut' there and I left quickly". (Elinor Young, in Harris, 2006, p. 217)

> "It was weird, to be in a room surrounded by people who looked like me. I had mixed emotions—happiness to be in the company of Iranian people, sad to feel that I could not really connect, and uncertainty about how to be . . . I felt very uncomfortable, almost like I had gate-crashed a family party. I didn't feel I had anything in common apart from my Iranian looks and, yet, I really wanted to connect with them". (Jade, in Harris, 2006, p. 43)

Accessing one's adoption records is a significant step to take. Yet, the official adoption story, the narrative in adoption agency documents, as with all knowledge, "may be misleading or inaccurate and can only be partial at best given the complexity of real human lives" (Baynes, 2008, p. 48). It follows that any knowledge about an adoption is partial or unfinished. Different perspectives will enhance it and add a more rounded picture.

> "I have had to dig and excavate, for as an adoptee, nothing can be assumed or taken for granted". (Sarah Francis, in Harris, 2012, p. 168)

Often, the language in historical adoption records is couched in racism, reflecting the era in which they were written. However, accessing records and receiving an adoption support service "could help to change complex feelings of shame about being black or minority ethnic; it could also help reframe the adoption story and the role (or exclusion) of black birth fathers in the adoption 'decision'":

> "You know, I started to feel not ashamed of who I was because, for many years when I was growing up, I felt ashamed that my father was Black. I felt ashamed that my mother's family were from Ireland ... but I've started to like myself a bit more ... I can understand more about me, where I came from, and that my dad wasn't the ogre he was painted to be, that he was actually quite a decent bloke". (Sarah (age 31), in Harris, 2014b, p. 350)

Accessing adoption records and obtaining the original birth certificate might also lead to late discovery of black or minority ethnicity.

> "My birth certificate also shows my birth father's name ... I saw that it was a very Indian sounding name. Naresh Kumar were hardly the names of a white Caucasian male. I chose not to think about this at the time as I still thought that I was white". (Jenny Mohindra, in Harris, 2006, p. 196)

It might also lead to learning that the information recorded is incomplete and the realisation that finding the sought-after relative will not be easy:

> "I do not even have a name for him or know which island in the Caribbean he was from. Unfortunately, no one in the black society could remember any black man ... in Port Talbot in 1974". (Leyton, in Harris, 2006, p. 201)

Some adoptees discover through their adoption records or contact with their birth mother that they were conceived through rape. This knowledge can be devastating and have an impact, at least initially, on the adoptee's sense of identity.

> "She was single ... and conception was due to gang rape. The reality crushed me. I couldn't justify my existence and my identity became intrinsically linked to violence". (Jo Burnett-Sharpe, in Harris, 2012, p. 36)

> "She had only been 17 when I was born, and it was in her second email that she told me about the rape. I felt upset and angry and wished I could crawl out of my skin because it felt dirty. Curious friends kept asking about my birth father and I hated being reminded". (Amina Clarke, in Harris, 2006, p. 188)

With time, after "the initial shock and grief" (Burnett-Sharpe, in Harris, 2012, p. 36), their thoughts might change and give rise to new questions about their mother's welfare and which parent they resemble. For some, it might help to explain their birth mother's response on being contacted:

> "Knowing the truth helped me to understand her ambivalence about meeting me". (Amina Clarke, in Harris, 2006, p. 188)

While some, as adults, establish contact with a sought after birth parent or relative, others experience a "refusal" of contact, which might be perceived as a second rejection or abandonment. The adoptee will need to mourn and grieve for the lost relationship, before considering contacting other birth relatives. Others will discover that the sought after birth parent or relative is deceased. Similarly, they will need to piece together what is known about their parent or relative and grieve.

With time, many adoptees realise they have a choice in how they respond to no contact, and the ability to reframe their life script from one characterised by loss and separation to one defined by connection and family:

> ". . . I realised I had choices. I could let the need to find the missing part of myself control me. I could bury it and hope it never came back to haunt me. I could hope to find a balance between the two". (Burnett-Sharpe, in Harris, 2012, p. 37)

> "I seem to have re-written my 'script' . . . I have a family. I have roots and I belong". (Deborah Weymont, in Harris, 2012, p. 196)

Where contact is established, the lack of familiarity with birth family/community culture, language, and accent can affect post-reunion processes (Harris, 2014b). Other difficulties may occur connected to a mismatch in expectations about the role the other person will take in their life or adhering to birth family culture or religion.

> "I feel desperately disappointed by both my natural parents for very different reasons. Perhaps my expectations have been unrealistic. My father has let me down because he has refused to acknowledge my existence, apart from two cursory telephone calls. My mother has withdrawn into a shell of secrecy and denial". (David Gilbert, in Harris, 2006. p. 174)

> "I found it hard to accept that she was my mother. I didn't feel that we had anything in common . . . I think from my mother's point of view she was just so pleased to see me after such a long time—it was simple, her daughter was back in her life. I, on the other hand, didn't feel like that, I already had a mother; I didn't need another one . . ." (Sharon Beazer, in Harris, 2006, p. 226)

> "I respect my birth family but chose to live my life differently". (Elinor Young, in Harris, 2006, p. 222)

For others, despite renewed contact, secrecy might remain, with relatives not being informed who the adoptee is. Although challenging, contact could provide an insight into what life might have been like.

> "Only her mother and her sister knew who I was. I learnt then what it was to be a secret. I got a glimpse of what might have been. The food I might have eaten, the language I might have spoken, the religion I might have followed and the places I would have seen. They all seemed so alien to me at the time. I wanted to belong, but I just knew that I didn't". (Nick Pendry, in Harris, 2006, p. 192)

Of course, not all adoptees will be interested in searching for their birth mother or birth father. Some might be interested in connecting with siblings. Others might express no interest in searching for information or birth family. A small minority will seek support regarding abuse and neglect experienced within their immediate and extended adoptive family (Harris, 2014a).

Becoming a parent and grandparent may give rise to powerful emotions, from heightened loss of one's birth mother to a sense of belonging:

> "Being a parent gave me a physical connection with another human being through sharing the same genes. This in turn gave me a tremendous sense of belonging. I started to feel that I was a real person

within a family, being more than just a relation awarded by the courts to two complete strangers . . ." (Frankie Pearce, in Harris, 2012, p. 50)

"The birth of my grand-daughter, Pella, has forced me to change the way I think about myself—from someone who is defined by separation and loss to someone who is defined by my connections and the gift of family". (Deborah Weymont, in Harris, 2012, p. 194)

Some transracially adopted adults have spoken (Dewan, 2003; Harris, 2006, 2014a) about mental distress, ranging from panic attacks about their racial identity through to suicide attempts as children and as adults, and becoming formal users (and survivors) of psychiatric services.

Transracial adoptees might view adoption-related issues as the underlying reason for their mental distress.

"People would stare at me—I was the only mixed race girl in my school—and I had never experienced racism and prejudice before. I started feeling self-hate, anger, pity, confusion and self-doubt. The pain had to come out, starting with painkillers, then laxatives, cigarettes and, finally, by cutting my skin on my wrists with keys and my own nails. Suicidal feelings soon followed". (Jade, in Harris, 2006, p. 41)

"Each time I see a new psychiatrist or therapist, the same issues repeatedly surface. The same questions asked, the same irreconcilable differences seem to remain: my absent father, my distraught and confused mother . . ." (David Gilbert, in Harris, 2006, p. 176)

The lack of understanding and appropriate support within mental health services has been highlighted.

"When I have been 'ill', many of these periods of emotional distress and confusion have resulted from issues of identity and colour, not having come to terms with 'black and white' and identity issues arising from being transracially adopted. Unfortunately, very little time or concern was given to these issues for many years by the professionals I saw. As a result, I was being treated with medication but not having a chance to look at my real concerns". (Darshan Davies, in Harris, 2006, p. 203–204)

Further, mental health service users could have additional concerns, such as strategies for maintaining positive emotional health while searching for and, possibly, meeting birth family (Harris, 2014b).

Some transracially adopted adults have spoken (Burnell et al., 1993; Dewan, 2003; Harris, 2003, 2006; Kirton 2000) about meeting others and have suggested that a tailored support group might provide opportunities to help them share experiences, strategies, and difficulties, reduce isolation, and receive empathy, support, and understanding from other transracial adoptees (Harris, 2014a). Practitioners (Dagoo, 1992; Hayes, 1996a,b; Mallows, 1989, 1999; Sheckleton, 1990) have similarly highlighted the importance of support groups and activities. Meeting other transracial adoptees can reduce feelings of isolation and difference:

> "Going to the group almost blew me away: it was the realisation that I was not on my own. Growing up, I was so isolated and thought that I was the only one, but I was not . . . They made me identify issues and areas I hadn't thought about and probably wouldn't have without that help". (Elinor Young, in Harris, 2006, p. 218)

Counselling or psychotherapy provides an opportunity to examine adoption-related concerns. However, many transracial adoptees report difficulty in finding someone knowledgeable about transracial adoption and greater difficulty finding a Black therapist.

> "The only counsellor who really helped me was an Asian woman . . . who did not judge me for my cultural knowledge and acknowledged my pain and anger without being threatened by my 'opinions'. In that safe space, I was able to explore my feelings about ethnicity, race and class and to realise important elements of my relationship, both with my adoptive family and my birth family". (Amina Clarke, in Harris, 2006, p. 188)

> "For two years the expertise of a black female psychotherapist enabled me to uncover so much internalised racism, helping me to understand and overcome feelings of low self-worth and self-loathing". (Dewan, 2003, p. 124)

Conclusion

In this chapter, I have identified some key experiences of transracially adopted children and adults. Transracial adoption is a lifelong experience. It is complex, challenging, and, at times, very painful.

Feelings of rejection and not being good enough, cultural dislocation and alienation, grief and anger are common. As adults, the search for birth family is often linked strongly to a search for racial and cultural identity. However, finding the sought-after person is only the beginning and never the end. The search is, in fact, a search for self. Yet, despite establishing contact, many transracial adoptees will not feel they fully belong due to the absence of shared culture and upbringing and sometimes language and class, while others will experience a "refusal" of contact or discover the relative is deceased or uncover information that challenges their sense of self.

Many adults are able to reflect on what they have gained by being transracially adopted, including, for most, stability, love, security, educational opportunities, and cultural capital. This, however, cannot be separated from the challenges, racism, and discrimination, and multiple losses and grief. In providing support, we need to provide a space where they can explore whatever is important to them. This requires acknowledging their losses and grief, their childhood and adult experiences of racism and discrimination, their feelings about self, and helping them to create a coherent narrative about their origins, their history, their life, and who they are. This will involve discussing issues of race and ethnicity, racism and discrimination, gender and class, sexuality and sexual orientation, family, identity, and belonging. Some of these concerns are shared by all adoptees. However, in a society where dominant discourses erase or deny "race" and racism (Dei & Calliste, 2000; van Dijk, 2002), it is the salience of race and racism throughout the lives of transracial adoptees that makes the experience of transracial adoption distinct. Further, with the government emphasis on increasing the number of adoptions and without delay, and the recent change to the legislation, arguably transracial adoption might become the preferred placement option for black and minority ethnic children. Today, the children for whom we are finding family not only have complex histories of abuse and neglect, but many have ethnic backgrounds that span several communities of origin or heritage. The challenge will be to achieve permanency for these children without ignoring significant components of racial and ethnic identity and downplaying the impact of racism in British society. In effect, to avoid creating another generation of transracial adoptees who will feel displaced and alienated from their communities of origin and lacking in the social, cultural, and linguistic knowledge and skills to feel comfortable within their birth families and/or communities of origin and to challenge racism.

> "I have had to question every aspect of my identity, my religion, my right to be British, a history to claim, the meaning of ethnic identity and race, the importance of genetics, the meaning of family, how to form relationships, and my place amongst peers divided by ethnicity and class". (Amina Clarke, in Harris, 2006, p. 180)

> "I guess my mother's only fault was thinking that my colour didn't matter that it is only skin deep. I'm not sure what world she lives in but it isn't mine". (Nicole McKenzie, in Harris, 2006, p. 69)

References

ABSWAP (1983). *Black Children in Care: Evidence to the House of Commons Social Services Committee*. London: ABSWAP.

Adoption Register for England (2011). *Adoption Register for England Annual Report 2010/11*. Leeds: Adoption Register for England.

Barn, R. (2013). 'Race' and adoption crusades in 21st century Britain. *Huffington Post*, 13 February. Available at: www.huffingtonpost.co.uk. Accessed 15 February 2013.

Barn, R., & Kirton, D. (2012). Transracial adoption in Britain: politics, ideology and reality. *Adoption and Fostering, 36*(3–4): 25–37.

Baynes, P. (2008). Untold stories: a discussion of life story work. *Adoption and Fostering, 32*(1): 43–49.

Beresford, P. (1999). Making participation possible: movements of disabled people and psychiatric survivors. In: T. Jordan & A. Lent (Eds.), *Storming the Millennium: The New Politics of Change* (pp. 35–50). London: Lawrence and Wishart.

British Association for Adoption and Fostering (2013). *Children and Families Bill: Written Evidence from the British Association for Adoption and Fostering*. London: BAAF. Available at: www.baaf.org.uk. Accessed 13 July 2014.

Brunton, L., & Welch, M. (1983). White agency, black community. *Adoption and Fostering, 7*(2): 16–18.

Burnell, A., Dagoo, R., Gorham, A., Iain, & Debbie (1993). *Thoughts on Adoption by Black Adults Adopted as Children by White Parents*. London: Post-Adoption Centre.

Burrow, A. L., & Finley, G. E. (2004). Transracial, same-race adoptions, and the need for multiple measures of adolescent adjustment. *American Journal of Orthopsychiatry, 74*: 577–583.

Butler-Sweet, C. (2014). 'Acting White' and 'acting Black': exploring transracial adoption, middle-class families, and racial socialization. In: V. B. Treitler (Ed.), *Race in Transnational and Transracial Adoption* (pp. 204–225). Basingstoke: Palgrave Macmillan.

Caballero, C., Edwards, R., Goodyer, A., & Okitikpi, T. (2012). The diversity and complexity of the everyday lives of mixed racial and ethnic families: implications for adoption and fostering practice and policy. *Adoption and Fostering, 36*(3–4): 9–24.

Dagoo, R. (1992). Getting together groups for transracially adopted adults, and for birth mothers. In: A. Burnell, D. Reich, & P. Sawbridge (Eds.), *Adult Counselling and Adoption* (pp. 48–52). London: Post-Adoption Centre.

Dance, C., Ouwejan, D., Beecham, J., & Farmer, E. (2010). *Linking and Matching: A Survey of Adoption Agency Practice in England and Wales*. London: BAAF.

Dei, G. F. S., & Calliste, A. (Eds.) (2000). *Power, Knowledge and Anti-Racism Education: A Critical Reader*. Halifax, Canada: Fenwood.

Department for Education (2012). *An Action Plan on Adoption: Tackling Delay*. London: Department for Education.

Department for Education (2013). *Further Action on Adoption: Finding More Loving Homes*. London: Department for Education.

Department for Education (2014). *Children Looked After in England (Including Adoption and Care Leavers) Year Ending 31 March 2013. Statistical First Release SFR 36/2014*. Available at: www.education.gov.uk.

Department for Education and Skills (2013). *Children and Families Bill 2013: Contextual Information and Responses to Pre-legislative Scrutiny*, Cm850. London: The Stationery Office.

Department for Education and Skills (2014). *Children and Families Act 2014*. London: The Stationery Office.

Dewan, V. (2003). A truer image. In: A. Douglas & T. Philpot (Eds.), *Adoption: Changing Families, Changing Times* (pp. 120–126). London: Routledge.

Evan B Donaldson Institute (2008). *Finding Families for African American Children: The Role of Race and Law in Adoption From Foster Care*. New York: The Evan B Donaldson Institute.

Feigelman, W. (2000). Adjustments of transracially and inracially adopted young adults. *Child and Adolescent Social Work, 17*(3): 165–184.

Frazer, L., & Selwyn, S. (2005). Why are we waiting? The demography of adoption for children of black, Asian and mixed parentage in England. *Child and Family Social Work, 10*(2): 135–147.

Gill, O., & Jackson, B. (1983). *Adoption and Race: Black, Asian and Mixed Children in White Families*. London: Batsford.

Greenwood, S., & Forster, S. (undated). *Tell Me Who I Am: Young People Talk about Adoption*. Manchester: After Adoption.

Harris, P. (2003). 'Am I alone in this grief?': user support for transracially adopted and fostered people. In: H. Argent (Ed.), *Models of Adoption Support: What Works and What Doesn't* (pp. 129–146). London: BAAF.

Harris, P. (Ed.) (2006). *In Search of Belonging: Reflections by Transracially Adopted People*. London: BAAF.

Harris, P. (Ed.) (2008). *The Colours in Me: Writing and Poetry by Adopted Children and Young People*. London: BAAF.

Harris, P. (Ed.) (2012). *Chosen: Living with Adoption*. London: BAAF.

Harris, P. (2014a). Meeting the adoption support needs of adopted adults who have been abused in their adoptive family: lessons from historical placements. *Adoption and Fostering, 38*(1): 50–60.

Harris, P. (2014b). 'I started to feel not ashamed of who I was': transracially adopted adults and adoption support. *Adoption and Fostering, 38*(4): 346–360.

Hayes, M. (1996a). Post-adoption issues in transracial and same race placements. In: R. Phillips & E. McWilliam (Eds.), *After Adoption: Working with Adoptive Families* (pp. 176–183). London: BAAF.

Hayes, M. (1996b). Transracial adopted people's support group. In: R. Phillips & E. McWilliam (Eds.), *After Adoption: Working with Adoptive Families* (pp. 184–188). London: BAAF.

Howe, D., & Feast, J. (2000). *Adoption, Search and Reunion: The Long-term Experience of Adopted Adults*. London: The Children's Society.

Ivaldi, G. (2000). *Surveying Adoption*. London: BAAF.

James, M. (1986). Finding and working with families of Caribbean origin. In: V. Coombe & A. Little (Eds.), *Race and Social Work: A Guide to Training*. London: Tavistock.

Kirton, D. (2000). *'Race', Ethnicity and Adoption*. Buckingham: Open University Press.

Kirton, D., Feast, J., & Howe, D. (2000). Searching, reunion and transracial adoption. *Adoption and Fostering, 24*(3): 6–18.

Mallows, M. (1989). Abercrave weekend: exploring the needs of transracially adopted young people. *Adoption and Fostering, 13*(3): 34–36.

Mallows, M. (1999). Meeting the needs of transracially adopted young people. In: R. Barn (Ed.), *Working with Black Children and Adolescents in Need* (pp. 98–106). London: BAAF.

Ministry of Justice (2011). *Family Justice Review: Final Report*. London: Ministry of Justice, the Department for Education and the Welsh Government.

Moffat, P. J., & Thoburn, J. (2001). Outcomes of permanent family placement for children of minority ethnic origin. *Child and Family Social Work, 6*(1): 13–21.

Ofsted (2012). *Right on Time: Exploring Delays in Adoption*. Manchester: Ofsted.

Owen, C., & Statham, D. (2009). *Disproportionality in Child Welfare: The Prevalence of Black and Minority Ethnic Children within the 'Looked After' and 'Children in Need' Populations and on Child Protection Registers in England*. London: Department for Children, Schools and Families.

Parliament UK (2013). *House of Lords Select Committee on Adoption Legislation, Adoption Legislation, Oral and Written Evidence*. London: Parliament UK. Available at: www.parliament.uk. Accessed 18 April 2016.

Patel, T. (2009). *Mixed-Up Kids? Race, Identity and Social Order*. Lyme Regis, Dorset: Russell House.

Patton, S. (2000). *Birth Marks: Transracial Adoption in Contemporary America*. New York: New York University Press.

Phoenix, A., & Simmonds, J. (2012). Negotiating multicultures, identities and intersectionalities Editorial. *Adoption and Fostering, 36*(3&4): 3–7.

Prevatt Goldstein, B., & Spencer, M. (2000). *'Race' and Ethnicity: A Consideration of Issues for Black, Minority Ethnic and White Children in Family Placement*. London: BAAF.

Quinton, D. (2012). *Rethinking Matching in Adoptions from Care*. London: BAAF.

Rowe, J. (1991). An historical perspective on adoption and the role of the voluntary agencies. In: J. Fratter, J. Rowe, D. Sapsford, & J. Thoburn (Eds.), *Permanent Family Placement: A Decade of Experience* (pp. 7–17). London: BAAF.

Rushton, A., & Minnis, H. (1997). Transracial family placements. Annotation. *Journal of Child Psychology and Psychiatry, 38*(2): 147–159.

Samuels, G. M. (2009). 'Being raised by white people': navigating racial difference among adopted multiracial adults. *Journal of Marriage and Family, 71*(1): 80–94.

Samuels, G. M. (2010). Building kinship and community: relational processes of bicultural identity among adult multiracial adoptees. *Family Process, 49*(1): 26–42.

Sawbridge, P. (1998). The Post Adoption Centre: what are the users teaching us? In: M. Hill & M. Shaw (Eds.), *Signposts in Adoption: Policy, Practice and Research Issues* (pp. 232–245). London: BAAF.

Selwyn, J., Frazer, L., & Fitzgerald, A. (2004). *Finding Adoptive Families for Black, Asian and Black Mixed-parentage Children: Agency Policy and Practice, Executive Summary*. London: NCH.

Selwyn, J., Quinton, D., Harris, P., Wijedasa, D., Nawaz, S., & Wood, S. (2010). *Pathways to Permanence for Black, Asian and Mixed Ethnicity Children*. London: BAAF.

Selwyn, J., Wijedasa, D., & Meakings, S. (2014). *Beyond the Adoption Order: Challenges, Interventions and Disruptions*. London: Department for Education.

Shekleton, J. (1990). *'A Glimpse through the Looking Glass': A Summary of Personal Experiences and Reflections of a Group of Transracially Adopted Adults*. Discussion Paper No. 8. London: Post Adoption Centre.

Small, J. (1982). New Black families. *Adoption and Fostering, 6*(3): 35–39.

Small, J. (1986). Transracial placements: conflicts and contradictions. In: S. Ahmed, J. Cheecham, & J. Small (Eds.), *Social Work with Black Children and their Families* (pp. 81–99). London: Batsford, in association with BAAF.

Soul Kids (1977). *Report of the Steering Group of The Soul Kids Campaign: London 1975–1976*. London: BAAF.

Thoburn, J., Norford, L., & Rashid, S. P. (2000). *Permanent Family Placement of Children of Minority Ethnic Origin*. London: Jessica Kingsley.

Thomas, C., & Beckford, V., with Lowe, N., & Murch, M. (1999). *Adopted Children Speaking*. London: BAAF.

Thomas, N., & O'Kane, C. (2000). Discovering what children think: connection between research and practice. *British Journal of Social Work, 30*: 819–835.

Trenka, J. J., Oparah, C., & Shin, S. Y. (Eds.) (2006). *Outsiders Within: Writing on Transracial Adoption*. New York: South End Press.

Triseliotis, J., Feast, J., & Kyle, F. (2005). *The Adoption Triangle Revisited: A Study of Adoption, Search and Reunion Experiences*. London: BAAF.

Van Dijk, T. A. (2002). Denying racism: elite discourse and racism. In: P. Essed & D. T. Goldberg (Eds.), *Race Critical Theories* (pp. 307–324). Oxford: Blackwell.

Wilkins, P. (2000). Story telling as research. In: B. Humphries (Ed.), *Research in Social Care and Social Welfare: Issues for Debate and Practice* (pp. 144–153). London: Jessica Kingsley.

CHAPTER ELEVEN

Positioning and respectful professional interventions for working with the legacy of Irish institutional care

Valerie O'Brien

Introduction

Since the late 1990s, there has been an outpouring of stories of abuse and maltreatment of residents in Irish institutional settings. The use of institutional care for children and adults in need crosses many cultural and geographical boundaries. Two major differences exist between institutional care in Ireland and that provided elsewhere. First is the extent of the practice and, second, the delay in change and the slow pace of commencement of family-based care. Paradoxically, Ireland now has one of the highest rates of family-based care in the world (O'Brien & Cregan, 2015).

A significant part of this chapter is given to an analysis of the context in which the institutional care of children occurred in Ireland to enable professionals to have a better understanding of:

- what occurred in Irish institutional settings and why;
- the impact of the institutional experience for people and their families, with a focus on transgenerational issues;
- the extent to which an emigration experience intersected with the institutional experience;

- the complexity involved for therapists and professionals working with people with an institutional experience;
- the importance of professionals' sensitivity to resilience and strengths;
- the non-homogeneity of the people involved and the need to be careful to avoid processes that may be experienced by users as stigmatising, pathologising, and as inherently disrespectful as were some of their experiences of institutional care.

This chapter is drawn from four major bodies of work which include:

- auto-biographical accounts of people that experienced life in various institutions;
- the Commission to Inquire into Child Abuse, 2009 (or CICA), which is referred to throughout the chapter as the Ryan Report;
- two Irish studies that captured clients experiences:
    - SENCS (2003) study which assessed the quality of services provided by the National Counselling Service set up in 2000 by the Irish State and partly sponsored by religious institutions. The service offers individual counselling sessions, without charge, to those who have experienced abuse in childhood.
    - Carr and colleagues' (Carr, 2009; Carr et al., 2010) studies of people who gave testimony about their institutional and subsequent life experience at the Ryan Commission of Inquiry;
- literature reviews of historical and contemporary child welfare practice, the effects of abuse, and effective service and therapeutic intervention.

The work also draws from the author's clinical work and supervision of those working with this population. It is this context that inspires me to review the legacy of the past in order to try shape better futures through reflection.

My positioning

The journey to develop an understanding of the institutional care of children, which can be of benefit to professionals and the clients of their services, has been challenging. I begin with a short explanation of my own positioning and how this is an influence in writing this account. I hope this will be helpful in locating the work.

I am an Irish woman born in 1960, a time when Ireland was beginning to change. While the pace of change was to be slow and arduous from my youthful perspective, none the less, it was a period that provided me with the opportunity to live a life that was largely denied to previous generations of Irish women. Access to tertiary education was a key to change. My willingness to challenge what was taken for granted by others, and a zest for experiences that were just about in reach, provided situations in which I could take risks, make mistakes, and shape possibilities.

My curiosity about Irish society was aroused by hearing stories of times gone by; however, I had a keen appreciation that many remained untold. I was well informed of both urban and rural social life around a small country town in Ireland by a mother who had many intergenerational stories and was willing to shine a light on the dark spaces. I understood that even strong connections could be quickly severed if individuals transgressed from what was seen as "normative". My education was in a Catholic Convent School (Sisters of Mercy) in which the potential for change was juxtaposed with reminders of Catholic doctrine. My views were shaped by the emergence of a social justice perspective, and my sense of righteous outrage was evoked frequently in response to situations of disadvantage and discrimination that I could see.

I had a strong desire to get away from what I saw as the constraints of a small town and the shackles of Catholicism. I succeeded, largely through determination, in realising a possibility that had been barely imaginable: to study social science in University College Dublin. Parallel involvement in feminist and political movements provided me with experiences through which I was to gain a broader understanding of my local history as well as a curiosity about why things occurred as they did. Training as a social worker at the LSE in London was followed by training as a systemic therapist and supervisor, which provided me with a skill set and conceptual base for working with various groups of people.

I have taken the opportunity to gain understanding of the events, processes, and contexts that surrounded institutional care of children and families in Ireland. I have also had an opportunity to consider my own relationship with these events, a relationship that involved unearthing family and community secrets and cultural stories that were painful and fascinating in equal measure.

In bringing a focus on this topic, I am guided by a number of points. First, the legacy of the past is interwoven with state, church, community, and family processes. Second, while I think it important to give voice to stories of the past, I am also conscious that there are many people whose lives were characterised by resilience, positivity, and achievement. Despite the poverty, the trauma, the abuse, and the pain of the institutional settings, hope, fulfilment, and love were to the fore in many lives subsequently. It is crucial that therapists and professionals critically examine their own relationship with the stories told and untold, irrespective of whether they hold an "insider Irish" or "outsider" position. As professionals, the extent to which we are shaped both by past and current discourses and simultaneously involved in shaping them is well recognised in the field (Flaskas et al., 2007), and, thus, the ethical responsibility to undertake this work is more important than ever.

What occurred

The Ryan Report (2009) states that an estimated 170,000 children were placed in institutions in Ireland between 1936 and 1970. The report cautions that the trends have been established from limited data sets. Approximately 105,000 children were committed to institutions by the courts and an estimated 25,000 were placed in institutions on a "voluntary" basis by local authorities (Raftery & O'Sullivan, 1999). The institutions had their genesis in the 1868 Industrial Schools Act. Under this Act, Industrial Schools were intended to provide practical training rather than an academic education for children who were neglected, orphaned, or abandoned. In the early twentieth century, there were seventy-one industrial schools in Ireland with 8,000 children, but this declined by the 1940s to some fifty-two industrial schools accommodating 6,000 children. By 1969, thirty-one industrial schools were still in operation, catering for some 2,000 children (Ferguson, 2007).

The Ryan Report shows that children from low income and large families, single parent families, orphans, and mentally ill children were more likely to enter the institutions. Carr and colleagues' (2010) study showed that 72% of the children were admitted from their family homes, while a further 14% were admitted from institutions such as children's homes and mother and baby homes. The extent to which agencies that had responsibilities towards children in need were also involved in keeping up the numbers of children to enable the institutions to continue is also illustrated by Ryan.

Legacy issues associated with the treatment of children and their families by the child welfare system have been a recurring theme in Ireland for the past fifteen to twenty years. The investigation of abuse of children within institutional settings and by members of the Catholic Church (Murphy, 2009; Keenan, 2012) has resulted in both public outrage and debate on the country's failure to protect vulnerable children. The issue of child abuse and children's rights has occupied a high position on the political agenda, culminating with the recent creation of a full Government Minister and Department of Children. The agenda has been propelled by the emergence of the latest scandal (O'Brien, 2014a).

What is known

The testimonies about what occurred in Irish institutions have been gathered and presented in Government Inquiries and through various accounts given in the media, books, and films. The evidence is frequently harrowing. Coleman's book (2010), which narrates eleven individual stories, illustrates some of the difficulties associated with separation, fragmentation of identity, and abuse experienced by the children. It also illustrates how traumatic events were remembered so clearly throughout the adult lives. The stories include the way the children left family homes: "I remember the woman taking the baby from my sister's arms . . . we were all screaming (p. 35).

The dehumanising effects of taking people's identity are illustrated: "The sisters told her she would be called Frances from then on . . . The nuns threatened a severe punishment for breaching the rules" (p. 184).

For another person: "He was known as 253" (p. 170).

These actions occurred in a country where membership of, and loyalty to, one's family, community, and nation were, and continue to be, of the utmost importance. In the accounts, there is constant reference to the hardship of work and what the children endured: "We didn't rake hay with rakes . . . we raked hay with our hands and you'd get thistles . . . and you couldn't even bend your fingers with the pain in them and in your bare feet" (Coleman, 2010, p. 44).

The theme of harsh physical work was compounded by neglect as well as physical, emotional, and sexual abuse, the effects of the abuse, and the callous indifference of the perpetrator is painfully shared: "It was done in an inhumane fashion. There was no pity, no nothing there for us. We were treated like animals" (p. 36).

Secret hope for retribution on their tormentors was dreamed of while in the institutions: "I wanted the fucker to burn in hell because we were taught about the fires of hell" (p. 203).

Another man gives a succinct analysis: "The animal that was working in the field was better looked after than we were" (p. 45).

The vindication of the truth of abuse allegations by the government investigation into the events led Irish historian, Diarmuid Ferriter, to conclude, "By presenting such an overwhelming body of evidence about what went on behind closed doors, the report provides a corrective to the atmosphere of secrecy and shame that surrounded these experiences for so many years" (2010, p. 333).

For the practitioner working with people whose lives have been touched by institutional care, the Ryan Report sets out in detail the manner in which decisions were made for children to enter the institutions, the effects of abuse, and the errors that the institutions made in responding to children's needs. Furthermore, there is now a sizable body of literature about the effects of childhood abuse and how these experiences can give rise to adult maladjustment and social, psychological, and emotional difficulties. The negative effect of such adversity is generally related to the severity, frequency, variety, and duration of the experiences.

In the next section, attention is focused on unravelling the context in which the particular form of Irish institutional care evolved for the benefit of professionals working with survivors. A key goal is that by attuning professionals to what occurred and why, a more appropriate service response and professional positioning will be provided. There is also the bigger hope that by appraising the stories of history, societies can avoid repeating the mistake of taking similar actions at a future time.

Factors that gave rise to the negative treatment of children

The position of children in society, the historic evolution of the state *vis-à-vis* colonisation, the dominance of Catholic social teaching, and the slow development of a professional input into the care of children are seen as key to our understanding the Irish institutional legacy. Historically, in Ireland, the position of children and their welfare was viewed as a matter of private responsibility, where parents were considered the sole and duty-bound providers of care and protection of their children (Considine & Dukelow, 2009). According to Ridge (2012, p. 387) this resulted in the "familialisation" of children, where "their needs and interests have remained hidden within the private sphere of the family". This "principle of family autonomy" (Richardson, 2005, p. 160), a basic tenet of Catholic teaching, was reinforced by the 1937 Irish Constitution, in so far as it identifies the family as the "primary and fundamental unit of society" and provides parents with "inalienable and imprescriptible" rights (*Constitution of Ireland*, 1937, Article 41.1.1). The family that was privileged, however, was, and remains, the family based on marriage.

Eugenics theory was a strong influence on the type of institutions that evolved. This ideology purports to show that those children with problems such as poverty, neglect, or abuse are biologically flawed due to the moral and biological makeup of their parents (Smith, 2011). Thus, children in need were treated as the "moral dirt" of society and were subjected to a form of "ethnic cleansing" (Ferguson, 2007, p. 125), accomplished by assuming control over them (Maguire, 2009). Mahood and Littlewood's earlier work (1994, p. 555) shows that "the moral status of abused children was seen as dubious and the challenge was to catch these children early and channel them into an appropriate regime of moral rehabilitation". This approach to treatment of children was not just an Irish phenomenon. It also occurred in England, where children in need were sent to Australia, Canada, and other British colonies (Humphries, 1996). However, the system of institutionalisation, which took a firm hold in Ireland, endured for much longer than in other countries.

The extent to which care was provided almost exclusively by religious congregations has its genesis in the evolution of the welfare system in Ireland and also reflects how the church positioned itself. There is ample evidence of the religious orders being involved in safeguarding their own interests, both in terms of saving Catholic souls, as well as the temporal needs of their institutions. There is also evidence that the burden of care was often found to be excessive during the period (Ryan Report, 2009). The state's peripheral involvement and its abdication of responsibility in resourcing, regulating, and inspecting institutions have been well portrayed. O'Sullivan and O'Donnell's (2012) work concludes that confinement across a range of Irish institutions was characterised by higher levels of coercive practices and was sustained for longer, compared to other jurisdictions.

As part of this historical exploration (O'Brien & Maguire Pavao, 2014), one has to ponder on the place of community and the much-cherished family during this period. The institutions were usually situated in towns and cities and, therefore, they had visibility and status in these communities. There is evidence of unwillingness, reluctance, or inability to intervene in the institutions on behalf of the disadvantaged children. While there are examples of individual testimonies whereby complaints were made to relevant authorities and children were helped to escape, the extent to which communities remained silent and largely inactive is part of the story that remains to be told.

The evolution of the professional sphere

During the first six decades of the twentieth century, the professional voice was largely missing from child welfare provision in Ireland. Instead, the "voice and power of Catholic teaching" was seen, according to Skehill (1999), as sufficient to meet the service needs of the day. Social work was slow to develop in Ireland and it originated with the 1970 Health Act, since when it has played an increasing role in child welfare (O'Brien, 2014a). This Act coincided with the publication of a government report, which examined institutional care and explored why the preference for family-based care, provided for in Boarding Out Regulations made in 1954, was slow to develop. This report was scathing of many aspects of institutional care provision and, in particular, stressed the ineffective nature of the state inspection system.

> In other countries the Inspectorate acts as a link between those in the field and those in Central Authority. In this way, the system ensures that no one school or centre is working in isolation, unaware of

developments in other regions. This has not been the position here. (Kennedy, 1970, p. 28)

The Kennedy report heralded the closing of large-scale institutions and forged the way for a change to family-based care for children in need. However, the stories of what had been happening in the institutions were to remain largely buried for another twenty years, other than for those professionals who encountered the consequences. The shift to family-based care has been pivotal in delivering this achievement (O'Brien & Cregan, 2015).

The role of popular media in telling the stories of institutional life

Investigative journalists, films, documentaries, newspapers, books, and radio have all played a role in opening up the extraordinary stories of institutional life in Ireland. The work of Raftery and O'Sullivan (1999), resulting in Raftery's powerful television documentary, *States of Fear* (1999), regarding the treatment of children in institutions, was pivotal to this awareness. The first episode opens with the statement, "The one good thing about Christmas Day was that there was no sexual abuse". This set the tone for the uncovering of the high levels of abuse that occurred in institutional settings (Prior, 1999). Raftery's work built on earlier documentaries such as *Dear Daughter* (Lentin, 1996) and *Sex in a Cold Climate* (Humphries, 1998) in which people who had grown up in the institutions told their stories. The documentary makers continued to probe other aspects of Irish institutional life, including clerical abuse, in *Suing the Pope* (O'Gorman, 2002), and the Magdalene Laundries, as depicted in *The Forgotten Maggies* (O'Riardan & Boland, 2009). These documentaries, and films such as *Philomena* (Frears, 2013), contain powerful telling of individual stories. Biographical accounts have also played an important part in bringing forth lived experiences. Books such as *Nothing to Say*, by Mannix Flynn (1983), *The God Squad*, by Paddy Doyle; *Freedom of Angels*, by Bernadette Fahy (1999), *Childhood Interrupted*, by Kathleen O'Malley (2005), Colm O'Gorman's *Beyond Belief* (2009), and Tyrell and Whelan's *Founded on Fear* (2006) have played their part, among others. Some of these authors tell stories of reluctant publishers, which again indicates the difficulty in overcoming the silence that surrounded these institutions.

Following Raftery's (1999) work, the public outpouring of the accounts of institutional life began in earnest. People told personal stories on radio and in print. The nature and scale of revelations prompted a community and societal response, and, finally, a political one that had been long awaited by the people who grew up in the institutions. These survivors told stories of the culture of silence that allowed atrocities to reoccur over many decades; they gave harrowing accounts of what actually happened; they spoke of the effects of sexual, physical, and psychological abuse and especially the impact of their powerlessness to save other children; they spoke of the cover-up by the responsible institutions.

The stories of those who experienced care and kindness were slower to emerge. Such stories of resilience, I would contend, have yet to be fully told, though some are now making their way via support groups on to web sites that are run by survivors, principally in Ireland and the UK.[1] Like family and community involvement in mother and baby homes, this aspect might not sit easily with the ineffectual state/evil church narrative about institutions.

Despite the transformation of recent years, one aspect of recent developments is a definite barrier to our progress, because it contributes to the silencing of institutional stories. I refer to the "gagging clause" laid down in the Residential Institutions Act 2002. This prohibits recipients who accept compensation under the institutional redress scheme from speaking of their experiences and provides for fines and even prison sentences if offences occur. An attempt to overturn this provision via a Private Member's Bill (The Institutional Abuse Bill) in 2009 was defeated. The prohibition continues to be a source of great distress for many.

The political response

While there were initial attempts by political figures to distance themselves from the past following the publication of Raftery's work, the public groundswell of outrage created a seismic shift. The harrowing accounts by adults of what happened to them as children, the part played by religious congregations, and the totally ineffectual response of the state led to a quick shift in the political response. The government offered apologies in 1999; a Commission of Inquiry was set up and a Redress Board provided compensation to the survivors, provided they undertook not to make public the terms of settlement. The publication of the Reports of the Commissions of Inquiry into abuse of children within institutional settings and by members of the Catholic Church and, more recently, into the deaths of children within the care system (Shannon & Gibbons, 2012) resulted in continued public outrage on Ireland's failure to protect vulnerable children. These accounts have had a cumulative effect and contribute to the resolve to break the culture of silence. Thus, issues of institutional child abuse and children's rights have occupied a position high on the political agenda for more than a decade now (O'Brien, 2012). Ironically, this follows several decades of Catholic Church-led pressure on Irish politicians to protect "unborn" children, leading to constitutional amendments aimed at prohibiting abortion in Ireland while women continue to have to travel abroad. The Catholic Church's moral high ground has been severely dented by the revelations of the events they presided over in institutions providing for vulnerable Irish children.

This has arisen alongside the focus on other institutional abuses, for example, in the Magdalene laundries (Inter-departmental Committee, 2013; Smith, 2007) and more recently on death rates in mother and baby homes (O'Brien, 2013). There has been a political readiness to explore single institutional issues, but there is still work to be done on how the network of institutions, the various religious congregations, and the state machinery operated in the lives of people, families, and communities.

Key context markers: what is known and the implications for services

While the topic has received huge attention in recent years in the stories told (Powell et al., 2013), there is little by way of reliable study or data on the children who lived in the institutions. Even less is known about what happened to them in later life as adults. There is no reliable estimate of the number of people that are still alive, or at what point they are in their lives. The paucity of baseline data on admissions and biographical information makes it impossible to devise reliable statistics now.

Drawing on 1,007 people who provided information to the Commission of Inquiry in 2009, and adjusting for the time lag between data collection and 2015, but not accounting for death rates, Higgins (2010) calculates that 38% of the population who were in institutions might be between sixty and seventy and the remaining 62% are over seventy years of age. The majority live in Ireland (58%), but a significant number (37%) are in the UK. There are implications, therefore, for professionals working in both jurisdictions, and the focus on "insider Irish" and "outsider" is put forward to enhance and attune professional positioning and will help to work with the impact of both colonisation and emigration.

The socio-economic profile presented in 2009 is also worthy of note in getting a picture of the people. At that time, 45% of adults who had been raised in institutions were dependent on various social benefits, 33% were employed, and 22% were retired. The vast majority were educated to primary level, 10% achieved a tertiary education at later stages of their lives. Two thirds reported that they had worked throughout their lives, but most in semi-skilled or non-skilled jobs. Forty-four per cent reported owning their own homes, 36% had local authority tenancies and the remainder were in the private rented sector (10%). Up to 20% reported being in temporary accommodation of various types. This latter figure suggests a level of vulnerability which, when combined with other data, is a cause for concern.

Social relations

Carr's study (2009) gives a picture of the people who were in institutions. Ninety per cent had reported experiencing abuse. Forty per cent were still married in their first relationship, 11% had never married, and the remainder reported various stages of separation and divorce. Almost 90% had children of their own. Of this population, 95% reported that they had parented their children, and 5% reported that their children had spent time in care.

All described various life difficulties, including mental health (74%), substance abuse (38%), frequent illness (30%), unemployment (54%), and anger control in relationships (26%). Relationships, good supports, and a good attitude were factors cited by many as helping them deal with these challenges.

There are concerns among survivors and people working in this field that the profile projected in the above studies is not representative. There are difficulties in accessing the stories, as the political context could be silencing survivors, just as they were silenced as children. Higgins (2010) indicates that there is evidence that the majority have led "normal lives of work, relationship and children" (p. 15). She also maintains that many have lived lives of relative poverty and disadvantage, directly related to their childhood in institutions. She maintains that the people who did not manage to build stable lives "could be among the most marginal in society both here and in the UK, a situation exacerbated now by their ageing" (p. 13). A cohort, mostly men, have complex and challenging needs, substances abuse issues, lack family supports, and are known to homeless, mental health, and prison services. Among survivors in general, many report feeling misunderstood by health and other professionals. Significantly, they express fear about needing institutional care as they enter older age and their health deteriorates. This is referred to by Janet in Chapter Eleven.

The emigration factor: issues for professionals working with Irish clients

There is evidence that people who left the institutions were part of the waves of Irish emigrants to the UK, while a smaller number went further afield. There is limited information about the numbers involved or specific details of the institutional population. If meeting the service needs of disparate groups is to be addressed, the history of the Irish abroad, and especially in the UK, should be considered. While many Irish people have been highly successful in the UK, the history of the colonial relationship, the impact of the "Troubles" in Northern Ireland, and the corresponding impact on the Irish community in the UK are important contexts markers for understanding the relationship between the two countries and the communities involved. Consequently, it is important to keep abreast of general trends in respect of the Irish living in the UK, as it might be a useful starting point in appraising the needs of the former institutional residents group.

In the 2001 census, the Irish comprised the largest and oldest ethnic minority in the UK. By 2011, the numbers had dropped due to deaths, people returning to live in Ireland, possibly associated with the economic upturn from 2001 to 2007, and people reaching retirement age. Walls (2001) showed that the Irish population in the UK, which includes both first and second generation, had consistently poorer physical and mental health compared to the rest of the population. She stressed an urgent need to consider their mental health needs but, according to Garrett (2004, p. 1), this did not happen and he contends that "there has been an embedded failure to recognise the specificity of Irish people". Evidence of this was found in a recent study by O'Connor (2014), which explored the relationship between counselling and therapy professionals and their Irish clients. She suggests that, due to the myth of white homogeneity, the Irish continue to remain "outside the public discourse on ethnicity and are predominantly ignored in policy decisions, practices and debates". She also found evidence that negative stereotypes of the Irish still abound, with Irish clients experiencing exclusion, anti-Irish sentiment, and being subject to anti-Irish jokes and discrimination based on accent, name, and use of Hiberno–English. She also found that the transgenerational, intercultural issues associated with the colonial past were ever-present for the Irish client as the "elephant in the room" (p. 118).

Intergenerational issues

It is important to consider trends associated with life opportunities and experiences of the second generation Irish population in the UK. There is evidence showing that the task of establishing a coherent identity proves problematic for this group. Hickman (2005) noted that many people are rejected in both countries as not being either fully Irish or English. These broad trends, which remain largely invisible, are important for professionals to take into account when working with people from an Irish background. It is especially important, however, where clients' parents have institutional histories, especially when the risks associated with intergeneration trauma and abuse are considered. The fact that Irish residents in the UK who grew up in institutions remain invisible compounds the difficulties for many of their children and grandchildren when they are users of services. Clients might not be comfortable telling the story of their parents, as it could reinforce negative Irish stereotypes. By remaining silent on such backgrounds, they might leave professionals ignorant of processes that are occurring. Clients might come from families where the stories remained largely silent. To open the stories of the past runs the risk of opening too many family sores. For others, the effects of a parent's institutional experience were pivotal in the lives lived.

Survivors: intercultural and older person issues

What is the likely impact of the intercultural/emigrant experience for people who also have negative experiences in institutions when they are users of health and social services? The testimonial accounts illustrate how a sense of shame, injustice, anger, or loss, arising from institutional experiences, have prompted many people to remain silent. This could be further exacerbated by the "absent but present" processes O'Connor found that occur between Irish clients and the professionals working with them. The clients assumed that professionals lacked awareness of Irish cultural heritage, transgenerational trauma, the intercultural emotion legacy, and their current experiences of racism or discrimination (p. 119). On the other hand, O'Connor found that English professionals felt a "a sense of threat, shame, guilt and stuckness" (p. 122) in relation to the intercultural issues when working with the Irish clients. These themes were particularly present when they were dealing with transgenerational, relational trauma and its affective legacy. O'Connor's study also sheds some light on the strategies clients used to avoid a focus on the intercultural elements. Strategies such as silencing a traumatic relational past and hiding or adapting the "Irish cultural self" are used by clients to defend against a "felt sense of potential discrimination but also to avoid the internalized shame, self-blame, guilt, anger, sadness and loss". Interestingly, these are strategies also found in the trauma literature. The intersectionality between the intercultural and trauma findings has implications, not only for the generation who lived in the institutions, but also for their family members who have been born into this legacy. Furthermore, it has implications for professionals working across cultures described below.

Enhancing service response

While gaps remain in respect of the current profile of people who lived in the institutions, their experience of service use and outcomes desired require consideration. First, the population in question is not homogenous, but it is ageing and many are part of second, third, and even fourth generation families, while some are socially isolated. These differences need to be considered, and the range of experiences of persons accessing services need to be kept in mind. Second, people rarely disclose that institutional care has been part of their past when accessing services or presenting problems. Furthermore, Higgins (2010) noted that it is unlikely to emerge while they are in receipt of services, unless a particularly strong relationship is built up between service and survivor. Third, where services have been accessed and people have disclosed this aspect of their past, the opportunity to co-ordinate responses at a multi-disciplinary level is limited. Yet, when we consider some of the sub-sets of the population involved, co-ordination, communication, and co-operation are crucial if outcomes are to be optimised for clients. Fourth, turning to the client experience of counselling services, there is evidence that people encountered different levels of competence, and the institutional experience and its effects were largely ignored in the work. Clients attributed the responsibility for this to both themselves and the professionals (SENCS, 2003). Higgins, on the other hand found that some professionals do not understand the effect of these experiences and she expressed a level of concern "at the lack of expertise among psycho-therapists and 'helping professionals' of the effects of abuse and the dangers that their interventions could do more harm than good" (2010, p. 13).

A number of measures are suggested aimed at improving service outcomes and client engagement, based on both the work of Higgins (2010) and the research on which this chapter is based. Some services might be specifically connected with the institutional legacy, while the majority will be offering services in which the institutional experience is not headlined and, thus, a range of professionals and diverse services are likely to be involved.

The stated mission of the organisation is a good starting point. Mission statements generally speak to organisational delivery models that aim to be respectful, adaptable, flexible, and transparent, client-centred, non-discriminatory services. Services should examine their mission statements against the issues that have been identified for this group of people, asking, "Does the way we say we are providing services fit with the needs of the people involved?" Second, services could evaluate if a learning culture is embedded in organisations, and if they routinely engage with service users regarding what they think is needed. Third, in terms of improving client engagement, it is important for services to examine if there is a sufficient knowledge base and understanding in respect of affects of trauma and the place resilience plays. Historical legacies, the affect of institutional experiences, their impact through the generations, and the tasks and transitions involved in older age need to be woven into the work.

Conclusion and recommendations to enhance professional work

This chapter aims to give professionals, and people with an interest in this subject, an overview of the past and a consideration of how therapeutic work needs to engage people who were involved in institutional care in Ireland. While it is written with this context in mind, it is likely that there are parallels here for people from other jurisdictions who experienced both institutional abuse and professionals working with them. The processes that continue to push people who experienced institutional trauma to remain silent should be uppermost in the professional's mind. Key to the work is role clarification, relationship building, and development of a "reflective and critical voice", taking into account an appreciation that the professional might be working with a range of referrals. It is likely that, while there is a level of knowledge about this population, much remains unknown. Curiosity on the part of the professional, and a commitment to social justice, will remain key to successful engagement. The question of how experiences can be spoken, heard, seen, and understood is key. Professionals need to have an understanding of the past, while, at the same time, appreciating that the pictures may vary greatly.

The opening up of one's own stories, and how the professional positions herself, is key to enhanced service delivery and client engagement, as I learnt from my clinical experience and research endeavours. In particular, through an exploration of my own story, as an Irish woman reared in 1960s Ireland, I worked hard to remove the shackles of a Catholic and rural upbringing. However, in this process I ran the risk of failing to respect how clients might still yearn for the very features of life that I was rejecting; thus, the iterative process is a crucial anchor.

In my clinical and supervision work, I have learnt that the processes and relationship fields involved are complex, emotional, sometimes polarised, and characterised by varying levels of ambivalence (O'Brien, 2014b). The extent to which stories of resilience can be woven into the work and how professionals might influence the wider discourses surrounding the institutional experience to encompass greater telling and hearing stories of strength and survival as well as pain and adversity is important.

At a clinical level, the therapist should be attuned to dynamics that lead the client's story to be seen as an individual and private issue principally, and not connected to the context from which it originated. There is a danger in this work that, while we talk resilience, the discourses perpetuate victimhood. Therefore, we must be vigilant to attend to the various experiences and groupings involved. To this end, I iterate Higgins' (2010) view that, at the end stage of life for those who experienced first-hand the legacy of the past, people should have their needs met in a respectful manner. I would go a step further and say that, as professionals, we have an ethical responsibility: to explore our obligation to advocate for change at political and service delivery level, especially when the vulnerability of many people and their families and the great injustices meted out to them are considered.

Note

1. Examples of such groups are as follows:

   Irish International Abuse Survivors Support Group Site. What We Do. Available at: http://irishabusesurvivors.com/wordpress/what-we-do/.

   Irish Survivors in Britain: Linking up Survivors, Groups, Networks and Services. Who We Are. Available at: www.irishsurvivorsinbritain.org/who-we-are-2/.

References

Carr, A. (2009). The psychological adjustment of adult survivors of institutional abuse in Ireland report. In: *Commission to Inquire into Child Abuse Vol. 5* (Chapter 3). Dublin: Stationery Office.

Carr, A., Dooley, B., Fitzpatrick, M., Flanagan, E., Howard-Flanagan, R., Tierney, K., White, M., Daly, M., & Egan, J. (2010). Adult adjustment of survivors of institutional child abuse in Ireland. *Child Abuse and Neglect, 34*: 477–489.

Coleman, K. (2010). *Haunting Cries: Stories of Child Abuse from Industrial Schools*. Dublin: Gill and Macmillan.

Considine, M., & Dukelow, F. (2009). *Irish Social Policy: A Critical Introduction*. Dublin: Gill and Macmillan.

Constitution of Ireland (1937). Dublin: Stationery Office.

Doyle, P. (1989). *The God Squad*. London: Corgi.

Fahy, B. (1999). *Freedom of Angels*. Dublin: O'Brien Press.

Ferguson, H. (2007). Abused and looked after children as 'moral dirt': child abuse and institutional care in historical perspective. *Journal of Social Policy, 36*: 123–139.

Ferriter, D. (2010). *Occasions of Sin: Sex and Society in Modern Ireland*. London: Profile.

Flaskas, C., McCarthy, I., & Sheehan, J. (Eds.) (2007). *Hope and Despair in Narrative and Family Therapy: Adversity, Forgiveness and Reconciliation*. London: Routledge.

Flynn, M. (1983). *Nothing to Say*. Dublin: Lilliput.

Frears, S. (Dir.) (2013). *Philomena*. Film, distributed by Pathé.

Garrett, P. M. (2004). *Social Work and Irish People in Britain: Historical and Contemporary Responses to Irish Children and Families*. Bristol: Policy Press.

Hickman, M. J. (2005). The limitations of whiteness as the boundaries of Englishness: second generation Irish identifications and positionings in multi-ethnic Britain. *Ethnicities, 5*: 160–180.

Higgins, M. (2010). *Developing a Profile of Survivors of Abuse in Irish Religious Institutions*. Dublin: St Stephens Green Trust.

Humphries, M. (1996). *Empty Cradles*. London: Transworld.

Humphries, S. (Dir.) (1998). *Sex in a Cold Climate*. Documentary distributed by Testimony Films, Channel 4.

Inter-departmental Committee, Irish Government (2013). *Report of the Inter-Departmental Committee to Establish the Facts of State Involvement with the Magdalen Laundries*. Dublin: Department of Justice.

Keenan, M. (2012). *Child Sexual Abuse and the Catholic Church: Gender, Power and Organizational Culture*. New York: Oxford University Press.

Kennedy, E. (1970). *Reformatory and Industrial Schools System Report*. Dublin: Stationery Office

Lentin, L. (Dir.) (1996). *Dear Daughter*. Film, Crescendo Concepts.

Maguire, M. (2009). *Precarious Childhood in Post-Independent Ireland*. Manchester: Manchester University Press.

Mahood, L., & Littlewood, B. (1994). The 'vicious' girl and the 'street corner' boy: sexuality and the gendered delinquent in the Scottish child saving movement. *Journal of the History of Sexuality, 4*: 549–578.

Murphy, Y. (2009). *The Commission's Report into the Catholic Diocese of Cloyne*. Dublin: Government Publications.

O'Brien, V. (2012). The place of family group conferencing in child welfare in the Republic of Ireland. In: *The Quiet Revolution. Aggrandising People Power by Family Group Conferences* (pp. 183–198). Amsterdam: SWP.

O'Brien, V. (2013). Adopt an open approach to a historic secret. *Sunday Times*, 17 November, p. 17. Available at http://hdl.handle.net/10197/5220.

O'Brien, V. (2014a). Navigating child welfare and protection in Ireland with the help of the fifth province. Feedback. *Journal of Family Therapy: Special Issue on Supervision, 1*: 91–117.

O'Brien, V. (2014b). Navigating kinship networks with the fifth province. *Human Systems, 1*: 1–21. Available at www.ucd.ie/t4cms/WP35.pdf.

O'Brien, V., & Cregan, M (2015). Fostering the future: a change agenda in the provision of alternative care. In: A. Christie, S. Quin, & P. Walsh (Eds.), *Social Work in Ireland* (pp. 88–105). London: Palgrave.

O'Brien, V., & Maguire Pavao, J. (2014). The last word: Irish American adoptions. *Irish America*. Available at: http://irishamerica.com/2013/12/the-last-word-irish-american-adoptions. Accessed 23 January 2014.

O'Connor, L. (2014). Tir ns Scaile (Shadowlands): an exploration into the intercultural dimension of the therapeutic relationship. PhD thesis, Middlesex University and Metanoic Institute. Available at http://eprints.mdx.ac.uk/14419/1/LOConnorThesis.pdf. Accessed 19 June 2015.

O'Gorman, C. (Dir.) (2002). *Suing the Pope*. Documentary, BBC, 13 May.

O'Gorman, C. (2009). *Beyond Belief*. London: Hodder & Stoughton.

O'Malley, K. (2005). *Childhood Interrupted*. London: Virago.

O'Riardan, S., & Boland, G. (Prod.) (2009). *The Forgotten Maggies*. Film, launched at Galway Film Festival.

O'Sullivan, E., & O'Donnell, I. (2012). *Coercive Confinement in Ireland*. Manchester: Manchester University Press.

Powell, F., Geoghan, M., Scanlan, M., & Swirak, K. (2013). The Irish charity myth, child abuse and human rights: contextualising the Ryan report into care institutions. *British Journal of Social Work, 43*: 7–23.

Prior, J. (1999). Participant in *States of Fear*, Raftery, M. (1999). RTE Archives. Available at www.rte.ie/archives/2014/0521/618546-states-of-fear-screenings-and-discussions-at-ifi/. Accessed 8 December 2014.

Raftery, M. (Prod. & Dir.) (1999). *States of Fear*. Documentary on RTE, 27 April. Available at: www.rte.ie/archives/2014/0521/618546-states-of-fear-screenings-and-discussions-at-ifi/. Accessed 8 December 2014.

Raftery, M., & O'Sullivan, E. (1999). *Suffer the Little Children: The Inside Story of Ireland's Industrial Schools*. Dublin: New Ireland Books.

Residential Institutions Redress Act (2002). Dublin: Stationery Office.

Richardson, V. (2005). *Families, Change and European Social Policy*. Dublin: Department of Social and Family Affairs.

Ridge, T. (2012). Children. In: P. Alcock, M. May, & K. Rowlington (Eds.), *The Student's Companion to Social Policy* (4th edn) (pp. 385–391). Oxford: Blackwell.

Ryan Report, The (2009). *The Commission to Inquire into Child Abuse*. Dublin: Government Publications.

SENCS (2003). *Survivors' Experiences of the National Counselling Service for Adults who Experienced Childhood Abuse*. Dublin: Health Services Research Centre/Royal College of Surgeons.

Shannon, G., & Gibbons, N. (2012). *Report of the Independent Child Death Review*. Dublin: Department of Children and Youth Affairs.

Skehill, C. (1999). *The Nature of Social Work in Ireland*. New York: Edwin Mellen Press.

Smith, J. (2007). *Ireland's Magdalene Laundries and the Nation's Architecture of Containment*. Notre Dame: University of Notre Dame Press.

Smith, K. (2011). Producing governable subjects: images of childhood old and new. *Childhood, 19*(1): 24–37.

The Industrial Schools Act (1868). Dublin: House of Parliament.

Tyrell, P., & Whelan, D. (2006). *Founded on Fear*. Dublin: Irish Academic Press.

Walls, P. (2001). *Religion, Ethnicity and Nationality in the Census: Some Thoughts on the Inclusion of Irish Ethnicity and Catholic Religion*. Available at: www.radstats.org.uk/No078/walls.ht. Accessed 15 January 2015.

CHAPTER TWELVE

Never too late

Janet, Mark Brownfield, and Sara Barratt

Introduction (Sara Barratt)

I work as a systemic psychotherapist in general practice. Mark Brownfield, her GP, referred Janet to me in 2011. This chapter is written by Janet, Mark, and me, with a contribution from the agency. We describe the work we have undertaken to help Janet to find some recovery from her childhood in a residential school and in care. It has been a privilege to work with Janet, for whom it took so much courage to talk about events that had been locked inside her for so many years, and brings to light the contested notion of memory. Her account can be difficult and painful to read and the passage of years has not diluted her feelings about the past. As part of our therapy we used EMDR, which is helpful in the treatment of post-traumatic stress (Shapiro & Maxfield, 2002). Essentially, the importance of our work was the creation of a system working together to create a safe enough environment to support Janet in talking about her early traumatic experiences and their effect on her adult life. While this chapter is primarily about systemic work with an older adult whose childhood experiences blighted her adult life and that of her children, it is important to note that the context of care in the 1940s was harsh, professionals did not consider that children might be suffering sexual abuse and, if they did, there were no structures in place to protect them. It was not until the 1948 Children Act that things started to change, although, as we know, in some ways nothing has changed and there are adults who still feel entitled to abuse children without fear of being held accountable.

Janet

I am seventy-four years old and live with my husband of forty-five years, Jack, in a mobile home park. I have three children, two from my first husband and one with Jack. I don't see my two elder children and only see my youngest daughter whom we moved to live close to, when she wants something.

I can't remember a time when I wasn't frightened. This started with my experiences of being brought up in what is now known as "care". Jack shouts at me a lot and scares me; recently, I shout back and throw things at him. I have seen lots of psychiatrists in my life and have tried to kill myself several times. I was never able to speak to the psychiatrists; I was mute because I knew they would want to talk about my past. Throughout my life I have wanted to disappear and can't cope with people I don't know wanting to talk to me.

In 2011, my GP said that there is a therapist working in the surgery who might be able to help. I didn't want to see anyone other than him. He kept telling me he thought it was a good idea so in the end I gave in. He said he would come with me for the first session. I don't talk to people at the best of times so when I walked in I was terrified and wanted to leave. My doctor and Sara said they understood and eventually I sat down. Dr Brownfield said he thought I had had a very bad time as a child and that it might be very difficult to talk to anyone about it. Eventually, they put me at ease and, in that first meeting, I started to talk for the first time about what had happened to me.

Mark Brownfield, Janet's GP

My first ever consultation with Janet was for an ingrowing toenail in May 2005. How could I have ever have known what a terrible story hid behind the eyes of this timid lady in her sixties?

As a general practitioner, I consider myself a holistic doctor, taking an interest in all domains of a patient's life. It is a style that comes naturally to me and is, I think, successful in every way but time keeping. Covering the physical, emotional, domestic, social, and sometimes spiritual agenda takes much more time than our allotted ten minutes.

On the surface, Janet presented as a "born worrier", constantly seeking reassurance and, as a practitioner, it was easy to feel that I was always slightly failing her. From her notes, I was made aware that she had been abandoned as a baby and fostered for all of her childhood.

Over the next six years, I met with Janet frequently, dealing with myriad complaints, among which were low back pain, gastric ulcers, irritable bowel syndrome, and, always, chronic anxiety. She was keen to reduce her use of diazepam and together we managed to halve her daily consumption over a six-month period in 2006. There was something preventing her from relinquishing the final 2 mg taken at night to help her sleep.

Janet's anxiety showed some familiar patterns. It was always worse on the lead up to ambitious holidays arranged by her husband (often cruises) and also around important family times, such as Christmas. In addition, she was frequently worried about her health. Janet had what was believed to be a small stroke in 1997 and was fearful of the next, and possibly fatal, event.

Looking back now, I can see that Janet rarely consulted any other doctor in the practice. She spoke fondly of her previous GP and I assumed it had taken a long time for her to trust him. I was unsure of the reason why and, on reflection, I sensed that Janet needed some kind of protection. Years passed with very regular consultations dealing with multiple health issues. These included conditions such as a blood disorder that has required chemotherapy to control her platelet count and a stomach ulcer that was treatable, but made preventing future strokes with blood thinners quite problematic.

In the first few months of 2011, Janet's anxiety levels increased. She became breathless both on exertion and at rest and there was nothing on examination to explain this. In March, it was Jack who spoke to me. I was never sure how the conversation had started; did I quiz him, was he sent by Janet, or had he come of his own accord? He explained that Janet had been abandoned by her mother as a baby and put into care. It was not so much that the penny dropped, but I was now able to see clearly how her current behaviour might be the result of deep emotional scarring. Ten days later, Janet saw me and asked if Jack had said anything. Sensitively, I opened up the conversation.

My notes are relatively brief and essentially refer to themes of lifelong rejection. It was clear that Janet was expecting to be rejected again and I was aware of just how delicate was the path we were walking. It was my hope that she could feel safe in her relationship with me, but my concern was that it had been a very long time, if ever, since Janet had felt safe.

Almost immediately I thought of Sara Barratt, a systemic psychotherapist working in the practice, whom I have known professionally since before joining the partnership seventeen years earlier. Over the years we have shared many patients and, with the explicit permission of the individuals themselves, have communicated regularly about our understanding of their issues. It is a confidential, but enabling, arrangement which seems to allow the patient a triangle of security in which trust can exist. I wished for Janet to be able to benefit from Sara's extensive experience with abuse.

From time to time, when patients are particularly vulnerable, I join Sara for the first consultation with a new client. It was important that we had such a joint session with Janet and I remember having to coax her into the room where the three of us would sit. The tension was palpable. It was going to be very difficult for Janet to start talking about something she had kept secret for most of her life and she could not be rushed. However, to our amazement, in that very first meeting, the disclosure started—in limited amounts to begin with, but gradually in more detail, she began to talk. It was clearly distressing for Janet to be remembering the events and terrors of her childhood, although something she said later made it probable that she was going to try to see it through: "I don't want to go to my grave without telling someone."

Sara

When I first met Janet, she came into the room with Mark and said she could not stay. We tried to calm her and, when she sat down, she started to talk and talked about the events of her childhood as if she would not stop. She said she would come to see me again and I was unsure as to whether she would be able to, as sometimes clients who disclose a lot in a first session can start remembering more traumatic events and are frightened of returning because they are worried that talking would make things worse. However, Janet did return and surprised herself that she could trust me enough to talk about the distressing aspects of her life. The first sessions were spent on her preoccupation with her children; the recent breakdown of her relationship with her son led her to relive the rejections of the past and she started to talk about what happened to her in residential care. She agreed that I could contact the agency responsible for the home and they were very responsive, agreeing to go through her records with her. It felt important that we created a network of support for Janet in which the GP, agency worker, and I could work together to help her create a coherent story.

Janet

Most of my troubles come from being brought up in a home. I was born in 1940, when the country was at war and there were not many people who wanted to look after abandoned children. I had lots of memories of that time and lots of flashbacks to being abused. I started to talk about them with Sara and although I couldn't believe I was talking about things that happened to me seventy years ago, once I started I couldn't stop. After a few meetings, Sara got in touch with the agency that I had been with and they visited several times to talk about their records of my childhood. So they, my doctor, and my therapist all worked together to try to help me with the terrible things that had happened.

There are a lot of different stories. There is the GP's story, the agency story, and my memories, which have expanded since I started working with Sara; they don't always fit together.

The agency says that when I was taken in by them, I went to live with a foster mother until I was five and a half years old, when I moved to a residential school and that they have no records of that time apart from noting that, at Christmas 1948, my foster mother, who was quite elderly, had moved to a derelict cottage with no facilities. It was cold and damp and dark and I remember having to bathe in the kitchen while she and her friend watched and laughed at me.

This is all that was written about me from when I was eight months old until I was eight and a half. I don't remember much of my time in the foster home before I was five. My foster mother had several jobs so I spent time shut out of the house. A nice couple lived nearby who were kind to me and wanted to look after me, so my foster mother didn't like me talking to them.

Sara

As time went on, Janet was reliving the abuse from the past; the carer who abused her would appear in her nightmares and her life was dominated by flashbacks. She would wake Jack up, dreaming that he was attacking her and there was a lot of tension between them. I started to talk to Janet about EMDR, as the reliving of past events was overwhelming and the search for a "safe place" where she could take herself in her imagination to help her feel calm was very important in helping her manage her daily distress and anger.

Janet

What I remember of being in the home was of being cold, scared, and alone. I wet the bed and remember hiding under my bed because I knew I was in trouble. The staff would drag me out by my hair and I remember spending the day tied to a toilet seat with the door open with a sign round my neck saying: "I wet the bed". I don't remember being given food or water and at night I was taken back to my wet bed. The other children would pass by and laugh at me. I think I wet the bed because I was always frightened.

The worst thing was the abuse I suffered from the caretaker. I was one of the youngest and when we had to change in the changing room, the other girls could run faster so they would run away and he would trip me up and make me touch him. Once when I ran away from him and hid in the garden, the staff found me and locked me in the changing room with him. He hurt me, made me touch him, and then raped me. The staff found me scrubbing myself in the toilets in the night and dragged me back to bed. When I showed them the blood on me and asked for a bath they refused and did nothing. I believed they knew what was happening to me. The staff also beat me for wetting the bed. No child would be my friend because they were frightened to be nice to me. We all got beaten and, if we didn't eat or like the food, we were tied to a chair until we ate it, even if we were sick. I have always had trouble with eating. This carried on until I went back to the foster home when I was eight.

I can't remember much of my life in the foster home. I remember waking up one night and my foster mother was touching my private parts.

The agency says that a social worker visited and recorded that someone else fed me while my foster mother worked. She had three jobs and was very deaf so I could not talk to her and she didn't talk to me. I spent most of the time I was with her on my own and often sat all night by the canal.

When I was eleven the agency records say that I had enuresis, that my foster mother said I had always wet the bed, so I was given medicine and referred to a doctor. When nothing changed I was admitted to hospital and they say I didn't wet the bed there. Of course I didn't—I felt safe. They also wanted me to go back to the home for secondary school. I didn't want to go. The record says that I told the social worker I wanted to go, which is not true. They say I seemed happy to go to the school, while I remember being carried from the coach kicking and screaming. I was taken straight to the infirmary and was told that I was mad. I was really frightened and thought the abuser would start up again. No one told me things had changed. I can only remember being terrified and wanting to get away. From my memory I thought I was locked in the infirmary for being bad. The agency records say I had written to the social worker. They don't say what I wrote but I think I told her I didn't want to be in the home; they say that I just wanted to go home, so after two weeks I went back to my foster mother and started a new school. It was a horrible place but, for me, safer than the home. Even the agency says that the house of the foster mother was tiny with a rat-infested toilet a long way down the garden.

The agency wrote that when I was fifteen I had a new social worker and that I wanted to go to catering college, so she took me to visit. There were problems with the foster mother who didn't want me to go out in the evening: she complained that I urinated in vases in the bedroom. This was because I was scared to go to the toilet with the rats. There was a lot written about me at this time. The social worker wrote that she thought I was holding something back, that I volunteered no information, and that I would only answer yes or no to questions. She also recorded that my foster mother was hard on me. I can see now that this social worker cared and was worried about me; she suggested that I could move to another foster family but I was scared and couldn't trust anyone. Neither could I believe that things could change for the better. The only people who were kind to me were the neighbours of my foster mother and I didn't want to lose touch with them. My foster mother continued to touch me and make me undress in front of her friends while she discussed my body and its changes. Once she reported that I hit her when, really, I took hold of her hands to stop her touching me. I was also still bedwetting and was referred to child guidance but didn't want to go as I couldn't trust anyone enough to tell them what was upsetting me.

The agency says I was asking about my birth mother; because I was very distressed and had lots of arguments with my foster carer, the social worker delayed telling me that she had found my birth mother when I was sixteen. She didn't want anything to do with me because she was married with another daughter and didn't want her husband to know about me. I now know that my mother had written regularly to the agency asking how "the little girl" was until I was four, when I think she married. I find it very upsetting that she didn't call me her daughter, as if I was nothing to do with her.

At that time I was also referred to psychiatrists, as I was still wetting myself day and night, and they said I should have psychotherapy. I had several appointments with someone but I was mute so they said they couldn't help me. I stopped wetting myself when I left my foster mother when I was twenty-one and married my first husband. I don't understand why. I never had a boyfriend until my first husband. I was terrified of sex but I wanted a baby of my own. We lived with his mother and they continually criticised me. After my second child was born, I left and lived with the children in digs until I met Jack.

Adulthood

My adult life has been hard. The only time I had sex in my forty-five years with Jack was to have a baby and we have a daughter. I have suffered from depression all my life and have tried to kill myself on many occasions. Jack has always shouted at me but he was very pleased to have his daughter, so this made him less angry for a while. My first husband and his mother turned my eldest daughter against me and she went to live with them and my son stayed with us. I have always been timid and haven't spoken to people other than to the patients in my job as a nursing assistant. I don't quite understand why I was so keen to help others when no one helped me, but I enjoyed my job and it got me out of myself.

My son, who was brought up by me and Jack, is now married and his wife said he has to choose between me and her; he chose her. I haven't seen him for six years but two years ago he started to phone me, keeping it a secret from his wife. Then, six months ago, Jack wrote one of his letters saying that I am ill and that they should come and see me. He didn't tell me he had written it, and then I got a phone call from my son saying I had to choose between him and Jack. How could I do that? Jack is my carer and I can't manage day-to-day life without him, so I no longer hear from my son and am upset that I will never see him again. I think about this a lot, as we were very close, so I talk about it with Sara because she understands how I feel. My eldest daughter phones occasionally and I start to hope that I will see her but she then lets me down. When I call, her husband answers but she won't come to the phone—so I do try but then get very upset by the rejection.

Janet: the therapy

I was surprised that I managed to talk to Sara about all the things that had happened to me; I relived the abuse, with flashbacks of the caretaker tripping me up, grabbing me, and raping me. I still have a fear of men with beards. When Dr Brownfield recently grew a beard, I didn't tell him but he really frightened me and I was relieved when he shaved it off. I still believed the caretaker would punish me for telling someone, even though I know he must be dead.

At first I couldn't sleep. I had lots of nightmares and was remembering more and more of the cruelty, of being raped day after day, of having my legs bandaged when we went out walking so that people could not see that they were cut and bruised. I felt very bad and sad and thought about killing myself most days.

After several months in therapy, talking about my childhood and the upset of my children not caring about me, with the therapist phoning me, and the doctor seeing me between those appointments, I felt for the first time that someone cared about me. I was angry with the agency and with my mother for putting me in that place. When I was fifty-two we found my mother; Jack and I went to see her and she didn't want to know and asked us to leave. I have a half-sister, but dare not contact her for fear of rejection. I expect my mother must be dead now. After Sara contacted the agency they met me several times and we went through the story of my childhood together. I learnt that my grandparents had wanted to see me but my mother did not give them permission. I hate her for that, for letting me suffer so much on my own.

During the work with the agency, when they talked with me about my records I got more upset in the therapy and I had to tell my husband I had been abused. He came to some sessions but was very angry with me. He said I had lied to him because I hadn't told him what had happened to me. And he was angry that we had a marriage without sex. Sara explained the effects of abuse, why I may not have told, and that this may be why I was so afraid of sex. Jack just got angrier, not only with me, but he kept writing to the agency wanting compensation. It was horrible because he was just worried about compensation while I was reliving all the abuse that had happened to me and remembering more and more.

Dr Brownfield

While Janet, once or twice with Jack, continued in therapy sessions, I would see her in between. She told me about the approach to the agency that ran the children's home for access to the records that were held about her. Jack was keen on seeking compensation and this made Janet angry. She had frequent nightmares, and was angry and distressed during the months following disclosure. Later in the year this would switch to depression, much of which was due to discoveries that were being made through meetings with the agency that ran the care home and she was linking her memories with the records. Jack was caught up in his personal conflict, defined by his generation, where individuals had to bite their lip and pretend to be coping with whatever problems they faced. Despite this, he was deeply troubled by the fact that Janet had not been able to share her story with him, especially as her experience had such a profound effect on the intimate aspects of their marriage. For the first time, he understood why there had been a need to make allowances for Janet in all aspects of their domestic and social life. He felt an unreasonable, but very real, anger.

On the surface, Jack was able to channel his energy into advocacy in the form of letter writing. Sometime after his letters to the agency that ran the children's home, he challenged Janet's son to justify his rejection of her and to recognise the importance of their relationship. They were all well meaning, all personally justified, but rarely with Janet's approval.

Janet

After some time of working with me, the agency social workers, my husband, and the doctor, we started EMDR (eye movement desensitisation and reprocessing) (Parnell, 1999) to try to help with the flashbacks and nightmares, which terrified me. First, we had to work on finding a place where I felt calm. Safe is not a good word for me but even in my foster home, when I went to sit by the canal, water has always made me feel calm and we spent a lot of time finding a safe place and making sure I could use it when things got difficult at home.

I really wasn't sure that I'd be able to go through EMDR work on the abuse, so I started with working on other upsetting events in my life. The first sessions were about times when I felt used by different people in my family; for example, I hadn't heard from my eldest daughter for several years. Out of the blue she called because she was in hospital following a stillbirth. I went immediately and was the only one to see the baby; I dressed the baby, cuddled him, and was alone with him before the nurses took him away. Then I went home and didn't hear from them again for years. I cried and cried and felt so alone. I think I was also thinking that no one was there with me when I was a baby and sometimes I wish I had died when I was a baby.

I had quite a lot of therapy sessions and the difficulties we worked on were often the times when I felt rejected by people in my family until I managed to start to talk about what happened in the home. I then started to talk about other things and, for the first time , told someone about the scrubbing. I had done it all my life, ever since the staff in the home found me trying to wash the blood off me. Whenever I have felt bad I have scrubbed myself with Dettol until I bled. It happened several times a week and I was always sore. We did a lot of work on this in the therapy. I had never told anyone about it and Jack never guessed as I was always careful to lock myself in the bathroom. I managed to stop by calming myself with breathing deeply and slowly and taking myself to the safe place we spoke about it EMDR. I didn't sleep and needed lots of phone calls between sessions so that I could feel safe but, after a long time, I spoke about the abuse and felt very pleased with myself that I had trusted someone enough. I do now really believe that I am safe but I just don't know how to talk to people and I think they are looking at me. Even at the surgery, where I go a lot, I won't wait in the waiting area but behind a screen until Dr Brownfield or Sara come to find me.

Sara

We used EMDR which, after a very few sessions, turned the reliving the terror and abuse into memories; this was alongside trying make the image of the caretaker smaller; we gave him a silly name and a different description so that, when Janet started to worry that he would harm her for having disclosed, she was able to tell him to go away and the name made him less powerful. It was important that the agency showed that they believed Janet and that they worked very closely with us. Jack felt cheated by not knowing what had happened to Janet. He attended a couple of sessions so that we could try to help him understand the impact of abuse, but he was fuelled by anger, which made it hard for him to reflect on the impact of Janet's experiences. Alongside the work on abuse, Janet feels that she had a lifetime of rejection and that her birth mother's rejection of her was the basis of all other rejections, particularly that of her children. We have thought about this in terms of mourning for the life she might have had as a child, an adult, and a mother. Midgly and Vrouva (2012, p. 125) quote Quinodoz (1996), asserting that it is not possible to mourn something that has not been experienced. In my personal and professional experience, the grief that comes with mourning a relationship one has never had has an intensity of emotion that can be inconsolable and, for Janet, that intense loss of family is relived every day.

Janet

We still do EMDR sometimes when I have flashbacks or, more recently, to help me attend hospital appointments. I have lots of health problems and have always walked out of appointments when I am scared. I have been able to go for a colonoscopy, which I would never have done before. Dr Brownfield phoned the treatment team and said I could only allow female doctors and nurses to treat me. I went to meet them and they showed me what would happen. I had never been for any appointments where someone was going to interfere with my insides. I really didn't want to do it but then also thought that, if I didn't, it would show that my abusers had won.

The nurse specially changed her shift to be there and held my hand. I said time and time again that the only thing that was important was that I would be asleep. I said it six times. Guess what—they put the needle in wrong and I was wide awake. I know they wanted to be kind but they got it wrong. They said they were sorry afterwards but I thought, "Why do these things only happen to me?" *But,* I was proud that I told them what I wanted and it is different that I can see they were trying to be kind. I have never before thought people may want to be kind to me. This is a big change, but I can be very upset when people I trust don't get it right.

Dr Brownfield

At home, things were difficult. Janet was at her most vulnerable when Jack was at his most aggressive. I spoke to Jack about the dynamics influencing his behaviour and feelings and he appeared to accept them at face value. He has seen little of me since.

I have continued to support Janet in the triangle of (relative) safety that exists with Sara and myself. This configuration of professionals and patient has augmented Janet's own resolve to somehow defeat her abusers and has enabled her to follow through, with encouragement, a number of medical procedures which previously would have been out of the question. Progress is evident to those who are professionally committed to her and none of this would be worthwhile unless we believed it was evident to Janet as well.

Janet

I am proud that I have spoken up for myself with the agency that brought me up and am pleased that they have believed me and supported me. I am standing up for myself with my husband and I have stood up for myself with my children. I am still upset about losing my son, but am trying to tell myself that I can't do anything about it. I am recovering because the GP, the care agency, the therapist, and the hospital doctors all took me seriously and talked together. I no longer have nightmares or flashback and have found ways, using some of the EMDR ideas, to avoid hurting myself, and to help myself feel calm.

I am also better able to stand up for myself. I am finding ways to stop my husband shouting. I try to walk away and I ask him to stop (although I still sometimes throw things) and there are times when we get on quite well.

I felt so relieved to have told someone. I always told myself I didn't want to go to my grave without having told anyone and I am so proud that I haven't.

Sara

I find it incredible that Janet, who has lived her life in fear and depression, has managed to lay so many demons to rest and to find her voice. In the years we have worked together, her voice is stronger and firmer and she is letting those around her know what she wants. She can even sometimes chat to her neighbours rather than scuttling indoors to avoid any contact. Of course, there are times when events get on top of her and she thinks of "not being here", but she has ways of managing that and, despite her increasingly poor health, now recognizes herself as a woman who can use her voice and have others listen to her. As Janet and Jack are coping with increasingly poor health, Janet is also terrified of being unable to manage and having to live in residential care, which she says she could not consider. Her great fear of being in any institution confirms Valerie O'Brien's comments in Chapter Eleven.

The agency

Janet's recall of abuse at the home is shocking and, when she first spoke of her memories, care was taken to compare her experience with that of others who had been in touch with the agency in order to see whether the abusers could be identified.

The agency has not been able to identify the staff she describes or to build a fuller picture from accounts by those who were her contemporaries. It is clear that her unhappiness in her foster home in adolescence was identified, but attempts to move her were unsuccessful, for the reasons Janet explains. The degree of harm she suffered made it difficult for her to trust anyone and, thus, as she so painfully describes, she was also unable to make use of the support offered at a specialist community mental health clinic. Janet has been very courageous in beginning this process at this stage in her life and we very much support this.

References

Midgley, N., & Vrouva, I. (2012). *Minding the Child: Mentalization-based Interventions with Children, Young People and Their Families*. Hove: Routledge.

Parnell, L. (1999). *EMDR in the Treatment of Adults Abused as Children*. New York: Norton.

Quinodoz, D. (1996). An adopted analysand's transference of a "hole object". *International Journal of Psychoanalysis, 77*: 323–336.

Shapiro, F., & Maxfield, L. (2002). EMDR: information processing in the treatment of trauma. In Session: *Journal of Clinical Psychology, 58*(Special Issue: Treatment of PTSD): 933–946.

CHAPTER THIRTEEN

Co-creating a coherent story with adults who have been fostered or adopted

Val Molloy

Adults who have grown up separated from their birth family through adoption, or by being brought up in care, might experience a number of difficulties when trying to make sense of their lives. Connections have been broken, information might be missing or withheld, and memory might have become subject to loss, suppression, selectivity, and revision. The importance of keeping an open dialogue with children about the circumstances of their lives was not recognised in the past, so children lacked the opportunity for an ongoing discussion which could take account of their growing need for information and developing capacity to understand complexity (Brodzinsky et al., 1992). Instead, many felt they were left alone to cope as best they could with the task of making sense of their circumstances. Adults who grew up in institutional or foster care, or who were adopted in the days when anonymity prevailed, can find themselves in great difficulty when it comes to piecing together their personal histories to create a sense of personal continuity and connectedness. I have worked for many years in an organisation which has been involved in caring for children in alternative care and this chapter describes the work I have undertaken in co-creating life stories with adults who were placed in foster or adoptive families by our organisation.

In this context, the existence of records and the possibility of gaining access to the information they hold is of huge importance (Feast, 2009). Some people need basic biographical details and confirmation of significant events and separations, while others are seeking to clarify confused memories or a muddled childhood chronology. Some are hoping to trace and make contact with lost family members as a way of assessing the importance of blood ties. Records could provide answers to long held questions and allow access to events that are no longer held in the conscious memory but which, nevertheless, have had an effect on the psychological development of the individual. The search for accurate information is part of a more complex search for a meaningful sense of self, and the professional's contribution to this relationship plays a part in helping the client to achieve this end. While not a strictly therapeutic relationship, it may, nevertheless, be an opportunity for growth and part of a "healing" process.

The decision to seek out records is seldom made without considerable thought, since it brings individuals face to face with a range of painful issues that might have been part of their life experience: rejection, stigma, loss, and feelings of difference. Some enquirers have family encouragement and support on this journey, some need significant professional support in managing the impact of the process, while others appear to cope easily. As a worker, it is important for me to understand the significance of the enquiry, validate the need to find answers, and provide context for past events (Feast, 2009).

Records are rarely coherent and, in gathering information from records, I piece together the connections and disruptions and develop a hypothesis about the impact of these experiences on the client's attachment relationships. At the first meeting, it is important to hear what the clients are hoping for, what they remember and have understood about their lives, and consider any particular vulnerabilities and the level of emotional support available to them. Since only a small proportion of the general population have personal experience of care or adoption, the client might not have found others who understand the impact of his or her history. Such feelings of difference can be very undermining (Brodzinsky et al., 1992), so, while for some, one or two meetings will feel sufficient, others might welcome additional time to process the information the records hold and work with me to make sense of the impact of this new information. In situations of more complicated loss in a disrupted childhood, the grieving that is a normal response (Bowlby, 1980) might be more difficult to resolve and it might be necessary to consider whether additional therapeutic help can be accessed.

When looking at historical records, information about fathers is usually scant, although the "searching" adult is usually more concerned for information about mothers in the first instance as, in my experience, this primary biological connection resonates and stirs a range of emotions, whereas the connection to birth fathers is usually less strong. Curiosity about fathers might present more forcefully at a later stage, sometimes leaving the individual facing the problem of having to live with unanswered questions.

In the following case histories, we see recurring themes of loss, secrecy, and confusion and their impact on the lives of the adults concerned. I searched our records for answers to help mitigate the effects of the past.

A childhood in care

Carol first sought access to information from her care records when she was a young, married mother. At the age of ten months she was placed in the care of a charity by her mother, a single woman who, in the days when unmarried motherhood carried significant social stigma, could no longer manage, and had grown up in a foster family. Her mother made these arrangements on the basis that she hoped one day to provide a home for Carol, and that care within a foster family would be only temporary. As part of this plan, she intended to remain in touch with her child.

The charity chose a family with teenage children for Carol because they could manage regular visits from her birth mother and facilitate restoration when the time came. In the event, Carol's mother was never able to make a home for her, and neither could she agree to her adoption, so Carol spent her entire childhood with her foster parents, who became Mum and Dad to her. Her birth mother visited and remained in touch in a somewhat unpredictable way. The agency supervised the placement throughout Carol's childhood, as well as working to keep in touch with her birth mother.

The records helped me understand the details of Carol's childhood from both Carol's and the agency's perspective. The initial decision to use more mature foster parents made sense on the basis that, having their own older children, their prime motivation was not to build their family. The intention was to avoid some of the tensions that can arise between foster parents and birth parents when the plan is restoration and contact takes place in the foster parents' home (Lindsey, 1995). The fact that the plan changed, but that contact continued, was a different matter. In such situations, the adults involved should put the needs of the child first (Kaniuk, 1993), but considerable feelings of rivalry and tension were not managed or contained by the parent figures in Carol's childhood and she had grown up with significant feelings of confusion and insecurity about where she belonged.

Carol first contacted the agency to ask for help in setting up contact with her birth father; when talking about her childhood, she spoke about her anger and disbelief about the foster parents she had been given. She could not understand how they could ever have been regarded as suitable. She said her foster mother was anxious, rigid, and critical, and she had never felt loved or accepted by her. She described a warmer relationship with her foster father, but experienced him as weak in relation to his wife. The intermittent contact with her birth mother had never provided closeness or security.

As a worker representing the agency "responsible" for Carol's family life, I found it hard to hear the sadness behind her anger, to begin to offer some explanation for the decisions that had been taken in the past, and to validate the significance of her experience. It was helpful that, from her adult relationship with her birth mother, she could understand why her mother had been unable to provide for her and why restoration had been deemed inappropriate. She also recognised the dilemma around whether to disrupt her placement in order to move her to a different permanent family with younger parents. However, her sense of what she had missed in childhood was clear.

This feeling of loss was reinforced by her relationship with her birth father, whom she had traced and contacted for the first time. He had then failed to sustain the contact, leaving Carol feeling badly let down, as though her existence had been denied. Acting as intermediary, I spoke to the birth father, who said he was unable to maintain a relationship with Carol since his present family did not know about her. Sadly, I was unable to persuade him to consider Carol's needs or move him from this position. This disappointing outcome seemed to add fuel to the anger already being carried by Carol, who broke off contact with the agency, leaving me feeling that we had once more failed her.

This brief contact had thrown into relief Carol's childhood sadness and pain, and her resulting ambivalence towards the agency. In one sense, Carol had experienced continuity in childhood and, through her ongoing contact with her birth mother, had the opportunity to understand something of her background. However, because of difficult relationships with her foster carers and the lack of a secure attachment figure, the central issue of loss remained.

Some years later, Carol was in touch again, requesting a copy of the written record of her childhood. She wanted the documents to be posted, which seemed to indicate her continuing ambivalence towards us. It was reassuring to hear that she had undertaken a period of counselling since our last contact and that she had found support elsewhere. However, I felt reluctant to post out records, knowing from experience that a first reading is best undertaken in the context of professional support. While agreeing to show the records, I pointed out that historical records had not been written with any expectation that the child who was the subject of the record might one day come to read them. I suggested that Carol might, therefore, find it helpful to meet to discuss the nature of the record and use a further opportunity to describe her own memories of the events of her childhood. She agreed, and we had several meetings to go through the record of her childhood. I found that the intervening years and, no doubt, her work with a counsellor, made a more reflective discussion possible.

Reading records is never easy. Clients might experience them as a stark and impersonal account of events that have affected them throughout their lives. Many years of living are compressed into a few hours of reading. Past practice is examined and might be found wanting, leaving both worker and client with the task of managing their feelings about this and trying to find some shared understanding. The language used in historical records might now seem inappropriate and unprofessional, provoking a range of emotions in both client and worker. The focus, however, should be on building together an account of childhood events that feels authentic and coherent. Carol used our meeting to examine once more the social work decisions made during her childhood, and to understand better the role played by her birth mother in these plans. At the same time, she "set the record straight", describing a childhood of anxiety and mixed messages which included the confusion of having two mothers, and explicit or implicit threats around being sent or taken away. I could recognise what this had meant for her and acknowledge that, despite the high level of contact and commitment from the agency, she had often felt lost, unhappy, and unconnected.

Some time later, Carol told me how difficult it had been to read about herself, and how raw it made her feel. She had not been able to return to the reports she had taken away for some time but when she was able to read them she noted how much of the record seemed to be about administrative matters and about the adults rather than her. She expressed ongoing sadness that records did not seem to hold the answers to her preoccupations and I was left feeling some of this sadness and that, for Carol, the process of mourning past losses was not yet complete. I hoped that she would use the opportunity of further work with her counsellor.

For some adults who have faced repeated or long term adversity in childhood, the task of resolving the impact of such experiences can only be attempted in therapy, which might go alongside the process of accessing information from records. Evelyn, for example, first returned to the agency responsible for her childhood care when she was in her forties. At the time, she was undertaking a long period of therapy, suggested by her GP following the breakdown of her marriage. Evelyn wanted to clarify the circumstances of her birth, a subject she had not been able to discuss with her mother, whom she had met in later life.

Evelyn was born illegitimately in the 1930s and initially placed by her mother in private fostering and then in the care of a charitable institution where she lived with her second foster mother. A settled few years ended with the death of this foster mother and a consequent move to a third family. She was then educated from five to fifteen years in a residential school. Not unusually for those days, Evelyn received no help in understanding and adjusting to this childhood of sudden disruption and loss in which she found the only constant thread to be her experience and love of music. Aged fourteen, Evelyn was introduced to her now married birth mother, but the years apart and the impact of lives that had gone in different directions meant that the relationship they established over the ensuing years never became more than "polite and friendly" (Siddons, 2002).

In therapy, Evelyn began to build a different model for close relationships and to explore her confused identity: "My therapy led me to understand that I had never had a proper relationship and that I had operated on a primitive level . . . I became aware that I lacked a sense of home inside myself. I recognised that music held me together and gave me hope." It provided what Winnicott calls a "continuity of going on being" (Siddons, 2002).

In returning to the agency during her therapy, Evelyn used details from records to clarify the circumstances of her mother's decision to part with her—a subject she had never raised with her. We also discussed the recorded details of the various moves she had experienced as a child and the reasons for these, and worked together to develop a coherent narrative of time and space. Some years later, in a second piece of work, I gave Evelyn letters which had been written by her birth mother, who died some time earlier, to enquire after her during the years of her early childhood. Evelyn had had no knowledge of these letters as a child, but they offered evidence to her as an adult that she had been held in mind by her mother during those early years. As she continued to weave together the threads of her life, Evelyn joined a network of those who, like her, had grown up in the agency's care, meeting again individuals she had known at school. Alongside this, she accepted a role as a voluntary helper with the agency and it became possible to share an acknowledgement of the deficiencies of past care and the sadness of childhood, yet, at the same time, manage an ongoing relationship with the charity which had previously acted as a parent. Now in her eighties, Evelyn describes this as an experience of "full circle", a life in which, all in all, she is settled and happy, with interests and friends, but where sadness and regret can be acknowledged. As a worker, I felt humbled by her story and by those of others I have worked with who, in old age, have reached a place of resolution.

Early adoption

Many adults who were adopted in infancy have faced similar issues as those who were in care. For many, the secrecy of their adoption was a burden that denied adoptees the information they needed about their sense of identity and belonging. Being adopted can, of itself, colour a child's self-esteem and identity (Brodzinsky et al., 1992), and the absence of openness compounded such difficulties, leaving many children and young adults with no means of exploring and resolving what being adopted meant for them personally.

Fay was born illegitimately and placed with foster carers who went on to adopt her. She was their only child. In her fifties, Fay returned to our agency to seek information about her adoption. She seemed diffident and shy, unused to expressing her feelings about deeply personal matters. She explained that she had not known that she was adopted until another child mentioned this to her when she was about ten years old. Fay struggled to describe the impact of this discovery, leaving me with a sense of the deep trauma involved at the time. Fay had found the courage to open up a conversation with her parents but their response was limited and she sensed that this was not a topic she could return to. The foundations of her childhood were rocked again a few years later when her father died unexpectedly, a loss that she and her mother felt keenly. Fay referred to "troubled" teenage years but, coming through these, she went on to establish a happy working life. Occasionally, she had tried to find out more from her mother about her adoption, but either her mother knew very little or had found it hard to discuss. After her mother died, Fay began to think about how else she might get information. She had not discussed her adoption with anyone in her network and her nervousness at having reached this stage of her life with such a secret seemed to me to reflect both the trauma of discovery and a burden of shame imposed by secrecy.

In asking about the records, Fay had expected to hear a straightforward story of teenage pregnancy, but the circumstances of her birth were more complicated and distressing than this in that she learnt that her birth mother had been raped and that she was born as a result of this. As she slowly took things in, Fay's response was matter of fact. She indicated that she now understood her birth mother's situation and the decision to part with her, but she expressed no feelings about what she had learnt. However, I understood something of her turmoil about what adoption had meant for her over the years when she said that, as a younger woman, because she knew nothing of her genetic background, she had decided she would not marry and have children herself. For her, this decision now seemed vindicated. Fay did not prolong our first meeting and, despite having been given difficult information to digest, declined the offer of another, saying that she now knew all she needed to know. I felt that she could not wait to leave.

It was some years before Fay returned to talk some more. Her strategy to put the past "to the back of her mind" was no longer working. She described symptoms of distress and disruption to her life, which suggested that the shock of learning about her adoption as a child had been reawakened by the second shock of discovering more of the circumstances. This time, Fay was able to share more of her worries and asked the questions that had come to mind since our last meeting, speculating about her birth family background. She was curious about what information her adoptive parents would have been given, and how the secrecy and "not telling" had come about. She did not blame them, but wanted to understand it better. Fay put on a brave face to deal with the fact that the record could not answer all her questions.

We continued to meet for a number of months and Fay remained preoccupied and sought opportunities to resolve the matters still troubling her. These included the painful thought that, in the circumstances, her birth mother could not have wanted her. "Everyone likes to feel that they are wanted." She began to wonder whether she might be similar to or different from her birth mother and asked for reading which might help her think about the impact of being adopted and, though the original symptoms of distress had subsided, she acknowledged that if they returned she might need additional professional help. In our contact there was sometimes what felt like painful silences when I wondered whether she found our meetings helpful, but I was conscious that there was, so far, no other person to whom Fay had talked or with whom she could undertake this journey. We continued to explore what seemed to be gaps and inconsistencies in the agency record as part of a slow and sometimes overwhelming effort to establish an account which held together and made sense to her. As she began to achieve this, her confidence grew. She began to talk more about herself and her achievements and interests, to reflect on her present life as well as the past, and to reaffirm her sense of self.

In her goodbye contact with me at the end of this piece of work, Fay wrote, "I feel sympathy for my birth mother but I don't feel connected to that family except through genes. For me, being adopted was always wondering, and not knowing who I was. I felt there was a ghost in my life. I now feel that I am who I am and it is the person you become in life that is most important. Finding information has resolved many issues that affected me throughout my life and I now feel some kind of freedom."

For many adopted adults, the search to connect with the past and to construct a coherent personal history is a much less painful process. There are also those who say they have all they need in the sense of self they have developed within their adoptive family. This might confirm secure family attachments, or it might say something about other preoccupations in life and a lack of mental space. Sometimes, there is a wish to avoid a sense of divided loyalties in that, like Fay, some adoptees do not embark on thinking in depth about the family of origin until their adoptive parents have died. Evaluating the meaning and significance of blood ties is perceived to be a less complicated task when concern for the feelings of others is not a current issue.

When Raymond approached the agency holding his adoption records, he was in the position of having a supportive wife and family. Like others, he had experienced early separation from his birth mother, but had faced additional adversity with the death of his adoptive mother when he was a young teenager. From Raymond's account, his father was unable to cope with this bereavement. The bedrock of family life had gone and Raymond was thrust early into responsibility. Raymond spoke warmly of his adoptive mother and letters written by her to the agency during the adoption process (still on record) conveyed to me a sense of her love and commitment to him. It seemed likely, therefore, that Raymond had had a good attachment experience in the years before her premature death.

Raymond indicated that he had always known that he was adopted, but that usually life was too busy to think about this. Now, however, there was additional encouragement from his children, who were curious about their father's background. His wife was more ambivalent, not wanting to see him "hurt" again. When this was discussed, it became clear that, like many people, Raymond found it hard to imagine circumstances in which he would give up a child. His own committed parenting was evident as he talked about his family, and this personal sense of responsibility made his birth mother's decision hard to fathom, which was why he needed information. He was not thinking of tracing his birth family, but expressed a wish to "put things to rest".

It emerged from the records that, like Raymond, his birth mother, Mary, had lost her mother as a child. Her teenage pregnancy had occurred later in the context of a once steady relationship, which had come to an end before the pregnancy was discovered. On hearing this, Raymond's attitude softened. He identified with Mary's bereavement and her lack of family support. He became concerned that she might still have no one in the world, and that, now an old lady, she might need him.

Raymond became anxious and preoccupied, responses, which are not uncommon to those in his situation but which, given his confident presentation, I had not fully expected. He no longer had reservations about tracing; indeed, this now felt urgent to him, wanting to know that Mary was all right and to tell her that her decision for him had been the right one. Having lived life so far with questions he had put to the back of his mind, he became overwhelmed with emotions. I assured him that this was normal, and he took the opportunity to air his preoccupations both with me and in supportive discussions with his family. Given his unexpected level of anxiety, it was important to explore Raymond's expectations of what might come from his urgent wish to trace, and to help him think about potential stumbling blocks, including that members of his birth mother's family past and present might have no knowledge of her first baby. Approaching Mary would be a delicate matter, which would need to respect her confidentiality until circumstances were clearer. If she were no longer alive, it would be an equally delicate task to approach half siblings who might not know of his existence and who might find it hard that their mother had gone to her grave carrying a secret she felt unable to share with them.

From public records it was possible to establish that Mary was still alive and that she had two more children, which, to some extent, allayed fears that she might be alone in the world, but Raymond still had a strong desire to move towards contact. However, when a discreet letter from the social worker brought an immediate response by telephone from Mary, her circumstances were not straightforward. She was sure that her other children did not know about her first baby as she had never opened up the subject with them. Having parted with Raymond in the days when anonymity for adoptive mothers prevailed, she had expected to hear no more and seemed unprepared for the possibility that he might seek her out one day. She wondered about his motivation and was preoccupied with her own problems, so did not ask for details of his life and indicated that she would need some time to think.

In such situations, the expectations and hopes of each party do not always coincide. Mary had plainly established a life in which she had hoped that, by holding on to her secret, she would leave the past behind. She was shaken, after so many years, to find that this was not so. The sadness for Raymond was that he had twice lost a mother while still dependent on that mother, and this meant that I needed to think with him about the fact that, whatever Mary might be able to offer, it was unlikely to replace what he had lost as a baby or as a teenager. This was not to deny that it was legitimate for him to be curious about his background and to hope for some answers to his questions around genetic connectedness. He wanted to know who he looked like, and felt keenly that establishing whether he had anything in common with his birth family was a task to be completed before he could finally settle his questions about identity and belonging. In accompanying him on this journey, I provided a space for his complex feelings and frustrations to be discussed as the situation unfolded. Raymond felt prepared for any outcome, but the process on which he had embarked was a complicated one in which it was impossible to predict the feelings that might emerge.

Thus it was that Mary's measured response was hard for Raymond to accept. Intellectually, her caution made sense, but emotionally it struck at the hurt caused by his earlier sense of rejection. Mary was also going through a difficult time. Owing to distance, we had only telephone contact, during which she spoke of the shock she was feeling and the strain on her health. She had undertaken to discuss things with her children but then delayed these conversations. I acknowledged that the present dilemma was reawakening a difficult time in her past and the painful decisions she had faced then, but suggested that society judges such situations less harshly now and perhaps her children would do likewise. Although this proved to be the case, the decision Mary came to was that she could not manage any contact with Raymond, saying that the strain of recent weeks had been too much for her.

Raymond was not surprised at this outcome, but it was hard for him to accept, particularly as it implied that Mary had no interest in him. He wondered whether anything else could be done, and whether Mary might listen to further reassurance and persuasion. I felt under some pressure from him but also believed that there was a boundary to be held over what might or might not be helpful; Mary, too, had rights, and her decision was not untypical for women of her generation for whom the trauma of parting with a child has never been resolved. Mary had implied that she had some health difficulties and we know that early pregnancy and childhood loss of a parent can be factors in later depression (Harris & Bifulco, 1993). Without knowing more of her circumstances, it would be unreasonable to press her too far. However, by way of completing the contact with her, and in order to help Raymond feel that a door might still be left ajar, I wrote once more to thank Mary for being in touch in such difficult circumstances. This letter prompted a call from her daughter, made with Mary's consent, in which more details of her mother's life were given. Raymond's half-sister expressed sympathy for Raymond, and the information she passed on helped him to see that Mary was in a more vulnerable situation than he had realised. He continued to feel disappointment, but the deeper sense of rejection eased.

Questions about family likenesses and genetic heritage were still unresolved and, while Raymond accepted that Mary could not be approached again, he spoke to me about his wish to write to another half-sibling whose address was on public record. What might be gained from this course of action had to be weighed against the risk of further distressing and alienating Mary and, given the nature of my own contact with her, I did not judge myself in a position to write to another family member. Raymond did not feel the same constraint but asked for advice on how to word his letter Fortunately, this letter had a positive outcome and met with a friendly response. As time went on, Raymond met his half-siblings and, finally, more than a year after the initial approach to her, Raymond received a phone call from Mary.

I had been uncertain that the outcome would be so positive and I had been conscious of actions being taken that I could not necessarily endorse, given the duty of care to Mary as well as Raymond, whose half siblings fortunately played an important intermediary role. In reflecting subsequently on his search, Raymond had no regrets; it had been important for him to put names and faces to his "lost" family and he had learnt details, which helped Mary's initial response to his request for contact to feel less personal. The relationship with Mary was only ever cordial, but he could accept this, and the warmer contact and sense of genetic connectedness with his half-siblings became important to him. Equally significant had been the fact that his family had supported him and shared the intensity of the process.

For Raymond, this search had been essential, because records alone had been insufficient in assisting him with gaps in his story and with establishing a deeper sense of meaning and identity. He still felt that there was a missing connection in his birth father, but earlier feelings of loss and rejection were now resolved and his sense of what adoption had given him was clearer.

Summary

We have seen that the effects of being adopted or growing up in care are lifelong, and the resulting task of building an identity and a coherent life story must be addressed in different ways as life progresses (Brodzinsky et al.,1992). Accessing personal records may play a significant part in facilitating this process, and takes place most helpfully in the context of a relationship with a worker who is able to allow the space for feelings and preoccupations to be heard. The process should be one with the aim of achieving a realistic and factually accurate recognition of childhood experience, and of piecing together the continuity of one's personal history.

When representing the agency with responsibility for past decisions, the worker holds a symbolic significance, which might allow the development of a different relationship to that which previously existed with the dependent child. Historical distance allows the worker to be separate from what happened in the past so, while the task of providing context for past events is important, defensiveness can be avoided. Sometimes, one or two meetings are sufficient to achieve a positive outcome, but there are times when work can only progress over a longer period: for example, where there is difficult information to process or a complicated history to resolve. It could also be the case that the negative aspects of past care feel too closely associated with the agency for the ex-care or adopted adult to invest in a relationship with its worker. In such circumstances, it can be helpful to think about whether counselling or therapeutic help should take place separately. A social worker with experience of sharing records with adults has particular skills to bring to that task, including an understanding of the impact of childhood separation and loss. However, the relationship established as part of this work is not that of patient and therapist, even though there may be restorative aspects to what takes place.

The need to create a coherent account of life events is often expressed as a need to "put matters to rest". While the initial separation from one's birth mother might not be remembered as traumatic, having in the past frequently taken place in early infancy, later losses or experiences can throw that first separation into greater relief, and can influence hopes of what might be achieved through a search of records or the possibility of reunion. The intense emotions sometimes stirred when reconnecting with the past include confusion, anger, and sadness, and frequently also gratitude that information has been preserved and is now willingly shared. This process of "putting to rest" is one of mourning as a result of which, if losses can be accepted, it becomes possible to move on in life.

References

Bowlby, J. (1980). *Loss, Sadness and Depression, Volume 3. Attachment and Loss*. New York: Basic Books.

Brodzinsky, D. M., Schechter, M. D., & Henig, R. M. (1992). *Being Adopted*. New York: Anchor Books.

Feast, J. (2009). *Access to Information for Post-care Adults*. London: BAAF.

Harris, T., & Bifulco, A. (1993). Loss of parent in childhood, attachment style and depression in adulthood. In: C. M. Parkes, J. Stevenson-Hinde, & P. Marris (Eds.) *Attachment Across the Life Cycle* (pp. 234–267). London: Routledge.

Kaniuk, J. (1993). Openness in adoption: practice issues. In: M. Adcock, J. Kaniuk, & R. White (Eds.), *Exploring Openness in Adoption* (pp. 7–24). Croydon: Significant Publications.

Lindsey, C. (1995). Systemic and developmental aspects of contact. In: H. Argent (Ed.), *See You Soon* (pp. 34–50). London: BAAF.

Siddons, E. (2002). Open Space: Reflections on institutional life. *Psychodynamic Practice, 8*(2): 229–236.

CHAPTER FOURTEEN

"It turns your whole world upside down . . . but still it brings immense pleasure": perspectives on kinship care

Julia Granville

In this chapter, I think about work in the area of kinship care. I start with some thoughts about the portrayal of kinship care and the language used to describe it and go on to explore some of the issues that arise in work with this client group. I draw on my experience of facilitating a support group for kinship carers over a number of years and include interviews with four members of that group. I also offer a clinical example from my therapeutic work to illustrate ways of working with the themes that emerged in the group. My work in this area has been as a member of the specialist Fostering, Adoption and Kinship Care Team (FAKCT), based in the Child and Family Department at the Tavistock and Portman NHS Foundation Trust.

All the interviewees have agreed to participate and chosen their pseudonyms. The clinical examples I have used are amalgams of clients I have worked with as a systemic family therapist and I hope represent faithfully the dilemmas and concerns of the many people in this situation that I have worked with over the years, while preserving their anonymity and confidentiality.

The context

Kinship care or whatever you want to call it

In the field of classic and contemporary literature in English, there are many references to what we would now describe as kinship care: Fanny Price sent away from her poor family to live with her wealthy relatives in Jane Austen's *Mansfield Park*, a context where she was constantly reminded of her inferior status; Harry Potter consigned to his Aunt Petunia's care, the cupboard under the stairs in Privet Drive, and the derogatory comments about his parents and their alien magical abilities; Dickens' David Copperfield, cared for by his eccentric yet kindly Great Aunt Betsy Trotwood; Dorothy's Aunt Em and Uncle Henry in the Oz books; Dave Eggers' autobiographical tale of the care of his eight-year-old brother Toph following the death of their parents, managing both to look after his brother in a rather chaotic, anxious, wild, but loving way and to negotiate his own young adulthood.

Sometimes, these stories depict kinship carers in the "wicked stepmother" mould; in others, a more love-filled picture is drawn. All these references in literature contain narratives of loss and longing, struggles with identity and allegiance, and some complicated ambivalence. Heroes, heroines, or villains?

Across many cultural contexts and times there has always been informal and sometimes formalised care of children by relatives or connected people. Such arrangements have supported parents in their work, education, or financially, taken care of orphaned children, or dealt with the many vicissitudes that can arise in family lives, and as a part of more communal forms of raising children.

In our world of changing discourses about the family, language plays a central part in constructing our ideas. The language surrounding kinship care is evolving; the term kin suggests a relationship by descent or consanguinity. The phrase "kith and kin" includes those related by blood and marriage (kin), those who are known through one's native land, and those who are friends and neighbours (kith) (*OED* and Oxford dictionaries online, 2015). The anthropological use of the term suggests ties that are recognised by relationship, descent, marriage, or ritual and through the performance of nurture or other forms of relating other than through biological, genetic, reproductive links.

So, within this notion is a combination of relationships through blood, marriage/partnership, those who are known, those with whom there is a sense of closeness and connection, and those with whom one is acting parentally, "doing nurture". It pleases me that the notion of kinship care incorporates the complexity of relationships, biological connections, affinity, affiliations, families of choice, so called "fictive" kin, and the different ways we organise our lives and relationships in different cultural and sub-cultural contexts.

Numbers

The number of referrals of kinship families to FAKCT has increased considerably over the past decade. In a previous account of our work, we noted the political contexts and discourses surrounding the greater use of kinship placements (Barratt & Granville, 2006). The statistics regarding numbers of children living in kinship care are unsatisfactory. There are no government figures on the numbers of children living in kinship arrangements, either under court orders or through the involvement of social services. Nandy and colleagues (2011) drew on the 2001 UK census household data and have estimated 173,200 (1.3% out of a child population of 13.3 million) are in kinship care. There was a range in the prevalence of kinship care between areas with up to four in 100 in some parts of the UK. This figure includes the known number of looked-after children placed with relative foster carers. In recent statistics, it is estimated that these number approximately 9,000 children in the UK, of whom 7,000 are in England (Department for Education, 2015). The remainder includes those placed through social care or court involvement, with or without court orders, and an unknown number of children whose families have made their own arrangements outside the remit of the authorities. These data also indicated that while the majority of kinship carers were grandparents, a larger number than previously thought were siblings. In addition, there was a significant number of aunts, uncles, cousins, etc. The census data did not identify situations where carers were family friends or non-biologically related connected people, so that the figures are necessarily an underestimate. The report confirms previous findings (e.g., Farmer & Moyers, 2008; Hunt et al., 2008) that many kinship carers experience a range of disadvantages in relation to age, poor health, and financial difficulties, often with significant issues of overcrowding in their housing. The findings confirm that a disproportionate number of children in kinship care come from ethnic minority and mixed parentage backgrounds. Hunt and colleagues (2008) and Farmer and Moyers (2008) offer survey studies and qualitative data comparisons of kinship and non-kin substitute care, suggesting generally positive outcomes for children, while support for these families varies in different parts of the UK.

My context

In writing this chapter, I want to acknowledge my own context and its influence on the positions I take. I draw significantly on myself, as a parent, biologically and through my partner, and also in some "quasi", yet important, parental/aunty way, through some close friendships. There is a small troupe of children, young people, and now adults to whom I feel myself intimately connected across the course of their lives into adulthood and their own experience of parenthood. Only two of them are biologically connected to me, and there is a range of connection between them and me and each other. How we name these relationships is sometimes uncertain and up for revision as the years roll on. Some of that is uncomfortable, and emotions about entitlement and claiming and not claiming of connections and their labels seem to be a part of this.

I am also now a grandparent. This has involved a reawakening of the joys and challenges of parenting young children and the powerful bonds of love that help me to understand the physical and, indeed, psychological efforts involved in being with young children later in life.

A number of years ago, I did a small-scale research study on the languaging of non-traditional family relationships, meeting with children in lesbian-headed households (Tasker & Granville, 2011). The families I met were working to find helpful, comfortable ways to talk about the complex web of biological and other relationships that honoured their significance and did not deny the ambiguity and complexity that was also present. This is often the experience for kinship carers.

How we connect, position ourselves, and are positioned, and then act, as people, therapists, and workers, in relation to the dominant discourses and normative models of the "ideal family" is essential to explore. For an interesting study in relation to lesbian-led families, see Perlesz and colleagues (2006). Such exploration enables us to work ethically, to engage with families of all sorts, shapes, and sizes, to explore and navigate the choppy waters of identity, the dynamics between tradition, norms, innovation, and experimentation in ways of "doing family". In work with kinship families, as with adoption and fostering and LGBT families, and, indeed, working across class, cultural, and ethnic difference, this consideration is the bedrock of sensitive, ethical practice.

Working with families

As a family therapist and in our Kinship Carers support group, I have worked with aunts, grandparents, uncles, their partners, cousins, older siblings, ex-partners of grandparents, parents of school friends, family friends. Sometimes, people step out of their usual role to care for a child, imagining that this will be temporary, while parents get themselves together. It might then gradually become apparent that this is needed for the long term. Some family members are already formally caring for the children and others are sought out by social workers or come forward to offer to care. There is a process of assessment and a court process with a range of different possible orders. Special Guardianship Orders (SGOs), introduced in 2005, are an option that offers stability and accords parental responsibility to the carers and limits birth parents' rights without extinguishing their connection in the way that adoption does. An SGO brings with it the right to request an assessment of needs and potential financial support.

Themes

Naming

One of the processes that kinship care families usually have to negotiate is that of creating a family language that can incorporate the naming and complexity of kinship relationships. Monica, Claire, and Ashakey described this in our conversation.

Ashakey: "When she came she was just beginning to verbalise. She said 'mum, mum, mum' and I answered. But I did have a real struggle with 'Who am I?' I didn't have time to process the whole thing, no one to talk it through with, how it would look. In the end, it happened so quickly . . . to close neighbours I explained, with some people I just ignored questions and let the assumptions go, if pushed, I would say she's adopted, I didn't want to have to explain special guardianship. I didn't know if I should let her call me Mum. I thought I was Aunty and then I just adopted 'Mum'. At school I have to say I'm not Mum, I'm her guardian. With other professionals it's 'OK, you're Aunty'."

The names used for carers by professionals, by the children they care for, by other family members, and by themselves reflects the entitlement they feel to take up and clarify their role. There may be an order conferring a title such as Special Guardian with its legal rights and responsibilities. Yet, with or without an order, this mandate might be more or less accepted by the carer, the children, the birth parents, and other family members. A child such as Ashakey's may call her "Mummy" but others might insist "Oh, you're Aunty" and someone in a position of authority, such as a hospital or GP, might only accept her as having parental authority with written evidence.

This inevitably challenges the nature of kinship care. In this Western, bureaucratised, normalising culture, despite the growing prevalence of families that are complexly connected, including close biological ties and ties of affinity, there is a continuing dominant discourse of family as mother, father, and their biological child. New discourses attempt to celebrate richness and complexity. Yet, differences from the norm continue to require explanation and to be mapped against that normative model. This could be both an external lived experience and an internal experience for children and their carers. What is it like for children to have to explain themselves, to feel themselves as different?

Claire talks about there not being many of her family around.

"I started out as 'Aunty', then the children gradually changed to saying 'Mummy Claire' and 'Mummy Jenny' (the children's birth mother), then it just changed to 'Mummy' and 'Jenny'. My sister was really angry. My parents still tend to refer to me as Aunty Claire. It's only recently that my parents have let that go. Only this weekend has my Dad referred to me as Mummy to the children."

Claire and Ashakey talk about the dilemmas of how to respond when the children call them "Mum"; whether to accept this or say they must use the agreed name. Social workers or others may "give permission" for the name Mum to be used, if this provides an important sense of security for the children, but some might also feel they have "stolen" the relationship from the birth parent. It might, indeed, be viewed or experienced like that by that parent or other family members.

For some grandparents, like Monica and Lucy, it feels simpler: Monica, "I'm Gran, always was, always will be, so it's easier"; Lucy, "I'm just Sean's Nan. Sometimes I say I'm his legal guardian or I might explain I have a special guardianship order. Only once I had to explain to an official. I do carry the order with me if I'm travelling. It's just accepted." Monica agrees, "She [granddaughter] regards me as her primary carer. Feels like we are a little family group. We are both clear. I use 'primary carer' with others. For instance, the dentist goes 'mumble, mumble, does her mother . . . father . . . mumble, mumble . . .' and I say, "Don't worry I'm her primary carer."

Perhaps being Nan fits more easily with our dominant norms, making it a less contested label. How much do people feel entitled to claim the word parent when aware of the potential challenge of not being the "real" parent? This might come from the child, from other family members, from outsiders, and from one's own internalised beliefs. How much harder when guilt, shame, responsibility, anger, blame, love, and grief colour the internal landscape?

Information

Several interviewees stressed the importance of having information at the time of making decisions. Lucy and Claire were clear what they would say to other potential kinship carers:

> Lucy: "Try and find out as much as you can about everything and think long and hard about what it involves."
>
> Claire: "Before you take the children, make sure you know what you're entitled to and fight for it. If you do see the children are struggling, do ask for the support that's available."

Later in the interview, Claire says,

> "The advice about what you're entitled to wasn't there, not really knowing where to turn for financial support. Obviously, I had to give up work to look after them. At first I was told I wouldn't get anything by the social worker who did the viability assessment. The information wasn't very clear. Applying for legal aid took really long and I only got it at the last minute. For nine months I had no advice. Only two days before the final hearing I got a solicitor. The court knew I was being assessed, but there was no one to speak for me. I didn't even know what a special guardianship order was, it was the first I had heard of it. I didn't really know what it would entail."

> Lucy: "Afterwards I heard other people talk about their packages of support and what was included. Well, I never heard anything about packages or whether I should have been putting anything forward. I didn't know anything like that was available."

Clear information is hard to come by and legal advice increasingly difficult to access. It is also difficult to fight for financial and practical support for a child that you also see as your own. What does it mean to be paid to care? Sometimes, grandparents are concerned that their grandchildren will be resentful if they know the financial arrangements. The need for proper financial support is evident and the cost of parenting children in local authority care is very high. Yet, there is often a tangled web of feelings about it. "You're doing it for love not money"; "If I ask for support/money, will they think I can't cope/take the child away?" "If the child were in care, they'd get x, y and z, and I'm just expected to manage." It is both hard to ask and hard to get and what is on offer is inadequate and constantly under threat because of limited and dwindling resources. It just does not feel fair all round.

Assessment and intrusion

There might be a long history of difficulties, repeated crises, and attempts to support the parents' care. Then, perhaps, something occurs and everything changes. Children could be removed or have been abandoned. Social services or the police might become involved, sometimes dramatically. In a state of turmoil, family members or friends take children in. Did they feel they had a choice? Most, when asked, will say that they felt there was no other option; they did not want a child to go into care or to be adopted and lose contact with the family. Yet, this is a momentous thing to do, with huge implications for people's lives and relationships.

> Lucy: "When going through the experience, it's such an upheaval in your life, it's very difficult to think clearly. . . . Your life is totally altered. You have to make a decision, do I or don't I?"
>
> Julia: "Was there anywhere to talk about that?"
>
> Lucy: "I had good support from friends, but only I could make that decision. I remember a lot of people saying you do have a choice."
>
> Julia: "Did you feel you had a choice?"
>
> Lucy: "No, no I didn't. But I think that's about me . . . I discussed it with friends and, though I didn't feel like it was a choice and I decided to do it, it was like what am I giving up here? My youngest child was thirteen, becoming independent going to school on her own. Finally, after five children, I was free. I was going to train to be a paramedic. And then it was Sean, who was two with behaviour problems."

Carers often experience the process of assessment as difficult. It takes a long time and explores areas of huge sensitivity. While they may recognise that this has to happen, it can feel like an unjustified intrusion into their family.

Lucy explains,

> "I found the assessment quite difficult, they went into every area of my life. I felt like I was on trial, that I wasn't really good enough to look after my grandchild. The other thing that was really awful for me was that I would be quite honest about the things that had happened in my life and then when we went to court everyone who was party to the court, the father's mother, everyone, had my whole life history in front of them. Your whole life is exposed. I didn't really realise that everyone would see it and have a copy of it to take away."

Social workers undertaking assessments need to understand how a potential carer makes sense of what has happened to the children, their relationship to the parents, and that they understand any possible risks. They need confidence that a carer will be able to help and support the child in the face of the experiences they have had and to honour the positive attributes of the parent while not downplaying the difficulties the child might have witnessed and lived through.

The potential carer has to be confident about their capacities to care into the future and meet the child's needs however much they might have been affected and disturbed by past experiences. This is often in the midst of crisis and distress, admitting problems, yet showing competence, resilience, and the ability to reflect.

Claire talks about her experience of the assessment period:

> "The woman who did it was really nice, but it dragged on and was really stressful. The situation was that the children were in care and that was really hard. Trying to juggle everything, the emotional side, the kids being in care. There was a lot of time we had to spend going over questions, I understand why they have to do it but it's very personal. It has to be done, but you're putting every bit of your life in front of someone . . . I don't think I ever thought I wouldn't get the kids, but when I started the assessment, I was twenty-four. There was an idea that at twenty-four I would be unable to go out and do things and that was a consideration. It seems so long ago now, I've had them eight years now!"

Support

All group members talked about the importance of the support group as a place where they could talk openly with others who would understand. Although their situations differed significantly, there was a sense of this being one place where they could talk openly about the struggles, the feelings, the joys, and frustrations.

> Ashakey: "It's not abnormal is it? Here, there's a kind of normality to it."

> Monica: "It's a great relief finding other people who are going through what you're going through . . . It's very helpful to me because my family, I can't talk to them about looking after this little grandchild. They don't think I should have done it and they're very hostile to it and to her. You've made your bed and you can lie in it . . . So coming here there's such an acceptance, it's such a relief really . . ."

The ability to talk openly about children's difficulties, their behaviour, their distress, was identified as central in keeping going by the group members and by many kinship carers I have worked with.

"Being able to say to a therapist, who is outside of your family and friends, 'She did this this morning!' and have someone help you think about it, what was going on, what might it be about, can be so helpful." Having someone else on the journey with you, who might not have the answers, but who you can say anything to, has been a lifeline for some of the carers. This was especially true where other family members were not supportive.

Carers who have looked after children for most of their lives can find it hard to make sense of their problems. "It can feel so hard to understand when you've had a child for most of their life and have offered stability and love that they can sometimes still struggle so hugely." I have found it invaluable to share some of the research on the impact of early and pre-natal stressors and early trauma, as well as the potential for change, plasticity, and development of resilience, well described in Graham Music's work (Music, 2011, and this volume).

Contact

Carers and their children are often negotiating some very difficult issues in contact with parents. For some, this is court mandated; for others, it is a positive choice. For still others, it can be disturbing and destabilising.

Ben, aged ten, wants to see more of his mum, especially for her to pick him up at school or to watch a school play. When she is well, his mum is young and pretty and he talks proudly about this. He does not want his Nan to come to assemblies. Is he embarrassed, or does it put him on the spot with actual or imagined explanations to his friends? He seems to be longing for "sameness" and "normality". It is especially difficult for children in kinship families when comparing their own family situations to that "norm", when there might be an existential sense of somehow not having been wanted or kept. Ben loves it if his mum comes with his granddad to watch him play basketball. Yet, she is often physically and emotionally unwell. She has periods of chaotic drug use and disappears regularly. Ben's grandparents struggle to know how to encourage contact and to monitor when his mum is so unwell that it will disturb Ben. They have to judge what to tell him and whether the irregularity and unpredictability of contact is harder than no contact. They also have to manage Ben's mum's fury with them if they say no. They have to handle it when she turns up at the door, especially if she is particularly vulnerable or unwell. Can they both help her and protect Ben, who worries about her a very great deal?

Andrea finds her grandson's contact with his mother almost unbearable because of the critical things she says to him during their six-monthly contact, when she often arrives late. In the past a social worker supervised the contact, but this was withdrawn. For a period, Andrea paid for an agency worker to do this. She recognises the need for her grandson to have some contact with his mother, but doubts the value of it, when it feels so focused on the mother's needs rather than her grandson's. With his dad, it's easier; they meet for lunch, but still she has to watch her handbag, as he has taken money, in all likelihood for drugs, in the past.

Impact on family relationships

Family relationships are often profoundly changed when parenting breaks down and other family members take on the care of children. The hierarchical organisation of the generations is shifted, which is confusing and uncomfortable for many. Different family members might not accept this. The sense of entitlement to parent and the acceptance of an alternative family member as a parent are not simple acts, but ongoing processes and negotiations that can be fraught and contested.

Lucy, Sean's grandmother, talked about feeling resentful, not of anyone in particular, more: "It's not fair, why me?" She described her other children's anger with their sister, Sean's mum, saying, "You must be so angry towards Sally [Sean's mum], she's turned your whole world upside down."

> "Sean was a big disruption to the family, my youngest felt she was no longer my baby, Sean was there and demanding all my attention and energy. She just became a little bit distant. To this day she and her brother don't really talk to Sally."

> Claire: "Taking on the children has been isolating."

> Ashakey: "I've had a lot of respect, people say you're doing a great job, but from a distance, I don't feel the same connection with my friends as I did. I'm not sure, is it just being a parent? Friends don't quite see the

way it's different from that, they think, 'So you're their mum, exclude all the other people!' Most people around me think that's how I should approach it, so every time there's a difficulty with contact or the extended family or behaviour problems, they think I should just cut it off. They don't understand the attachments."

Monica: "A couple of my friends have been very helpful, just listening. My family have been depressingly unhelpful. This little one [Monica's granddaughter], we're very fond of each other and actually it's working out quite well, but when I mention her, I see something ripple across my daughter's shoulders, I can see she really doesn't like it, perhaps she's jealous, I don't know, so coming here [to the support group] is really helpful because I can talk about her here."

Claire: "They try to be supportive, but for my Mum and Dad, it's really only when it works for them. We haven't seen my sister for a long time; she's not stable, lots of difficulties. My parents think the children should see their mum. They're not acknowledging me as a parent. It causes tension at certain times."

Monica: "With my family, I can't ever moan. If I do they just go well, Mum . . . we knew this was going to happen."

Claire: "No, I don't ever moan."

Talking with children: how, what, and when to tell?

Group members begin to build a trust between them and to share their histories in this confidential space. One recurring theme is how to talk with the children. They may try out different ways and words to explain drug use, alcoholism, depression and mental illness, chaotic lives, domestic violence. The group discusses how to manage this with sibling groups at different ages, levels of understanding, maturity, and vulnerabilities. We consider whether anything really is secret or unknown, and the effect of not saying as well as being open and answering questions explicitly. Shame and secrecy can begin to dissolve as experience is shared. There is laughter and wry humour and a large dose of common humanity as painful stories are processed. Anger and tears are shared and accepted without drama and fuss. My experience has been that through this process many carers become more confident in talking with the children. There are no definitive answers, just a space that is safe enough to have a go, with ideas and suggestions from others, sometimes other carers, sometimes the facilitators, but with a knowledge that everyone is on a similar journey and it's not a straight path.

> Lucy: "It was difficult because there was no physical problem, so it was hard for Sean to understand: 'well, how come she can't look after me?' I explained his mum wasn't well, she wanted to, but she wasn't able to look after you. Sean is more aware as he has got older of the reasons."
>
> Julia: "How does Sean understand it?"
>
> Lucy: "Well, Sally was very young, she was a teenager and wasn't able to look after a baby and she picked the wrong person. He knows his father was violent and that he went to prison and it was a bad relationship and that his mother didn't have the capacity to look after him. Same with his Dad, I have told Sean that I do believe his Dad loved him, but just didn't have the ability to look after him, hadn't had the opportunity to learn how to look after a baby, had had a really bad life and just didn't know how to look after you, to keep you safe."

How the stories are told raises the dilemmas of loyalties to different family members' versions of events. Carers have their own perspectives on the parents, depending on their pre-existing relationships, their ideas about what has happened, and their role in the family and the history. Talking to children comes with a lot of emotional resonances that can make any family member reluctant, wanting to shut down or avoid the issues. Gentle challenge and reference to the common struggle can begin to make this easier. Sometimes, however, this might not be material for the group, the painfulness of it being more readily talked through in therapy.

Family therapy with a kinship family.

Theory and practice

In this section, I present a clinical vignette highlighting my approach to the work and theoretical ideas that I have found particularly helpful.

Clinical vignette

Ryan and his family were referred to our service at the suggestion of Ryan's school, where there were concerns about his aggression to teachers and peers, reporting that he was unable to sit still, was making animal noises in class, running round school, and seemed to have no sense of danger,

At our first meeting, we learnt that Ryan's grandparents, Ann and Tom, had looked after Milly aged twelve and Ryan aged eight for six years, because of their mother Sarah's struggles with drugs, depression, and violence from her partner, Calvin. The difficulties had escalated after the birth of Ryan, culminating in the police removing the children after neighbours had alerted them to a serious incident of violence and their discovery of the children living in poor and unsafe conditions. After a brief time in foster care, the children went to live with Ann and Tom, who struggled with Ryan themselves at times. Ann took main responsibility for the children's care and found Ryan both angry and sad, finding it really difficult to get him to do things, like getting ready in the mornings, accepting "no" to things he wanted, and running off on the way to school. He would get tearful at bedtimes, crying and saying how much he missed his Mum. He had bad dreams and was scared to go upstairs alone. Milly, by contrast was described as quiet and clever and always helpful. However, there had been some upsets with friends and recently she had come home very late one night and Ann and Tom thought she had been drinking.

Therapeutic use of genograms

The drawing of a family tree can be both a painful and a joyful activity. It provides so many opportunities for talk and sharing when done collaboratively and with sensitivity. There is a potential to stir things up by making visible and concrete on paper the web of relationships, loyalties, and losses. Yet, there is a considerable therapeutic opportunity to help adults and children to look together at what is there, how it feels, and what it means. The genogram can enable children's and adults' experiences to be spoken about, and named. Children can be given a chance, perhaps for the first time, to ask questions. So often they have questions that have felt impermissible, risky, or upsetting to bring up. Adults often need support to make it possible for these questions to be asked. This was the case for Ryan, who had lived with his grandparents since he was eighteen months old. His father was not mentioned and, indeed, Ryan was not sure what his name was when we did the family genogram. Tom and Ann felt huge animosity towards Ryan's father and blamed him for Sarah's collapse into chaotic drug use and mental ill health. Having a genogram available at each session to add and refer to facilitated the process of dipping into and away from the family stories in a delicate dance, which was enacted in sessions explicitly and implicitly through word and gesture.

In kinship families, the relationships might not fit in a straightforward way with the somewhat normative representations used in the construction of genograms. It is good practice in family therapy, and especially important in these families, as in other non-traditional family constellations, to offer to families the opportunity to come up with their own ways to symbolise relationships if they wish. For children, it might be helpful to use an Apple Tree Family (Tasker & Granville, 2011) where they can place apples on a tree for each person they see as family, offering an inclusive definition of family as whoever you see as being in your family. This takes away the dilemma of representing biological and other connections and offers a good sense of who is important and core to the child. People who might be highly problematic, traumatic, or controversial are included or not, as the child chooses. As an early and safe conversation, this might well be a good place to start.

Talking about the story

A few sessions into our work, Ann and Tom said the children knew they could always ask anything, and that they had talked a couple of years ago about Mum being unwell. Ryan interjected, "No we didn't!" It seemed as if this conversation was not remembered and we talked about how sometimes you need to have lots of conversations over time. I asked Ann and Tom how they felt about talking now with the children. They said they knew it might be emotional for everyone but they wanted the children to be able to talk about anything they were worrying about or wanted to know. I asked if they had any ideas about what Ryan and Milly might want to ask. Tom thought Milly was worrying about Mum and why they had not seen her recently. I referred to the family tree and asked Ann whether she thought Ryan would have questions from that. Ann started to say that it was hard because there were things none of them knew and Ryan interjected, "Yes, my Dad!"

Supporting carers to make it possible to talk about these things is a delicate process. Seeing the family relationships before you in symbolic but explicit form can bring home the difficulties and the losses in a very immediate way. Choosing the right moment to do this is based on the therapeutic relationship at this point, the establishment, perhaps, of what Barry Mason refers to as "safe uncertainty", a state of trusting enough to be able to open the door to considering how and why things are as they are or might be, but with space to enable the possibility of new or different understandings to emerge (Mason, 1993). We need to give plenty of opportunity to talk about the process and check how family members are finding the exercise. John Burnham's ideas on relational reflexivity are an invaluable aid to us in this engagement (Burnham, 2005). How is this conversation for you? Are my questions helpful or not? How will I know when we have done enough for today? Are there other questions I would be better asking you? Are there themes we are missing that would be important for you/other family members to think about today?

Kinship carers have their own feelings and beliefs about the helpfulness of talking, which have to be discussed and understood. Sometimes, this is best done away from the children before a whole family conversation can be contemplated. For Ann and Tom, talking about Sarah's difficulties and about Calvin, the children's father, were emotive topics. They were very uncertain about how the children understood their mum's difficulties. They had told them she was unwell and that was why she could not look after them, but were worried about telling the children that she used drugs because they felt they were too young. They were unconfident about talking about mental illness and anxious about how the children could understand this. They were concerned the children might blurt either issue out at school and the stigma and taunting that might ensue.

Sometimes, Sarah was in a better state and the children had contact, but there were times when things were chaotic for her and they did not know where she was. On two occasions it turned out she was in prison, while the children thought she was in hospital. We were able to think together about what the children knew, imagined, and might worry about. We talked about secrets and how things can be half-known or sensed and the effect of this. We discussed when and how they wanted to talk with the children. They felt they needed to be honest within the children's ability to understand. Ann, however, was worried about the effect of her own upset and anger when talking about Sarah and what this would be like for the children. In response to a question, Tom said he thought they knew how she felt anyway, as they could read her like a book.

Identity

Ryan and Milly are of dual heritage. Ann and Tom make clear they are comfortable in wanting to support their identities. They do not have any contact with Calvin's family, however, so neither child has access to the black Caribbean side of their family. There has been some concern that Ryan regularly makes negative comments about other children's ethnicity at school and tends to pick on more vulnerable children. Ann and Tom find it very difficult to speak about the children's father and blame him for most of Sarah's difficulties. In our initial sessions, we explored what this could be like for the children, especially Ryan, as a child of mixed ethnicity and how this could be affecting his sense of what kind of boy to be. Was he internalising a view of black men as tough, aggressive, to be feared, or, indeed, admired or emulated? Was he managing his discomfort and even shame about his own vulnerability by attacking any signs of vulnerability in others? His grandparents were worried that his behaviour meant he might be "turning into" his violent, criminal father either because of an idea about his inherited genes or what he had witnessed. Unpicking this together was a route to loosen the potential of these ideas to form some kind of defining identity for Ryan that he could only act into.

Ideas on identity and stories from narrative therapy are particularly helpful. Perlita Harris (Chapter Ten in this volume) and Freedman and Combs describe listening to stories with a deconstructing perspective:

> we seek to open space for aspects of people's life narratives that have not yet been storied. . . . We hope they will experience their stories as something that they have a hand in shaping, rather than as something that has already shaped them. We believe this attitude helps to deconstruct the "factity" of people's narratives, and that such deconstruction loosens the grip of restrictive stories. (Freedman & Combs, 1996, p. 46)

So, with Ryan, exploring the different ideas about his difficulties as well as the stories around his experiences, the family began to develop more multi-faceted descriptions and explanations with him.

For Milly, the distress that slowly emerged was her idea about her mum not having wanted her enough, that she and Ryan were not sufficiently important for Mum to sort herself out. An impassioned cry came, "What's the matter with her? Why doesn't she learn?" Milly was gradually able to say how angry she felt and then how sad she was. Both children remembered the cuddles they had had with their mum, an image filled with cuddly toys and a puppy from early childhood that seemed part memory, part oft-recounted story, and part fantasy of longed-for closeness.

Drawing on attachment ideas and their use in family therapy (Byng-Hall, 1995; Dallos, 2006), it was important to support the grandparents' ability, within the temporary secure base of therapy, to help the children develop more coherent narratives that could encompass the barely consciously remembered trauma of seeing frightening violence towards their mother. We also began to have conversations together about seeing her suffering over many years the effects of drug use and depression, physically run down, emotionally volatile, at times in an absent state. We gradually found ways to talk about this and her "unhappiness and confused mind, which got her so she couldn't look after herself and make good decisions".

Family structure and relational dynamics

Addressing intergenerational stories, grandparents' relationships, parents' own growing up, as well as the early years of children, is almost always part of this work. I find myself moving between the past and present, exploring patterns and influences, picking up on both the resilient stories as well as the difficult ones and the accompanying emotions and influence on family lives and relationships. Ann talked about her mixed feelings about Sarah, fury, guilt, self-reproach, bewilderment, and incomprehension, wondering what was down to her divorce from Sarah's father, Sarah's choice of a man who was then violent, and from whom she could not seem to manage to separate, however bad it got. Ann and Tom were struggling to make sense for themselves about what had gone wrong so they could manage to help the children with this.

Ann and Tom's younger daughter, Laura, felt she had lost her Mum as well as her sister through all this. She haltingly recounted in our joint session that it was not reasonable, but she was resentful sometimes that Milly and Ryan took all her Mum and Tom's time and love. This had led to her withdrawal and Ann missed seeing her daughter and the support she offered with the children. The family thought it would be good to experiment with some mother–daughter time for Ann and Laura, and Tom agreed he would babysit.

Tom and Ann had rather different ideas about discipline and Laura was different again. Exploring these differences as positions on a continuum, encouraging each to get interested in why each other's positions were important to them, assisted family members in working together, in being less oppositional with each other about the "right way" to handle things (Campbell & Groenbaek, 2006). Working with positions in this way, often with them represented visually, became a familiar tool in the sessions. We used it to think about whether it was more important to focus on understanding the influence of past traumas or to concentrate on problem interactions and "parenting" in the present, to understand what behaviour meant as against finding strategies to manage behaviour. We also used it to think about the importance for children of having a dad around as opposed to having loving adults who care for you being the essential. We also explored the family's relationship to professionals, the school, and social services. It took some of the sting out of the conversation and seemed helpfully to introduce more flexibility in how the family looked at things.

We are often involved in working with the complex networks around the children and families. Using systemic ideas about positions, levels of context and meaning, and the way the issues can be mirrored up and down a system that has become stuck, accusatory, defensive, punitive, or neglectful, is a whole further area of discussion which, though fundamental to much of the work, is beyond the remit of this chapter, but is addressed by Wendy Lobatto (this volume)

Conclusion – end thoughts

I look back at this chapter and I think, have I just written a (rather long) list of the issues? What do we need to do about this? Then I think, actually no, the point is to try to understand what it is like, to be able to accept, to listen, and to allow the complications. Out of that emerges anything that might need to be done. I am aware that there are dilemmas for us as therapists, as workers with this client group. How do we choose where to direct the focus of our conversations with families? In engaging with family members, we negotiate together a wide or narrow focus, moving between problems and strengths, past and present. Our valency, the resonances for us, will influence the lenses we end up using most. Our use of self, our willingness to be in there with families in their pain and their triumphs, is the bedrock of our practice.

Acknowledgements

My thanks go to "Claire", "Ashakey", "Monica", "Lucy", and all the members, past and present, of the kinship carers support group, as well as to the many kinship families I have worked with over the years, for their individual and collective honesty, courage, determination, creativity, and resilience and the inspiration that this offered me. Thanks also to my warm and wonderful co-facilitators and colleagues.

References

Barratt, S., & Granville, J. (2006). Kinship care: family stories, loyalties and binds. In: J. Kenrick, L. Tollemache, & C. Lindsey (Eds.), *Creating New Families* (pp. 162–179). London: Karnac.

Burnham, J. (2005). Relational reflexivity: a tool for socially constructing therapeutic relationships. In: C. Flaskas, B. Mason, & A. Perlesz (Eds.), *The Space Between. Experience, Context, and Process in the Therapeutic Relationship* (pp. 1–17). London: Karnac.

Byng-Hall, J. (1995). *Rewriting Family Scripts.* London: Guilford Press.

Campbell, D., & Groenbaek, M. (2006). *Taking Positions in the Organization.* London: Karnac.

Dallos, R. (2006). *Attachment Narrative Therapy*. Maidenhead: Open University Press.

Department for Education (2014). *Statistical First Release 36–2014*. Office of National Statistics.

Farmer, E., & Moyers, S. (2008). *Kinship Care: Fostering Effective Family and Friends Placements*. London: Jessica Kingsley,

Freedman, J., & Combs, G. (1996). Opening space for new stories. In: *Narrative Therapy* (pp. 77–112). New York: Norton.

Hunt, J., Waterhouse, S., & Lutman, E. (2008). *Keeping Them in the Family: Outcomes for Children Placed in Kinship Care Through Care Proceedings*. London: British Association for Adoption and Fostering.

Mason, B. (1993). Towards positions of safe uncertainty. *Human Systems: The Journal of Systemic Consultation and Management, 4*: 189–200.

Music, G. (2011). *Nurturing Natures: Attachment and Children's Emotional, Sociocultural and Brain Development*. Hove: Psychology Press.

Nandy, S., Selwyn, J., Farmer, E., & Vaisey, P. (2011). *Spotlight on Kinship Care*. Bristol: University of Bristol.

OED & Oxford dictionaries online. Accessed May 2015.

Perlesz, A., Brown, R., Lindsay, J., McNair, R., De Vaus, D., & Pitts, M. (2006). Family in transition: parents, children and grandparents in lesbian families give meaning to 'doing family'. *Journal of Family Therapy, 28*: 175–199.

Tasker, F., & Granville, J. (2011). Children's views of family relationships in lesbian-led families. *Journal of GLBT Family Studies, 7*: 182–199.

INDEX